Fear Not

Fear Not

BY DAVID FABRICIUS
& CRAIG A WRIGHT

authorHOUSE®

AuthorHouse™
1663 Liberty Drive
Bloomington, IN 47403
www.authorhouse.com
Phone: 1-800-839-8640

Edited & Co-Authored by: Craig A. Wright, The Wright Firm, Inc. 09/2011

First published by AuthorHouse   10/07/2011

ISBN: 978-1-4634-4481-5 (sc)
ISBN: 978-1-4634-4482-2 (ebk)

CRI Counter Terrorism School of Las Vegas, Nevada USA

CRI Counter Terrorism School is a top counter-kidnapping and counter terrorism school based in Las Vegas, Nevada. CRI Counter Terrorism School offers federal military, law enforcement, corporate, and civilian courses.

www.critraining.com www.critraining/delta2.com

Printed in the United States of America

Any people depicted in stock imagery provided by Thinkstock are models, and such images are being used for illustrative purposes only.
Certain stock imagery © Thinkstock.

This book is printed on acid-free paper.

Contents

The 2.2 Full Spectrum Family Protection, Home Defender, Personal Defense, Riot & War Zone Survival System

"FEAR NOT is a no fluff, easy to follow format that not only identifies the problem, but presents us with a valuable and pragmatic solution."
Lee—Special Forces Soldier

Learn how to avoid danger and how to become a hard target. Be one that is very difficult to kidnap rape and murder or even to kill in rioting, battle zones or war. This is a fully integrated tactical defense and trauma medical system designed to save both you and your kids lives and for escaping various threats alive. It presents a practical guide for empowering women, couples and men on the street, in their cars and at home. If you ever wondered how you would deal with a violent criminal encounter or even riot / war zone conditions then this book is for you. It shows you exactly how to prepare and what to do second-by-second, minute-by-minute.

What you choose to do (or fail to do) tactically during the first 2 seconds and what you do or fail to do medically during those critical first 2 minutes, could make a 90% or greater degree of difference between survival or death.
DAVID FABRICIUS

"Choice is all you may ever have and never have." *Without proper training and practice, your choices will narrow dramatically. David's wisdom in* **FEAR NOT** *can give you the edge you need to optimize your choices and chances when confronted by imminent danger.*
C. A. Wright (Airborne, 8th SFG)

Warning and Disclaimer

The world by its very nature is a very dangerous place and has become ever increasingly so. Firearms, knives, violent criminal encounters and wars are all potentially lethal and so are all tactical and trauma medical procedures relating to it. Handling ammunition containing lead should be avoided as lead is known to cause reproductive harm, birth defects and possibly other serious complications. If you cannot avoid the use of ammunition containing lead, then at least wash your hands immediately after exposure. Ideally one should only use lead ammunition in well ventilated areas and open environments.

Reading this guide in it self cannot and is not adequate to gain the needed levels of proficiency one may want and need in a real world encounter with violent criminals. It cannot and is not intended to replace hands-on training and regular practice. The reader of this guide is being advised to seek and obtain practical, professional training in each of the skills covered in this publication.

By choosing to practice and use any or all of the information covered in this guide the reader fully accepts without any exception complete responsibility for any and all accidents, injuries or damages that may occur at any time and under any conditions. The reader is explicitly advised not to practice the tactics, techniques and procedures contained within without prior hands-on training offered by the author and his training associates. Readers who desire to receive training should contact the author directly for training availability and recommendations for instructors and training organizations. He can introduce you to some of the best-of-the-best.

The author assumes no liability for any injury, damages or negligence that may occur through the use of any or all information contained in this body of work. The author and all his associates and helpers expressly disclaim all liabilities, demands, claims, suits, losses, deaths, injuries, actions, costs of any nature, category or type whatsoever that may arise from the direct or indirect use of any information covered in this guide. This guide is not a replacement for in person practical training nor is it a substitute for a personal consultation about your rights and responsibilities with your own legal advisors. It is highly recommended to observe and then comply with all applicable federal, state, county and municipal laws, ordinances, rules, regulations and requirements. Please pay close attention to all the safety recommendations pertaining to the safe and responsible ownership and use of firearms as it is vitally important. You should learn and practice all tactics, techniques and procedures under carefully controlled conditions and with professional supervision only. This guide is not an all inclusive source on the subject matter covered. The reader is enthusiastically advised to consult additional, reliable sources and resources. This guide has been written with specific attention to having the safety of women in mind even though it is primarily intended for couples (families at home and on the street) and is also very suitable for good and honorable men.

Many of us have the opportunity to travel to foreign lands whether it is for business or pleasure. Circumstances beyond our control could put any one in the middle of a hot bed of violence. You may be a highly valued target or simply an asset by opportunity. No matter the reason, you will want to read this book, study it again, and then pray you never need to use the contents shared within. It could save your life if a battle were to erupt and get you out of an actual combat zone safely.

Note: All high risk action photographs in this publication were modeled with safe weapons only and under very strictly controlled and supervised conditions and executed by highly trained personnel. In high risk firing positions, plastic training weapons were used. Real weapons were utilized very selectively and with great care and responsibility by highly experienced experts only. Do not use a real gun, even if unloaded, to practice the scenarios presented and explained. Use an empty water pistol, water pistol with water only, or a professional plastic demonstrator gun in safe and controlled environments.

A water pistol or large syringe filled with ammonia and red pepper mix can be improvised to serve as a very effective self-defense weapon when traveling in places that are risky and where you cannot carry a firearm. Please do be cautious. Once loaded with our special mix it is no longer a toy. Treat it as a dangerous weapon and if used correctly into the eyes, mouth and nostrils of an imminent threat, it is. Test your mix and chosen water pistol or syringe for functionality before relying on it.

Important: Be sure that the training you receive does not set you up with false confidence or ideas that will get you or your family killed and possibly get you into serious legal trouble. Be aware that the medical trauma procedures discussed in this publication may only be administered in many countries by certified medical professionals who specialize in emergency trauma medical care. Stay legal and stay safe. This book is not intended as an "ultimate commando warrior or warrior reindoctrination" program but it is intended to offer more usable insights and options in really extreme circumstances than most 101 books on self-defense can offer.

Great effort has been taken to make sure the value of this information is sound. Do not attempt to use any of this information unless you are well trained, rehearsed and experienced or in an inevitable and imminent defend-or-be-killed last resort situation. The medical information here is not in anyway meant to replace appropriate and required education, training and certification in all relevant fields of study and practice. The publication is intended for academic study, informational advice and for some novelty purposes.

Know that with activities such as weapon disarming your risks are always very, very, very high. That is the reality. Also, please understand that I took no pleasure compiling this book and wish that there was no need for this kind of information in our world.

I prefer you never need to use any of this information on engaging a threat. I also do not want you to hurt anyone but likewise I do not want anyone to hurt your family or you. My

goal is constantly to help you avoid danger and confrontations, to give you non-lethal options and to teach you how to retreat and escape safely from threats.

However, my goal is also to prepare you to become a very hard target and to help you be better prepared to protect your family and to defend yourself from evil people in a legally justified way if you are ever forced to do so both in peace or time of war. In such cases I want you to be able to successfully use non-lethal techniques and if necessary even Wolverine like intensity, Coyote cunning and Special Forces level skills to take care of your dear ones and still survive unharmed.

FEAR NO ONE BUT GOD!

Distribution and export restriction:

The sale or reading of this publication to mentally ill individuals, foreigners or minors is strictly prohibited. Also, the U.S. Government [Directorate of Defense Trade Control] views the sale, export and transfer of defense related type services and products as an integral part of U.S. National Security and U.S. Foreign Policy and therefore restricts trade of certain goods. This publication may or may not now or in the future be subject to the aforementioned trade restrictions. Therefore, export of this publication to anyone outside of the United States of America may be deemed illegal if not now, in the future. The content in this book may only be authorized reading for U.S. Citizens and individuals with appropriate clearances.

Please determine and observe all relevant Federal Law and Trade Control requirements as they apply to you.

PROLOGUE

Over time I have had the opportunity to visit many places and many people around the world. From the great industrialized nations of the world to what some call the third world and beyond they all have much in common. By there very existence though and in every case, someone always seems to be in charge. We have leaders referred to as King and Queen, Emperor, Dictator, Monarch, President, Prime Minister and even Pope. I discovered perhaps the best traits in civilized man in their simplest form amongst some island peoples that lived in harmony both with each other and the environment. They had an understanding that one served to support the other in virtually all cases. Certainly they too had laws or rules and a tribal Chieftain but there's was not a government out of necessity but rather a hierarchy based on wisdom, knowledge and seniority. As Thoreau once related to us; "your world is but a microcosm of my world which together makes up our world and the macrocosm of all that's living combined."

They say our planet is ever shrinking and though this is but a rhetorical statement, we know that in some context it is true. We can board an aircraft and actually chase the sun to the ends of the Earth. With the push of a button we can see and speak to friends and family around the planet by bouncing signals through space. Through innovation we have been forever building bridges that hurtle us into other microcosms where as visitors we are sometimes not always welcome.

In many cases, various countries and their peoples have now grown used to strangers and their customs as long as there continues to remain a healthy dose of respect. For your own safety it is always important to be aware of the customs and laws of any strange or new society in which you find yourself. Now days, I suggest before you travel overseas that you do some concentrated study on the land, the people who inhabit and the customs that govern there before you book a ticket for a visit. Many standards accepted in one culture could be considered insults in another. One thing was for certain. **During my travels it was made tragically apparent to me that there are more good people the world over that are not prepared to help themselves out of difficulty than there are those who can.** We live in an unsafe world. Surely there were better days when we all felt safer and yes we were much further apart back then or so it seemed.

That thought takes me to **FEAR NOT**. Just by stepping out of your door each day, you are allowing yourself to experience all of the microcosms of your society simply by threading your way across town. Sure, we have standards and laws and police to enforce those laws but how can you really expect someone else to be there just at the right time and at the right place when things become bad and go tragically wrong? You can't! Sure we can spend a lifetime surrounding ourselves with ethics and positive philosophies but what happens when someone who has never heard of those things ventures into your space? Are you prepared to confront someone who has nothing to lose and everything to gain simply by imposing their will over yours? You may have to decide in a split second just what measures you are willing to take and how the outcome may evolve. Are you really prepared to make that decision? Some of us are.

FEAR NOT was derived as an act of kindness yet still unfortunately out of necessity. Approximately seven billion people inhabit the Earth. About 800,000 to 900,000 are kidnapped and taken hostage annually for some form of profit. (Sex Trades, Adoptions, Breeding, Slavery, or just Recriminations) Other crimes against humanity number in the tens of millions. Sometimes attacks are organized, but all too often they are simply just random criminal acts where an opportunity presented itself to someone of low moral character.

Some of the most experienced, proficiently competent and tactically trained men from some of the finest fighting forces around the globe have had some hand in helping to contribute to the material you are about to have revealed to you. Where you have spent a lifetime being the good neighbor, men such as these have been sent to other shores for years to see to it that everyone else also remains a good neighbor. Knowing the old saying that sometimes a good defense is the best offense is more than just words.

Within **FEAR NOT**, you will be introduced to the method for making you and your family safe and secure from almost any unwanted intrusion. (AAPE) It stands for Awareness, Avoidance, Protection and Escape. We could expand on this even more and call it (AAPPEE) for Awareness, Avoidance, Prevention, Protection, Escape and Evasion but for the sake of our discussions throughout **FEAR NOT**, we simply chose to call our training AAPE. Every facet and detail of AAPE is important and every skill that you can learn and become proficient with along the way to mastering AAPE could ultimately be the difference in you being a victim or a hard target. I wish I could predict the outcome of every incident that could ever befall you but you know and I know that would be absurd. What I do know is that with the information you are about to receive within the covers of this book you could be better educated, more aware and better prepared than 99% of all the people around you. You may not be the best fighting force to ever suit up, but by GOD you will be someone that the average run of the mill criminal will have wished they had never run into. Of this I can assure you.

In a life time, some of you have never had trouble or even been in trouble but that could change in just a moment and so could the rest of your life since it may rest with that outcome. That is not the issue here. What is or could have been done to prevent the situation or how you should handle the eventuality is. As I mentioned previously, it could be by no fault of your own. What you do control though are your actions and preparedness coming up to that moment and immediately following. Your police know and you should know that most crimes are crimes of opportunity. If you ever encounter an instance where a safe society breaks down and a crime is being committed against you in your home, on the streets of your town or any town; take this information seriously and you can learn to eliminate any violent criminal opportunity even before it starts. Take this book and keep it safe. Treat it as you would your Bible. I want you to refer to it often and know that these teachings will never go out of style nor probably change in their importance. If I could one day say that the future for everyone will be free from any criminal threat, then and only then would I be comfortable in saying put this book and these types of thoughts behind you. But, for now, I don't see that as a viable option. In fact, I am actually seeing the opposite becoming society's new norm.

I have no way of controlling this information once it gets published. You must know that our work here in **FEAR NOT** is not the ultimate knowledge we have to all serious and combined threats. That type of additional special training we will continue to keep to ourselves but offer it in the strictest of confidence and only to those that can meet our additional qualifications. This book was essentially written only for those who are good of heart. If that is you, then welcome. If it is not you, then I ask you to put this book down now and simply walk away. Our efforts here will be of little use to those who want to take advantage of others. Our goal is for our readers and students to be victimless. There are many options available for you to study and acquire life saving traits and techniques. I certainly would never want to intimate that we know it all. I also am not saying that this is the only book that you will ever want on the subject or that we offer the best and only training you should want to pursue. What I am saying though is that if you could only pick one book to serve as a guide or manual for this type of training, then you might just want to make that book **FEAR NOT**!

I welcome you to a long and prosperous life always surrounded by safe passage.

Acknowledgements

The author would like to acknowledge the contributions, photographs, advice and editing efforts of the following persons in their suggestions, recommendations and help in the evolution and development of this guide:

Doron Benbenisty—Founder CRI Counter Terrorism School
Former Israeli Special Forces, and Counter Terrorism Instructor
www.critraining.com

Joel Martinez—US Navy SEAL, Senior Instructor

James Williams—Sword Master, Specialist Strategy and Tactical Trainer **www.Systemofstrategy.com**

Wes Doss PhD.—Founder Khyber Interactive Associates, LLC. Founder 1 Inch to 100 Yards Warrior Conference. SWAT instructor. Crimson Trace Laser Training Director
www.khybertraining.com www.warrior-conference.com

C. A. Wright—U.S. Army Airborne 8thSFG, especially for his diligent editorial work, writing skills, attention to detail and his perseverance in seeing this book to completion

Tony—CRI Training Director, for reigniting my passion for trauma medical care and for all I have learned from him

The author would also like to thank the following people for their tireless efforts at modeling for the photographs and allowing him to use their images in this publication:

Cristy—for modeling for the pictures—Thank you very much. You are being appreciated

Doron Benbenisty—for the pictures used

Wes Doss and Hye Chong Doss for pictures they provided

Ken Haan for his contributions

Thank you also to Lee (TFR) and Ken Walther for their contributions

Additionally, the author would like to acknowledge the NRA, Front Sight® and all of the other organizations who promote the safe, responsible ownership and use of firearms through their marksmanship training and their work to protect our constitutional rights; more specifically, the Second Amendment right of individual citizens to keep and bear arms. The author would also like to thank the authors and instructors offering courses to civilians who have gone before him for their example and the insights he has gained from their work. A special warm thank you is extended to Massad Ayoob for his work and influence as an author and for what I gleaned from his work regarding the legal use of firearms in The United States of America.

I also want to acknowledge the continued efforts of the U.S. Dept. of Justice and their Bureau of Justice Assistance that organized the National Neighborhood Watch programs available to most every citizen in virtually every community across America. Although these programs are both local and national, they can be used as a way to tie together the very foundation of our own AAPE system. Awareness, Avoidance, and Prevention are the motto of the Neighborhood Watch. Utilizing and applying the training and resources of this truly outstanding program will ultimately improve anyone's abilities. Start by contacting your local police departments for information or USAonwatch.org.

The author fully acknowledges that this is not an all inclusive body of work on topics such as legal matters pertaining to safe firearm procurement, training, storage, gun safety, marksmanship etcetera. It has a more specific mission. You will find that the appendix of this book provides sections for both fundamental and very advanced ideas and seasoned practices on the topics of training, weapon safety, weapon handling, marksmanship and more.

ENDORSEMENTS

The intention of "FEAR NOT" is to share a collective knowledge and the necessary skills to help people deal with inherent real world dangers in our society. It is a must read if you ever intend to travel or live overseas.
Ken Walther, CIA Technical Ops (retired)

FEAR NOT is a No-Fluff easy to follow format that not only identifies the problem but presents us with valuable and pragmatic solutions.
LEE, A Special Forces Soldier

Travel overseas can be a very expensive proposition to say the least. FEAR NOT is a must read and retain book that will keep any trip from becoming even more costly!
Edwin Alan, Freelance Travel Writer

Every chapter is an eye opener but I personally want to recommend the chapter and outline on medical trauma and emergency care. It is important for you to familiarize yourself with even basic procedures because they could determine the difference in life or death.
Dr. Vicente Narciso, Board Certified General Surgeon
(40 years Trauma & General Surgery)

FOREWORD

By Doron Benbenisty

Founder & Owner of CRI Counter-Terrorism School www. critraining.com

Beyond all the tactical knowledge, wisdom and experience; I can summarize that at the end everything in Fear Not is actually promoting happiness. Let me explain. If the training provided in this book will help save even one person's life then that means that there is one less orphan and widow in the world.

Read it carefully, study it and apply it with care and mastery. Stay safe, take care of your family and keep training.

Doron Benbenisty—Founder CRI Counter Terrorism School

From Ken Walther, CIA Technical Ops (retired)

Having spent a total of twenty years overseas, working and living in over 100 countries, personal safety was of a high concern. The safety of our colleagues, friends and families often superseded ones own safety as they were often not as prepared, conditioned or knowledgeable on how to defend themselves in hostile situations. Many of our colleagues had Military service to draw from, as did I, and many of us were skilled in forms of martial arts and hand weapons. In such cases when your civilian contacts were accompanying you in areas of potentially hostile activity, it was normal to assume a protective or at least instructive role when in tumultuous situations. That is why **"FEAR NOT"** and paramilitary training is a must for working overseas.

Keep in mind that most countries in the world do not have 2nd Amendment rights like we do in the U.S.A. Yes, the *"bad guys"* are often armed making your decisions more critical. Our U.S. Government cannot override local laws, except in special circumstances, so count on being unarmed on foreign soil for the most part. However, since the U.S.A. still honors our rights to bear arms, we should defend those rights and learn to use a weapon and be prepared to protect your family and yourself. Remember, *"An armed man is a Citizen; an unarmed man is a subject"*.

The intention of the book, **"FEAR NOT"**, is to share a collective knowledge and the necessary skills to help people deal with the inherent dangers in our society. Most definitely it is true that your chances of encountering danger are much higher in foreign countries. Teaching and informing overseas American citizens has been a continuous challenge for decades. Our Agency, along with the Department of State, conducted safety and training indoctrination to our Embassy and Consular personnel as time and budgets would allow. Many of our expatriates and civilian employees had never been overseas and were both naïve and inexperienced in their foreign environments which made them easy targets in many cases. We instructed them in using common items and materials as *"equalizers"* or defense weapons and even built their confidence by showing the power they could develop using speed, decisiveness and surprise. The follow up would then be for the attendees to continue to practice in groups or enroll in regular self defense courses.

"FEAR NOT" is a book I would recommend to civilian employees in preparation for their overseas assignments. I would equally recommend it for our citizens to read and learn from on their home turf. I would also recommend that people be exposed to some common sense *"tradecraft"* to enhance their observation skills and how to *"read"* a potentially dangerously situation. Kudos to these men who want to help people avoid danger if they can, learn to react to dangers if they are involved and ultimately how to respond so as to survive and then protect their loves ones.

Ken Walther (CIA retired)

A Personal Note from David Fabricius

"David has an outstanding ability to help people overcome fear"
General C. Whermann Ph.D. (Ret.) Military Intelligence

Our world is becoming increasingly dangerous and living in America is even and very sadly becoming less safe. Wars are raging across the planet. Natural disasters abound. In one's home a higher level of awareness is wise and prudent. There are reports of between 6000 and 12,000 home intrusions each day in America. That breaks down to more than one in every four to six people being a victim of a home intrusion today. There is a violent crime being committed approximately every 15 to 20 seconds in North America. This may get worse if the economy remains challenged and declines further into a less favorable state.

After seeing how vulnerable people and single women are, especially in our increasingly dangerous world, I felt a calling which compelled me to help. Having had extensive and highly specialized past training in related subjects and knowing some highly skilled individuals from whom I have gleaned several very valuable lessons, I simply could not help but respond. I wanted to create a simple, inexpensive and highly effective system as my humble contribution. First and foremost I wanted it for my sister, my sister's daughter and her daughters. Next I wanted a practical and effective system for every other law-abiding woman, couple and man within my reach that has a sincere and lawful interest. I did not want to pass without documenting and leaving some of the useful knowledge and skills that I was privileged enough to learn over the course of my life. I feel uniquely qualified and positioned to make this contribution.

Many other people are equally as and more qualified and I encourage them to make their own contribution. This is mine. Let us each contribute the best we can according to the gifts, opportunities and calling each of us has been given. We each can contribute in our own unique way and without envy of one another. The sun shines equally for all of us. Let those of us who have uncommon skills in medical trauma first responder care and self-defense teach as many good and law abiding people as possible without conflicting amongst each other. There is much work to be done and every qualified teacher and instructor is needed. There are more who need our help than we can reach in our lifetime and the overall needs of humanity are urgent.

My mission with this writing was to create an integral system that is quick and easy to learn. I wanted it to be relatively inexpensive to implement, immediately usable and offer real-world applications to last a lifetime. What you are reading here is a system for overcoming fear.

Given the choice, I would always much rather teach people how to love one another and choose non-violent living rather than how to handle weapons. Sadly, sometimes events will dictate for us what is needed. I feel we are currently in a time such as that. I take little if any pleasure in teaching gun or knife related training and encourage you to always seek a path of non-violence. It is my prayer that you will never need what is being shared in this work.

Should you ever have the need to respond with force from an imminent threat as a last resort and have determined you are in a defend-or-be-killed situation, I want you to know that I have given you the most important and best recommendations I possibly can to survive that encounter. My goals are and remain to continually evolve this work so as to offer the best system in the world and not be from a place of ego, but rather from a position of caring.

Looking at the risk and threat women and people face in an increasingly dangerous and violent world made me realize that what is offered in this publication is needed by those I care about. This was how the 2.2 System was born. It is a uniquely integrated solution for emergency response situations where firearms, edged weapons such as knives or other dangerous threats are being presented. The 2.2

Family Protection & Personal Defense System provides you with a systematic emergency response plan and as a last resort an option to violent criminal encounters where an imminent life-threatening act is being presented.

Remember, the focus of this publication is very specialized. We intend to equip women and others with a second-by-second, minute-by-minute, first contact emergency response system for avoiding, escaping and surviving a criminal threat. It is also effective for fighting back if necessary. Its primary goal is simply to make you a hard target and be someone who is very, very, very difficult to kidnap, rape or murder. So I recommend you learn this system well. Study and practice until you master it and then "**Fear Not**".

Always proactively pursue excellence without any apology or excuses for doing so while keeping your faith and sense of prayer. In a world where mediocrity has become a very commonly accepted standard I want to challenge you to be a person of uncommon excellence in the areas that matter to you the most. Try to remain a lifelong master student of first response tactical defense drills as well as an effective student of medical protocols for trauma procedures.

It is only with humility, training and more training that you can improve your ability to effectively and successfully meet the intense demands and challenges presented by a violent criminal encounter. There is nothing pleasant and easy about a force-on-force close quarter combat type fight for your family's or your personal survival. It requires strength of character with great wisdom, exceptional capabilities and lightning fast reactions. Your actions are based largely on simple to execute but highly effective and safe to use devastating techniques and proven tactics.

Take full responsibility for your family and your own security and safety. Be their protector and personal security coach. Seek out the teachings of the best people to improve your skill. Invest time with my friends and me and my team of expert specialists. Read several of the books written by Massad Ayoob and others like him to give you the right mindset. Be a lifelong learner. Stay sharp. Get yourself a 12 gauge shotgun, a .40, .45 or 9 mm caliber pistol, a .44, .357 or .38 Special revolver and a compact or subcompact 9 mm G-19 or a .22 L pistol. Acquire three quality tactical flashlights, a quality tactical folding knife and a comprehensive trauma specific first aid kit. Get into the habit of wearing one handgun on your dominant hip and another in a quality shoulder holster. With a concealed carry permit you could daily carry your .22 L pistol in deep concealment along with a tactical folding knife.

Frequently dry practice drawing and presenting each of your handguns. Practice transitioning between your handguns and changing magazines. At minimum always carry you .22 L pistol and / or tactical folding knife. Routinely practice with your shotgun and also transitioning from your shotgun to each of your handguns in your multi-layer defense system. Be consistent in where you wear each firearm. Also learn at least 3 non-lethal self-defense skills really well along with at least 3 man stopping unarmed combat skills.

You must educate yourself extensively in family, home and self-defense laws. Educate and train yourself with professional help in gun safety and learn to shoot very well. Take repeatedly trauma first aid classes and practice all gun shot and knife wound related protocols and procedures. Become masterful at our AAPE system and be sure to learn in-person from my friends and me how to use the "FEAR NOT" in home, in car and on-foot first contact drills effectively.

I deliberately did not include everything you need to learn in detail within **"Fear Not"** as I do not want the bad guys to know everything to expect if they attack you. There are vital details that you must learn and practice in person with me and or my friends and team. That is how we will give you the winner's edge in worst case situations and conditions.

Before we move on, there are two vital considerations you need to be aware of.

1. Are you willing to use lethal force if forced to do so as a last resort to protect your family from being kidnapped, brutally raped or killed?

2. Are you willing to study, train and practice to develop the level of safe and effective gun handling skills you will need in such an extreme situation?

Your answers need to both be a definitive YES if you are going to read this information. If not, please stand down and burn or delete this information. If you answered yes, then we ask that you please invest special attention to the legal indicators and safety rules outlined in this book and always take full responsibility for all your own choices, decisions and actions.

Threat Test:

1. Is a firearm, knife or other dangerous or lethal weapon visible and obvious in the threats hand?

2. Is the threat close enough to kill or severely injure you or those with you that you are legally aloud to protect?

3. Is the threat showing clear intentions to kill or cause you or your loved ones severe bodily harm?

Can you avoid or escape the threat? If yes, DO! If no, then determine how you can deescalate the situation with minimal or equal force. As a civilian family guardian, your intention should be to only stop but not to kill the threat.

If left with absolutely no other option, then and only then, implement the threat stopping action that will best fit your unique situation in a effective enough manner to end the threat.

(Special Message)

Special Message from a Special Forces Soldier

I refuse to live in fear. Make no mistake, there's a lot to be afraid of out there. It could be from the spectacular such as natural disasters, violent crime, and terrorism, to the more mundane, such as an auto accident or falling down the stairs. If you think about it, there's a lot to be afraid of from an ordinary staircase. No matter how athletic you are; if you run full speed down a set of hardwood stairs in your stocking feet with your eyes closed, chances are that sooner or later you'll end up with a broken neck. So, you prepare and act in a prudent manner without even thinking about it. You wear non-slip soles, you use a handrail, you go at a safe speed, and you keep your eyes open. These are simply common sense measures that you take to prepare yourself. Similarly common sense measures can be taken to prepare yourself for someone or something that can do you great harm.

Which brings us to this book; finally someone has presented us with these measures in a no-fluff easy to follow format that not only identifies the problem, but presents us with valuable and pragmatic solutions.

Please divest yourself of any images of a camouflage fatigue-clad militia member spending his days rolling in the dirt shooting at paper targets of bad guys, and his nights improving his fortified bunker. David has provided us with a guide for everyday people to prepare for and handle life-threatening situations and it is my firm belief that the more prepared you are for these situations, the less likely you are to encounter them. Leave fear to others and prepare yourself for whatever life puts in front of you

"The brave man dies but once, the coward dies a thousand deaths."
Lee

Outcome Goals—Tasks, Conditions & Standards

It is my belief that it is always practical to clearly begin with one's core and desired outcomes first. Here are my intentions with this work.

Outcome Intentions & Goals

To help you develop knowledge and skills needed to avoid danger by becoming a hard target and one that is very, very, very difficult to kidnap, rape and murder along with inspiring you to continue your own education and life long training. This includes having very specific second-by-second, minute-by-minute first contact immediate action drills for in-home, in-car and out on-foot while knowing medical trauma protocols and procedures for dealing effectively with life-threatening situations.

Live with more peace of mind because you know that you know you are ready to deal with emergencies.

To let your loved ones really feel safe and totally protected in your presence because of your knowledge, through your awareness and from your skill set.

In our actual in-person training we have three very specifically intended level one outcomes measured as *"Tasks, Conditions and Standards"* in conjunction with the 2.2 integrated system that is foundational and generative to this entire body of work. There are also Level two and Level three outcomes.

Tasks, Conditions & Standards

I want you to know with total clarity what the most important survival action steps are and then I want to help you to become highly proficient in each of the critical action steps. My desire is for you to be able to take the most appropriate and most vital action steps at exactly the right time and in precisely the best way under high stress, high risk circumstances. My goal is to help you be calm, cool, methodical and effective when under a threat or attack. It is my belief that if a person can successfully complete the following three TCS tests, they will have developed a very valuable and high level baseline of knowledge and skills. These skills bring empowerment to achieve the three core intentions stated above. Avoid danger and become difficult to kidnap, rape and murder while living with a more merit based peace of mind, thus creating an authentic sense of protection for your loved ones.

Our goal as civilian non-combatants is always first and foremost to avoid danger. If danger finds us our plan is to talk, run or buy our way out. We always aim to de-escalate and placate situations or retreat and escape rather than to fight. If forced to fight to escape and stop the threat then we always aim to choose non-lethal options as our first response. If a pepper spray or stun gun or arm lock will stop the threat then we can choose not to use a lethal option such as a head grab and twist or a firearm. We believe in avoidance, minimum force and where possible non-violence.

Now, having said that, should aggressive predators attack us and in spite of our best efforts to avoid them or retreat from them we are forced to engage but our non-lethal efforts prove ineffective to stop the threat then we decisively respond with controlled aggression, surprise and speed. Responses such as a dynamic head twist or knife use or firearm use should always be your last resort only and are only appropriate in lethal worst case situations. If a simple arm lock, hand palm strike, forward kick, pepper spray or stun gun will stop them then that is what you should use as a self defense response for your families protection. Please understand that a pepper spray, stun gun, baseball bat, martial arts skills or even a knife may not be sufficient enough to stop the threat. Remember to be 100% sure of your target and legal position before you place your finger on the trigger of your firearm. Specialized training is essential if you are going to have the knowledge and skills you need in real world gunfights.

2

Here are our 3 fundamental tests for assessing your level of real world encounter readiness to quickly assess and respond to very dangerous situations. Once mastered, also master the Level 2 advanced TCS drill and deeply consider what I like to call the *"Mogadishu-readiness system"* for a full spectrum emergency response readiness. Mastery of these standards will add massive value to your capabilities.

Test 1 Task—Explain the most important firearm safety rules and specifically also how you will deal with a violent home invasion. What will you do if you come under attack while in your vehicle? How will you deal with an assault while on foot on the street? How will you ensure that you are a responsible gun owner? What does AAPE mean and how is it to be used? Explain and demonstrate both the legal requirements for responsible gun storage, carry and use, plus the AAPE System in detail. Apply and demonstrate the functional skills you need to affect a handgun and knife disarming, attack a training dummies head with a powerful and violent head twist, or strike a training dummy with three, rapid and seamless high impact strikes. (Ex. Kick, heel thrust, elbow strike/punch/heel strike combination and repeat the entire process with three knife impact actions such as two arterial/vein slashes and one vital organ stab combination).

Conditions—Low light, confined area and external stress induced pressure and inhibitors as may be expected when under attack and or wounded. (Ice water treatments for shock stimulation and other instructor induced stress)

Standards—Knock training dummy Bob down in under 2 seconds

Note: I believe that it is best to stay on your feet in both gun and unarmed conflicts. I am not the biggest fan of either prone firing positions or ground holds or grappling. It does have it's time and place but should be used minimally. However I want you to practice taking a training dummy or a tough and well protected sparing partner in an aggressive MMA style takedown.

Go in at a 35 to 45 degree angle and hit your opponent powerfully with your head or shoulder in the solar plexus while grabbing them with both hands behind both knees thus forcefully knocking him/it (Dummy) to the ground. Now fist and elbow pound his/its face and quickly move behind him/it and practice or rehearse a choke out drill. (Be very careful with practicing a choke out and include professional supervision.)

Please understand that unless you are a powerful person with extensive grappling and jiu-jitsu experience you are better off staying on your feet and in keeping at least a 20 yard or greater distance and using a shot gun, battle rifle, carbine or heavy caliber hand gun to control or dominate the situation.

Test 2 Task—After explaining the details of the 2.2 in-home and in-car and out on-foot drills you fire three accurate handgun rounds into at least one target at a distance of three to seven yards. At the next level we fire three rounds into each of three targets for in a real life experience that is typically the minimum number of assaulters you may face. You will repeat again at fifteen yards. Always practice using multiple targets in random numbers for in real life bad guys typically hunt in packs. Gangs are often greater than just three and could exceed twelve or more. For the test the instructors will use either one, three or seven targets randomly. Repeat this test 3 times using 3 different handguns such as first a .40 or .45 pistol, then a 9 mm pistol and finally a .38 revolver or .22 L pistol.

Conditions—Low light, confined area with instructor induced stress.

Standards—Accurately hit the heart/lungs/spinal cord with two shots, with a third shot into the lower brain, between the upper lip and mid forehead on one target only. For a higher personal standard fire one accurate stopping shot each into three individual targets in 2 seconds or less.

Test 3 Task—Perform an initial trauma wound head down medical assessment protocol and provide effective medical treatment for the five most important causes of preventable combat deaths—Blood loss, blocked airway, abdomen and torso wounds including tension, shock and trauma induced hypothermia.

Conditions—Low light, confined area and instructor induced shock

Standards—Accurately complete the entire trauma care *"first responder"* assessment protocol and the five procedures taught in less than 2 minutes.

These are high standards and they need to be! Mastery of these three demonstrations of competence given in a rapid yet seamless order will give you the integrated full spectrum mastery I believe you need. Skills defined here will be required to stand a fair chance of protecting and defending your loved ones and yourself against severe bodily harm or death at the hands of violent evil criminals.

Level 2—Advanced TCS

Task—Fire 3 rapid accurate 7.62 rounds standing at a distance of 100 yards, drop into a prone position and fire 7 more rapid accurate rounds, place weapon on safe and move fast and tactically to 75 yards, kneel and fire 10 more rounds. Transition to a 12 gauge shotgun and kneel at 50 yards. Fire 5 rapid accurate slug rounds, reload tactically with 5 buckshot rounds, move fast and tactically to 25 yards and accurately rapid fire the 5 rounds on 3 different targets. Transition to a .45, .40 or 9 mm pistol and empty the magazine with rapid accurate shots from a kneeling position, change magazine and move fast and tactically to 7 yards and empty that clip. Transition to a tactical knife and swiftly and aggressively move in on target with a direct stab into a vital organ or two 45 degree neck slashes and a heart stab. Then transition into a powerful head twist on a training dummy followed by a swift heel kick once the dummy is on the ground. Finally perform a complete, fast and systematic head-to–toes, sides and front and back medical self check and treat first a severe dominant leg upper thigh wound with a tourniquet, then a chest wound with an occlusive dressing and then a dominant arm biceps wound with gauze and a bandage. Use a minimum of seven targets and one training dummy.

Conditions—Low light with induced stress

Standards—All rounds must be placed in the heart, lung, spinal cord and brain area. Safety catches must be effectively and responsibly used. Shooter must demonstrate mastery of safety standards, use of cover, shooting positions, marksmanship, tactical reloading and magazine change, tactical movement and knife handling. Also demonstrate battle trauma first responder mastery. Everything in the entire task string must be executed in a smooth, fast and professional manner. Take this test once without night vision goggles and once with. Should you ever be forced into a war like situation you will have to be more proactive, more evasive and more ruthless than what I recommend for dealing with criminal attackers in just peace time. When a society breaks down and all hell breaks loose you need to be more Wolverine and less White Knight. You will unfortunately need to be more like a cunning and stealthy Coyote in order to survive.

Level 3—Advanced TCS

Level 3—is a confidential level reserved only for carefully screened law-abiding citizens in our Masters class? It deals with counter-kidnapping as well as more advanced war-zone escape and survival strategies and tactics for families of Forum leadership under such conditions and circumstances. If you had to survive and escape a kidnapping today what is your plan? What if you are caught in a developing war zone, how will you deal with that and lead your family and forum safely out of danger?

Two of my contacts managed to escape from kidnapped captivity and my lead trainer in Special Forces School twice survived intense ambush killing zones. It is possible but it takes faith, luck, prior training and the right mindset gained only from an actual experience and during quality training.

My recommendation to you is to seek out training from three to five of the best and the toughest training schools you can access. The more intense your training and the higher the standards of the school the better off you will be.

You must become masterful at scanning for danger and responding wisely.

Our core drill is to pray, crawl, talk, buy or run our way out of trouble when we cannot avoid it or hide from it. Next, we choose to position our family and self on high ground, in deep darkness, behind solid cover near several escape routes. Plan and rehearse this at home and in and around your vehicle. Prior preparation is vital. If as a last resort we are forced to engage we use the element of surprise if we can, plus speed and enough violence of action to only stop, but not kill our imminent threat.

We believe being a conscious observer is the key, as is the importance of carrying 3 to 5 layers of defensive gear. Look at the entire person with special attention to their hands, look at rooftop lines, windows, doorways, edges of every alley, shadows, in cars, for muzzle flashes and dust clouds. Be well trained, well equipped and alert. Have an **Immediate Action Drill** ready to implement if forced to retreat or engage.

As you lose the element of surprise increase your speed and intensity with "controlled aggression". Sadly, most violent situations will often require you to defend by attacking if you are to survive. Be systematic, calm, and act swiftly. Deal with the closest, most imminent and most dangerous threats first. This may require 1 to 7 proactive and precise heavy caliber rounds into the hearts, lungs and brain of each assaulter to stop them. You have to act with Wolverine like intensity to create chaos, confusion and fear in and amongst them to stop them. Use their shock and confusion to retreat and escape to safety. Stay within all moral and legal parameters and be willing to be formidable in the protection of your family and community against evil criminals.

As civilians we plan not to fight. We prefer retreat over getting engaged in combat. We must choose non-violence and peace. We hide in the dark behind the best cover in the best concealment we can find until the threat leaves. Having said that, it is wise to have a loaded 12 gauge pump action shotgun with #7 birdshot, 00 buckshot and slugs, or a M14 A1 or SKS battle rifle or AK 47 in your own well trained hands, or at least a .44/.357 revolver or .45/.40 pistol backed up by a 19 to 21 inch blade short Samurai sword, or 13" blade authentic Samurai inspired knife, and / or a powerful Ranger style hatchet. Remain concealed behind a rock or tree in the shade or darkness, and only if discovered, proactively protect your family and defend yourself with your shotgun, sword or hatchet as may be necessary and tactically wise. Never fight unless you have absolutely no other choice. Whenever forced to fight to stop an imminent life-threatening threat; be ferocious, methodical and extraordinarily capable. Your training standards must reflect this philosophy and the above principles.

Why We Care

We care because friends and families of friends have been attacked, kidnapped and killed. We care because I have a sister with a daughter and grand daughters. Our friends have been scared in war zones. We care because far too many good and innocent people have been killed by criminals and in unjust wars. Our elderly, single women and our children are far too vulnerable and we care because our world is changing and becoming more dangerous. There are far too many horrific real life encounters documented previously where helpless people have been kidnapped, abused, raped and murdered. Far too many woman, children and old people have been brutally traumatized by criminals or by invading soldiers.

Police records and history books are full of cases where woman, children and even men have been victimized. Equally, history books all around the world are full of accounts of how approximately 200 million civilians have died in civil unrest, wars, and through acts of natural disasters in just modern times. In most cases with training, intelligent preparation and gun ownership the outcomes could have been very different. We see cases where the victim was in their home, had their doors locked, owned big dogs, and even while the victim was talking with a 911 operator they where still grabbed, severely beaten, raped, or even worse kidnapped or murdered. This can all happen before police help could arrive. In cases where the police were very swift, effective and even caught the intruder/s, some victims were still brutally assaulted, raped or already murdered. Having a gun or at least a stun gun or a knife in your trained hands can make all the difference. I care deeply and do not want you to become a helpless victim of violent criminals. It is wrong and for most it is preventable. I want to enable you and empower you to protect and help your children, parents, spouse or yourself should you ever be forced to do so.

My personal concern is especially for single woman and their young children, and for older people living alone. They are such soft and easy targets for criminals and may not have the resources to purchase expensive gear and take expensive and long duration classes in self-defense. Therefore, I have included, promote and teach the use of inexpensive solutions such as the use of a water pistol, box cutter or scalpel as self defense hardware or the use of a bandana or tampons for medical trauma supplies. We live in dangerous and uncertain times, this knowledge is essential.

For a single women going out somewhere that could prove to be risky, it may be easier to conceal a sealed scalpel knife or box cutter in your handbag or underwear and get away with having it whereas a full size knife or revolver could certainly be noticed and difficult to explain. A pepper spray may be a valuable and better option in most cases and would be my first recommendation for women dating or that are socially active on any given night. Please take care by first knowing your rights and for your own sake and for the sake of your family attend our hands on training.

You should obtain a copy of the CRI ITS DVD by Doron Benbenisty which will acquaint you with how to handle extremely difficult or life threatening situations step by step.

Why People End Up Dead . . . In Gunfights

Most people, including those who carry guns professionally that die as a result of a shooting or gunfight die as a result of the following reasons:

1. They underestimate how serious things can get. They do not realize how well prepared they need to be and how well equipped professional bad guy's can be. They end up dead in gunfights because they are not *ready* with a firearm, body armor, an advanced medical trauma kit and enough of ammunition and skill. Lack of adequate, quality second-by-second, minute-by-minute tactical drills and trauma medical care training and gear, including ballistic protection and advanced trauma first responder skills and items. This includes thorough training in the AAPE/ "OODA" cycle/s, gun use, knife fighting and unarmed combat. People also end up dead because of having too small caliber weapon, not being good at effective threat stopping shot placement due to poor training or poor marksmanship and occasionally due to having too weak ammunition, poor functioning ammunition or even running out of ammunition. Many people end up raped, kidnapped or murdered from a weak mindset and they were under the impression that their pepper spray, baseball bat or martial arts training would be enough to protect themselves and their families. Don't be naïve and ignorant enough to believe that

2. Weak execution of tactics and / or trauma medical care procedures. Specifically in regard to stopping blood loss in extremities, dealing with an obstructed airway, treating torso problems such as a sucking chest wound and a developing tension pneumothorax, and treating shock and trauma induced hypothermia.

3. Not having the correct, specific, necessary and needed medical items on hand after being shot.

4. Not having a well thought out first contact plan and backup plan, nor an effective proven battle drill to follow as one's foundational action under virtually all circumstances. You must respond rapidly, drop into the most appropriate firing position and fire at least three accurate shots. Aim for the heart, spinal cord and brain or at least for the lungs, pelvis and thighs.

5. Overconfident, mediocre, complacent, slacker attitudes

6. Cheap unreliable gear that malfunctions at a crucial time of need.

7. Being outnumbered.

8. Not using and dominating the high ground, best cover and darkest area.

9. **It is their appointed time of destiny and someone shot them and they lost more than 25 % to 30% of their blood and or were hit in vital organs such as the brain or heart. "It is that simple."**

As a result most statistically get shot or stabbed in under 2 to 5 seconds of first contact with violent armed criminals and loose functional ability within 3 to 60 seconds after having been shot. Death often sets in within 2 to 5 minutes of the first wound. Training you to a self-reliant mindset and the carrying of well selected tactical and trauma medical items are the key to reducing ones risk. Knowing what to do, when to do it, how to do it and doing it well are all vital aspects if one is to survive a violent criminal attack. This level of skill and confidence can best be gained through skilled, realistic, rigorous, focused and intense hands-on scenario training repeated frequently. A high skill level with your hands, feet and elbows along with shotguns, pistols and revolvers and with knives and specialized medical trauma supplies is always your best insurance if you end up in a full on gunfight with violent, armed assaulters.

The sad reality is that you may need to be self-reliant in your response to an emergency. I recommend you do an internet search for the classic reference case of Warren vs. The District of Columbia. Here is an overview from the reports filed and my understanding of the circumstances. As you read about this incident, just imagine how different this case could have been if the women involved were as well armed and well trained as described within **Fear Not**. As you read, visualize three trained women with shotguns or handguns in a situation where the two intruders and assaulters only have one knife.

A Case Study: "Warren vs. the District of Columbia."

It occurred on Sunday, March 16, 1975. Two men broke down the backdoor of a rooming house occupied by 3 women at 1112 Larmont Street NW in the District of Columbia. One woman was in the lower level while two women were in the upstairs. The two women on the upper floor heard noises below and called the police. They were assured help would be dispatched and it should arrive shortly. At this point they could hear the woman below scream and cry for help. The intruders were sexually molesting and abusing her.

Four police cars were dispatched to investigate what was considered to be a simple burglary in progress. Some police officers drove by the back without stopping. Another did knock on the door but left after receiving no response.

Once gone, the women upstairs again heard the crying and scream of the woman below. The two criminal intruders were forcing her to perform sexual acts and were raping and beating her. They called the police again for urgent help and were again assured help would arrive soon. This time police help never came.

However, the two women upstairs later heard people moving downstairs and thought it was the police. They called down to the woman below just to discover it was the intruders they heard and they too were now discovered. This was the beginning of a 14 hour ordeal which now also included them. The three women were taken at knifepoint to one of the rapists apartment and there they were forced to perform sexual acts on one another, submit to a variety of sexual demands, and were beaten and raped for 14 hours.

The 3 women sued the city police and this became the well known and much talked about case of *"Warren vs. the District of Columbia."* The court ruled that the police were not liable in any way to any victims of any criminal act for their failure to provide police protection, in spite of an obvious "demonstrated failure" on the part of the police.

This philosophy and finding has been clearly evident in numerous other cases since. It comes down to something like this! "The police have no general duty to provide any protection whatsoever as a public service. It was said that *"Their duty is to protect and serve the state and further the interests of the state"*. It was not found that they were to specifically protect individual citizens or families against violent criminals where crimes are about to be committed or are even in progress! The daily task of the police consists of maintaining law and order by enforcing the law, protecting public property and generating income for their operations and jurisdiction.

The *"protect and serve"* slogan must be interpreted in the correct context. It makes for nice warm intentions but also is somewhat misleading regarding public relations. The police may be a deterrent for criminals but it is not a bomb proof guarantee or a certain reality when your family and you may need it most. There are many good police officers that will help you if they see you are in danger. Even with the best intentions, there are simply not enough law enforcement officers to help all of us 24/7, 365 days and nights a year. If the police force was double in size, it is always unrealistic to expect a police officer to be available within those vital first 2 seconds. The same applies for a paramedic first responder team trying to reach your injured family member, or you, in the critical 2 to 15 minutes immediately after a shooting, or gunfight.

There are cases on record where crimes where committed on the same street as the police station or even just around the corner from it on the next street. At best, they could only investigate afterwards in an effort to assign blame. They are not in the business of proactive prevention and protection everywhere at once. That is the reality. Having gone through Police Academy training and having served on a SWAT team, I understand and respect our police and that their job is not an easy one. I also understand and care as much if not more about your need and desire to protect your family.

Now, I fully understand how many women do not want to carry a firearm and deal with everything relating to that privilege. However, especially in today's world more women realize it is becoming increasingly important to be fully capable of a self-reliant response. Most authorities recommend a self-reliant capacity for at least the first 20 minutes to 72 hours for many types of emergencies.

To be truly capable of a more self-reliant response to an imminent violent criminal threat it is wise and prudent to be well prepared. This includes having the right gear when you need it. Let us take a look at that.

If those same three women had powerful dogs, shotgun, revolvers or high volume super strength pepper sprays or even just a box cutter or scalpel knives with adequate quality training in realistic personal protection the outcome of that incident could perhaps have been very different. A shot gun and a hand gun would have made all the difference for these three women. Two or three well trained and well equipped women can be a lethal force, especially when working together as a well trained team, and women often benefit from the element of surprise. After all, what criminal expects a woman to put up a SWAT or elite military quality strategy or tactic into her response to their assault and be equipped with and skilled in the use of what's on our list coming up?

Our Focus

Our focus is to optimize your ability to protect your family and defend yourself in hostile tactical environments. We emphasize our training for in your home, in your car and on foot in the street whether during peace, civil unrest or war time. Prepare yourself for violent criminal home intrusions, against kidnapping attempts and in the event of highly intense rioting or unfolding war zone battles. We care about significantly increasing your survivability and your ability to protect, defend and provide advanced first responder trauma medical care in chaotic, hostile, low light and confined or other conditions. Specifically, your training pertains to situations where your family or you come under attack by violent armed criminals or you get caught in a war zone battle.

This catalytic and foundational publication is not so much or in any way intended as a book on general gun handling, legalities, safety issues, etcetera since there are already so many outstanding books dealing with those subjects. However, to be responsible, these topics are well covered in the appendix attachments in the back of this publication. FEAR NOT is offered primarily to create awareness and wisdom in a practical mindset with realistic, real world practical skills required most likely for real world violent criminal encounters. It is being offered from a caring heart as a second-by-second, minute-by-minute, step-by-step first contact response guide. Its message is simple . . .

The first 2 seconds of contact are vital from a tactical perspective, as is the first 2 minutes of medical treatment after a wounding.

Here is what I have realized.

What you choose to do (or fail to do) tactically during the first 2 seconds, and what you do, or fail to do medically during those critical first 2 minutes, could make a 90% or greater difference between survival or death.

The goal here is to focus on what you need to know in those two all important windows of time.

In my view people perish needlessly due to inadequate training from what they should and can realistically expect during a violent criminal encounter. Due to this lack of wisdom and skill I offer a simple, step-by-step, second-by-second and minute-by-minute, what to do first contact action drill and defensive system. At the risk of being perceived to be "over the top" in my approach I want to rather over prepare you than under prepare you. It is my hope that you will see this message for what it is, a caring attempt to keep your family and you safe when the really bad guys show up.

There are numerous outstanding books loaded with valuable information and written by very experienced and highly celebrated authorities on many other important topics. Please be encouraged and diligent in your study of those sources and content. This is also not intended to be a classic, general, broad-spectrum, cover-it-all guide for beginners in the world of tactical family self-defense and first aid. Our mission is much more specific and advanced. The Appendices attached provide a comprehensive foundational introduction for people new to safe and responsible gun handling and more. Experienced folks will also greatly benefit from it and should occasionally refresh their memory with it. We trust that all this will serve you well.

The 2.2 System©

Here is what it means. It represents the first 2 seconds of a tactical response situation and the first 2 minutes of a medical trauma response combined as a full spectrum into one integrated emergency response system.

Again, please realize, understand and accept that,

What you do or fail to do tactically during the first 2 seconds, and do or fail to do medically in the first 2 minutes after a wounding can make a greater than 90% difference between life and death.

99 % of all the people on the planet are not adequately trained to respond quickly, effectively and appropriately enough to survive.

I want to change that for many people and especially for as many women and couples as possible. I want to teach you to do exactly what you need to know and do and then I want to recruit you to help me reach more people who want to learn how to best respond during those first 2 vital seconds of contact and the first 2 critical minutes of medical care. Know the 2.2 system and be prepared to potentially save your children, spouse and your own life and not be a soft target or become prone to kidnap, rape and murder.

First, you ideally need a system to eliminate having to think or how to decide what to do to avoid any danger. If that is not realistically possible then you need a way to respond to the threat at hand.

Whether you are armed or not, you need a devastatingly effective first contact emergency response drill and a proven trauma medical response drill (protocols and procedures) you can immediately apply.

Let's first explore the nature and experience of fear. Then let's embrace the 2.2 system and the most ideal gear for your use within that system and its specific immediate action drills. Remember you only have two seconds to affect your escape loop or to deliver an effective counter assault. Two minutes is the time you have to deal with the five most common reasons people perish after being shot.

AAPE System©

Here is our foundational acronym and system for staying and getting out of danger, be it from criminal threats or from the full blown threat of a war.

Women have strong intuition. You ladies should trust in it and use it more consciously. When you sense something is up and not quite right, go AAPE!

A = Awareness + Avoidance of all real and perceived risks. Be proactive. Be a keen observer of people, situations and conditions. Continue to avoid and evade high risks.

A = Assess your situation. Observe, evaluate and analyze your strategic and tactical threats, immediate, medium term and long term. Look and emotionally feel into developing threats, environmental hazards, surveillance and intelligence gathering in progress or strangers approaching. Scan left to right, high to low, close to far and multi dimensionally deep for threats, cover and escape routes. Assess people, see the whole person visibly and notice their hands as the threat comes mostly from their hands. Look at, into and through doorways, windows, edges of alleys, roof lines, in and beyond cars, for shadows and into shadows. Assess what resources are available to you. Rely on both your instincts and training. Improvise if you have to. Be audacious, intelligently flexible, adaptive and bold. Be willing to use diversion, deception and disguises to create confusion and surprise in support of your response. Realize that the average violent criminal encounters involving a shooting, gun or knife fight, will statistically occur most often under the following conditions:

1. During low light conditions and late at night

2. In confined or secluded areas

3.   At from arms length to 3 yards to 5 yards away. In war zones it could be 7 or 15 to 100 yards or so and even out as far as 1000 to 3000 yards or more.

4.   Involve multiple assaulters, typically three or more. Assaulters may include females. In disaster zones you may have to deal with large gangs plundering and in war zones you may even face highly specialized 2, 4, 6, 8, 12 or even 15 man teams. Military will sometimes mobilize entire battalions of hundreds of soldiers.

5.   It can happen instantly in just 2, 3, or 5 seconds. War zone battles can rage for hours.

Typically, on average, individual assaults involve only 3 to 9 shots, including yours. However, be ready for exceptions. It is also worth knowing that statistics are rumored to show that when law enforcement officers arrive and start shooting they miss as often as 3 out of every 4 shots. People do get killed in "friendly" blue-on-blue fire.

In most cases the killing is done with either a handgun (70% or more of the cases) or a knife (5%-10% of the time). In war zones it is most likely to be a rifle or bombs.

Fatal wounds are typically in the head, chest, abdomen, pelvis or legs and in about 30 % of the cases from the back of the head. Wounds through the sides of the torso can be especially deadly. In wartime situations all of the above statistics change and expand dramatically by becoming much worse.

P = **Position** yourself in a tactically advantageous position or location that will best support an escape and allow you to effectively engage the threat if either of those two responses become necessary. Be proactive and decisive. Be ready to respond immediately if you are forced to do so. In all out battle zones be willing to prevent the threat from moving into a position of control and dominance. Be ready to overload the threats life by swift, intense chaos created by you. This chaos is intended to stop the threat and to facilitate your escape to safety during their confusion and fear.

E/E = Escape or Engage. Escape as soon as you safely can. If you are well trained or armed, that is reason enough to make your escape. Evacuation, retreat and escape to safety without engaging are your first and best options, if it even is an option. If available, escape immediately using stealth, diversion, deception, disguise, distraction, speed, concealment, cover and if forced to do so in an extreme case, controlled non-lethal or lethal force. Do not hesitate if this is the only way you can safely get away. Ideally, do all you possibly can to avoid, deter or at least deescalate the situation as your first choice.

If you have no way to escape but have the option to do so, hide in the darkest place possible behind the best cover available. Be careful not to be in a backlit location. Know what they see at all times. Always be in a position of operating from an area of the lowest light possible. Observe and respond from there. When forced to engage, do so with lightning fast surprise and legally justifiable intensity. When forced to move, do so in an unpredictable, irregular pattern and unconventional rhythm. Should you need to use a flashlight, use it very sparingly, briefly and precise. Move to a new position immediately after using your light.

Engage, only if in imminent lethal danger with no further preclusion as your very last resort and when a safe escape is totally impossible due to the means, opportunity and jeopardy of your assaulter/s. In such legally justifiable cases, respond immediately with necessary force or equal force only. Only use enough force to stop the threat. Rapidly turn the odds in your favor by using the proven principles of surprise, speed and appropriate violence of action. If forced to do so, exploit your threats weaknesses as a result of their observed actions as you constantly AAPE them. If you have no other choice, immediately evolve the situation. Create massive chaos and a shock overload for your assaulters and escape in the midst of all that shock and chaos as soon as you can safely do so and then call 911.

Use and dominate the high ground. You may or may not choose to use a brief blinding white light if you have a 120 to 150 lumens tactical flashlight and trained skill in its use. In general, avoid lights stronger than 125 lumens due to the risk of after burn exposure since these lights get very hot and are not needed for most at home family protection situations. Also using a brief but intense strobe light mode at close quarters could be powerful if correctly used as it will affect their night sight, depth perception, spatial orientation and ability to see and interpret information about you. It may, or may not disorientate and overwhelm them enough to lead to their surrender or rapid compliance. But keep in mind it will also compromise and mark your position in the dark. You have to move if you use light.

Remember to only shoot if absolutely forced to do so by their imminent threat. Even then, only shoot with the intention to stop the threat, not to kill. Align your eyes, light and firearm with an ice pick/ jaw alignment technique when you shoot. In your training and practice, do not fire every time you draw and present your weapon. What you practice becomes coded into your software and eventually it will be instinctively hard wired into the firmware of your central nervous system and response actions. Also practice alternating the number of shots you fire to again remain flexible in real world situations and not be conditioned to any one fire string. Typically range between a series of one to three, three to five or five to nine shots per shooting string. Do not get over conditioned to just one set response. Some flexibility is essential.

Practice aim shooting, point shooting and instinctive shooting. Ideally use aimed shooting. However, many, if not most real life encounters are in distances of less than 3 yards and evolve very suddenly. This often forces the use of point or instinctive shooting techniques with minimal aim. Shoot to hit the heart, lower brain, spinal cord, pelvis and thighs. These methods are very risky and require good muscle memory built into you from extensive practice. Practice also the use of intelligent angles and consider always using hollow point or expanding full metal jacket rounds.

When you hold a pistol close to your body, hold it not too tight on your clothing as this may cause a malfunction with loose hanging garments. Do not risk that. Remain intelligently flexible and adaptive.

Be knowledgeable and skilled in the use of hemostatic agents to stop bleeding and an Israeli bandage both as a dressing and as a tourniquet. Also familiarize yourself through quality training with a 30 F Nasopharyngeal airway nose trumpet, improvised one way valve chest seal and exit wound seal and the use of a 14 gauge decompression needle catheter. You cannot survive simply by relying on external help to protect and rescue your family. Help may be delayed or never come. Prayer is immensely powerful but realizes that Source does not mind us dying. In fact, it is part of our predestined life plan and the grand plan.

If forced to engage you must be trained and ready. You must be willing to be intense, ruthless and lethal. You must have a 12 gauge shotgun and / or a .40 caliber pistol or another weapon of choice be it a .357 revolver, 9 mm pistol or .38 Special revolvers in your own trained hands. If you do not have any of these then you will have to be exceptionally skilled in martial arts but even then, having at least a handgun will be the best choice in high threat situations. Your ability to effectively present and use one or more firearms as and when needed is the most important key to your survival in any really nasty and dangerous situations.

I invite you to research the work of Col. John Boyd, USAF (Ret) and specifically his *"OODA"* cycle for outstanding and deeper insights. My AAPE system was in part inspired by Boyd's *"OODA loop",* and also by my own military training and other references. Understanding the concepts of AAPE and *"OODA"* are vital for combat survival against violent, armed criminals. Learn its philosophy, principles and practices exceedingly well. This is the base that should guide all our protective and defensive actions as well as all our offensive actions where needed. It is the key to situational awareness, forecasting, avoiding, positioning, deciding and executing any of your decisions and actions more intelligently and therefore more successfully.

Remember to be situational aware but also anticipate and notice what is unfolding so you can rapidly position yourself to most effectively escape or engage if forced to do so. It is always best to first try to avoid or to run, talk or buy your way out of a fight. If that is not possible, then engage as taught or as needed for that unique situation and set of circumstances. Also remember that a pepper spray, stun gun or baseball bat may not be effective and efficient enough to stop the threat. You will in most cases need or really need a shot gun, battle rifle, carbine or heavy caliber hand gun. Like it or not, that is the reality if you are to successfully protect your family in a real world encounter and emergency situation.

It is also important to make peace with the possibility and inevitability of human death, including that of yourself and family. It happens; it is part of the cycle of life.

We could expand this model out to read AAAPPPEEE—Awareness, Avoidance, Assess, Preparation, Positioning, Protection, Engage, Escape & Evasion but our acronym would sound like a cry of panic from a screaming African ape! Our focus is on what you can resort to and how should you respond to any imminent life-threatening danger.

Plan B

Life is not perfect and plans can or will go wrong often within seconds of first contact in a battle. Initially we recommend you have and systematically follow a step-by-step, second-by-second and minute-by-minute first response plan for dealing with violent criminal contacts while in you home, car or anywhere on foot which would include war zones. We realize though that you may be forced to adapt to various unique circumstances and conditions.

Every shooting and every gun fight is unique with its own conditions and circumstances. It is vital to remain open minded and to be able to respond with intelligent flexibility. Do not become rigid and dogmatic to just one way of responding. Should you ever follow our on-foot, in-car, or at-home first contact action drills and realize that due to a unique challenge you need immediate adaptation then respond as follows; Immediately and swiftly enter a new AAPE loop and a new improvised and adapted 2 second on-foot, in-car, in-home/building drill based on your unique situation. Proactively take the initiative to escape or dominate the situation.

Be open and willing to be extremely unorthodox in your firing positions, firing angles and tactics. This also applies in your medical trauma care procedures. Improvise if necessary. Be audacious with daring, guile and unconventional solutions. For example, use tampons or sanitary pads to stop bleeding if you do not have blood clotting agents, combat wound gauze and Israeli or other wound dressing bandages. For camouflage you can use charcoal from a fire and some mud. Paint all buckles mat black or olive green and cover them with dull gray, black or olive green tape to reduce noise. Do whatever it takes.

The typical need for a Plan B could occur with the sudden unexpected appearance of additional threats. This could be from your weapon running empty, malfunctioning, being accidentally dropped into an irretrievable area or there could even be a case of when the police show up and start firing upon the threats. They may even perceive you to be a threat.

AAPE the encounter with high situational awareness and rapidly get ahead of the events in an appropriate tactical loop using our AAPE framework as a drill. Either remain still and low beneath knee level and act dead if you have to or use surprise, speed and the appropriate force in generating a new loop. Use Wolverine like intensity and audacity with the intelligent flexibility and daring guile of a Coyote. The valiant and voracious threat of a Wolverine plus the stealth and cunning of a Coyote is a great combination to avoid a kidnapping or if attempting to survive an unfolding war zone.

In your escape out of a war zone wear civilian clothes for the area and that blend in with the crowd or a uniform of the strongest and most dominant controlling force. Then, when it's best to do so, go your own way and change clothes as necessary. Cover your head, avoid direct eye contact, remain silent, avoid official gathering points if they are set up by unjust people you cannot trust and move with a woman but do not endanger her . . .

What are your family plans and your Forum plan for dealing with violent home intrusions, a violent kidnapping, riotous chaos, violent looting or an unfolding war with intense battle conditions? What are your prevention and response/recovery/escape and survival plans? How about having to deal with the loss of a family member or Forum friend? How prepared will you be?

*Caution: Regardless of the plan you follow, always be mindful of over penetration risks. A 13 to 21 inch blade short samurai sword can be a very useful tool in close quarters battles where the risk of over penetration is high. A combat hatchet is also very powerful in a certain type of man's hands. Always be mindful of the type of wall materials and also intelligently utilize angles to avoid shooting unintentional victims. Hard concrete surfaces, walls and odd angels may cause a ricochet danger, especially if hard (ball) ammunition is used.

Soft tip ammunition, number seven (7) birdshot and body armor will provide a limited amount of protection against ricochet and over penetration risks.

Visualization Practice

Study, practice and rehearse the individual building blocks in each of these three tests. Also, frequently visualize and mentally rehearse yourself executing each of these individually and as a seamless combination with mastery. Commit yourself to being very alert with total situational awareness. See yourself scanning your environment efficiently as you mentally loop through our AAPE System. Notice your decisiveness. Note yourself successfully avoiding the threat and retreating to safety. Plan yourself talking your way out of potentially violent situations. Observe yourself implementing three different non-lethal options for family protection and self-defense with controlled aggression, surprise and speed.

Visualize performing a perfect disarming, first against someone with a handgun, then against a knife. Set your *"controlled aggression"* mindset and perfect execution of technique. Visually perform a swift and powerful combination of non-lethal, unarmed strikes effectively hitting the groin, trachea, eyes, jaw or temple of the head. Run through performing a powerful, dynamic and lethally violent head twist. Visualize performing a perfect legal concealed draw and firing three aimed and accurate shots hitting the heart, spinal cord and lower brain. Visualize yourself using a shotgun effectively, then a revolver then a pistol and performing a smooth, fast magazine change and then drawing and using your tactical knife. See yourself in a standing, kneeling and prone firing position. Visualize performing a successful trauma medical *"first responder"* five action procedure system seamlessly and time yourself in doing so. Then take the three foundational and one Level 2 TCS tests.

Repeat this frequently to build your skills and to stay sharp for any eventuality. Be Mogadishu ready and many other situations could be relatively easy to deal with. Visualize yourself dealing successfully with kidnappers, with violent home intruders and see your self successfully evading, escaping and surviving an unfolding battle in a war zone. Contemplate exactly what your best course of actions will be. What are your options? How will you lead? What will you take? How will you best conceal it? What will be your plan and three best destination options? How will you deal with a loss of life in your family or Forum? Your personal inner and outer strength, faith, caring and example will be the key to helping your family and Forum cope with any such horrific eventualities. Finally, visualize using high ground, dark areas, shadows and superior cover while going through our in-home, in-car and on-foot body guard and medical first aid drills. This mental practice is what conditions you to respond effectively without hesitance in a critical moment. Do it frequently and in great detail. Recommended Reading: **HEART OF THE LEADER**

As you go through this book, you will be exposed to methods and thinking that I sincerely hope will be foreign to many of you. For that I am grateful. It may seem repetitious at times but that is because we are talking about life saving measures. I want to give you every opportunity to retain what you are about to learn. "Practice makes perfect" is an old saying but so is "Carelessness makes widows and orphans". All of the information and training you are going to be exposed to is for real world life saving measures. It should not be compromised and will not be for everyone. That's fine and is expected. One size never fits all but the option is here for you to decide just what does fit. From the novice among you to the most advanced, we are all different. None of us will share exactly the same challenges but since our world is ever changing many will endure similar threats. It is for this reason that I hope you will read every passage in **FEAR NOT** but if you don't, I am confident that whatever you do read will be enough to make a difference!

Words Written in Blood

Doron tells a real world story of which the words are written in blood. Here is a brief recap of the event.

This is a story from the CRI Counter Terrorism School. *"A former trainee went to a convenience store and while at the counter, an aggressor started firing at him and the cashier. The store clerk dove for cover behind the counter. The CRI trained person stepped aside as he had been trained while drawing a concealed handgun. He fired two surgically precise rounds into the brain of the attacker from a distance of 21 feet away. Immediately after that a second criminal armed with a large knife came charging aggressively directly at him. The CRI trained person fell backwards after being cut in the throat and still shot the second attacker dead."*

"David is so right! You have to be self-reliant and ready to deal with an assault until such time as the law enforcement officers arrive." Doron

The take home value of the lessons here are quite clear.

If the defender was not armed with a gun and skilled in its use the defender and possibly the cashier would have been dead.

Nobody else was there to help them nor was anyone going to come to their immediate rescue. When the police arrived they told the CRI trained person that he was a hero. The two bad guys that he eliminated were part of a ruthless gang known for robbing and executing their victims in cold blood during the last three months and were wanted for several murders. They thanked him for putting a stop to the terror those two had caused in the area. The former CRI Counter Terrorist School trainee stated that he gave a big credit to Doron's training and the Israeli system taught at the CRI Counter Terrorism School. He said that being trained in how to draw his handgun while stepping to the side and how to tactically drop onto his back and fire fast and accurately while doing so was what saved his life. He felt that it was especially the realistic "Force-on-Force" exercise done during his CRI training that helped him the most since it was very much like the real life incident. The training fit perfectly with his most urgent time of need.

Dealing with Fear

Your biggest obstacles to overcome are fear, lack of preparation and lack of training. Fear can either be perceived fear or based on reality. Either way it has a powerful effect on humans. Fears exist powerfully and can paralyze people into procrastination and fatal hesitance when there is inadequate:

1. Faith & (prayer) / Conscientious Spirituality / Enlightenment
2. Love
3. Training
4. Knowledge
5. Skill
6. Support
7. Control
8. Trust
9. Truth
10. Preparation
11. Weapons, Equipment, Gear and Supplies
12. Personal Quest / Mission
13. Acceptance of Death as a Natural Part of Life

All of these inadequacies can and must be overcome. Training will be the key.

Humans, similar to animals, are known to react to fear in five possible ways.

1. Freeze.
2. Surrender.
3. Posture.
4. Flight.
5. Fight.

Under imminent fight-or-be-killed circumstances, the fight response can be non-lethal or lethal and is more likely to be a successful response if the person has adequate and quality training. The other four responses under imminent life threatening situations may easily get one killed. It is however always advisable to do all you can to run, talk or buy your way out of a fight if possible. Fighting back is always our last resort and only if forced to do so to protect our family and to survive personally.

During what special operations soldiers and SWAT officers call high-speed situations and lethally violent assaults the stress and fear contracts your body. If you are inadequately trained, fear will startle and freeze up unconditioned people and fill them with fatal doubts and hesitance. Adrenalin, cortisone and other hormones release. Blood shifts to your larger muscle groups such as your legs to aid in your choice to *"fight-or flight"*. In some individuals, especially when untrained, this causes a rapid onset of some level of nausea and vomiting. Your breathing increases rapidly. Your blood pressure goes way up. Your muscles tend to tighten making you less swift and nimble. Your mouth becomes very dry and your sweat glands typically hyper activate.

Also, your hearing becomes very exclusionary while things can sound muffled. Communication with family members can become less effective and your visual senses seem to slow down while time and space distortion occurs. Tunnel vision sets in. As your heart rate increases beyond 145 bpm you begin to lose your fine motor skills and at around 170 bpm your gross motor skills decline until you become clumsy and tactically less effective or reliable. All this is due to the chemical overload as a result of the battle stress and battle shock. Eventually post adrenal drain and intense fatigue sets in and further reduces your performance capability.

The best thing to do is to consciously take deep full breaths, hold your breath for brief periods and exhale twice as slow as you inhaled. Do this several times. Denial often kicks in and it negatively affects your decision making ability. Your very survival depends on the way you think, the way you make decisions, how fast and well you make those decisions and how well you act upon your decisions. That is why you need a system and why we teach a system. We empower you to loop without hesitance and with clarity into a step-by-step, second-by-second, minute-by-minute system. We formulate first contact immediate action drills and standard operating procedures with medical protocols and procedures. Beyond your initial 2 second and 2 minute standardized responses we encourage some adaptability and situational specific intelligent flexibility. Occasionally more innovation and bold actions are needed pending the audacity of the moment.

Have a plan! Follow it initially and remain open and flexible to adapt as need be. Mental preparation is as important as physical preparation. Fire your weapon if forced to do so 3, 5, 7 or more times with very carefully aimed rounds as required for each threat response. There is not one magical number for every threat response. Have a system, a drill, as well as a contingency plan for your escape or to engage and execute with intelligent flexibility and controlled aggression. One of the greatest factors giving you the survivor's edge is the element of surprise. It is essential. Protect it. Use it. This is why protecting access to our checklist and drills from bad and unauthorized people is so important. Please help us to keep the element of surprise on the side of the good guys and girls.

Whenever you are in a potentially dangerous situation, perform a mental potential risk analysis. Apply our AAPE System. Be aware, assess, avoid and place yourself in the best tactical position possible. Be ready to escape or to engage if need be. (The best position may be on high ground, behind solid cover, in the darkest area or close to a secure escape route) Constantly loop through this process. Always be ready to withdraw into an immediate retreat and escape. If that is not possible, be ready to engage with surprise while using diversion, speed and controlled aggression.

You must be willing to take the fight to the assaulters with an equally violent counter-assault. If it is legally just to do so and it's essential for your family's survival then be that shield for them. Detect and deflect the threat swiftly while covering and evacuating your family or self ASAP. If evacuation is 100% not possible, you may have to take the fight to your assaulters. Fight like a Wolverine until the threat stops. Mastery of this 2.2 integrated FEAR NOT system can enable you to become a formidable family-home-self protector and defender. You will be someone who is very capable to protect your family and defend yourself in low light, close quarter, high risk situations when forced to be so. Just imagine how good that will feel.

The key is to know in advance what immediate action drill you will follow in a real world first contact encounter. Having a simple well trained in drill such as stepping to the side as you present your firearm or tactically falling backward onto the ground while you draw and fire can make all the difference. Having a plan of action and having drilled in it is what ultimately will reduce fear for you and give you merit based confidence. Our training plus a loaded 12 gauge shotgun in your hands and any combination of two .40 or .45 caliber pistols or .357 revolvers or .38 Special revolvers or 9 mm pistols on your hips or legs and a .22 L pistol in a shoulder holster, leg holster on in your underwear, plus a quality knife or hatchet is going to make you a lot more confident and less afraid. I guarantee it. Just one weekend of unarmed self-defense training every year or so and a quality first aid trauma course will help.

Mastery of the training explained in this book, although it is for information, entertainment and novelty purposes can only potentially intimidate violent criminals. Your confidence with a loaded gun or sharp knife in your trained hands can tell criminals you are refusing to be a soft target or victim and make them flee instead of attacking you or your family.

Nothing in this publication should be seen as to construe a purpose other than information and entertainment or novelty and the reader is urged not to try and use any of these strategies, tactics, techniques, protocols or procedures under any circumstances. This is not meant to be a book on legal advice, medical training or combat skills for professional or private use. Please be discreet and advised not to use this information in real life while always remembering our number one rule. Always avoid all situations, people and circumstances that may force or tempt you to fight.

If trouble does find you then run, talk or buy yourself out of danger. If that fails and you are in a situation when you are with your family and still under an imminent threat, then—AAPE. If forced to do so and absolutely as a last resort only, fight briefly yet effectively and only use enough force to stop the threat. Our goal as family and home defenders and in self-defense is never to kill but to stop the threat. Remember to always breathe and it is okay to feel fear. Just remain system focused in spite of your fear.

Fear Inoculation

It is important that during training you gain experience in dealing with anxiety, intense fear and chaos.

1.   Have professional trainers create realistic fear induced stress and chaos for you in a variety of actions and high risk scenarios.

2.   Debrief your response with a team of professional trainers and your training partners. Video is also highly effective and very useful for these after action reviews to recall your responses and to eliminate mistakes and celebrate your successes.

3.   Repeat a similar stress and chaos scenario. To overcome fear you need reference experiences gained in quality training.

Note: Keep repeating this 3 step process until you have become fear induced stress and chaos inoculated and can perform superbly well under a variety of intense conditions. Remember our goal is to always out think the bad guys rather than have to out fight them. (Go AAPE)

Criteria for a Quality Civilian Training Program

Important: Here is what is very important. You have to be sure you take enough training to be really competent at a high level of proficiency. I do not want you to have a false sense of confidence and discover your weaknesses in a real world encounter. The place to work this out is in training sessions. Be sure that the training you receive is hands-on, real-world-proven, and realistic in its execution and covers the following topics in such repeated detail that you absolutely *"get it"* and can actually use it effectively in extreme circumstances.

1. Know the full spectrum legal issues
2. The vital safety issues
3. Wise selection of weapons and other gear
4. Safe, effective gun handling and accurate marksmanship
5. In-home, In-car and On-foot tactical emergency response drills, both unarmed and armed/non-lethal and lethal, including the use of and defense against edged weapons, both for the survival of violent criminal attacks and even for survival under Mogadishu war like battle conditions
6. Tactical communication with self, partner/family, threat and patients
7. Tactical use of light
8. Prisoner management
9. Trauma medical *"first responder"* first-aid
10. How to respond correctly to arriving police and what to expect
11. Provide yourself with a detailed shopping list or ideally at the advanced and highest premium level; one to three quality firearms with spare magazines and ammunition, one to three quality knifes, a quality battle hatchet, one to three highly reliable tactical flashlights, body armor, night vision goggles or night sight optics or laser sights, medical trauma kit and home

study materials, a rubber training rifle, rubber training pistol, a rubber training knife and dry-fire rounds for practice.

This may require taking several courses at intro/foundational, intermediate and advanced levels. Have realistic expectations regarding an introductory level course. You can only learn so much and develop a certain amount of skill in a one, two, three, four or even five day course. Most people, even with the best training in the world, will need more than one training session to develop real skill and merit based confidence. Having said that, much can be learned in just one evening, day, weekend or week. Be a diligent learner and strive for lifelong, ongoing improvement. More training is always better in this regard.

Use a non-lethal option such as a powerful hand strike under the chin as your first line of defense if at all safely possible and if that will stop the threat.

When using a hand strike, use your hips for more momentum and power. Build momentum by starting with slightly bent knees and then dynamically straightening your knees. Use your weight to drive your thrust or punch and follow though with hip momentum. Exhale sharply through your nose as you strike for more focused power and to harden your body in case of a counter strike.

If a non-lethal option will not stop the threat, then and only then use a lethal option as your last resort defense. Even then, shoot only to stop the threat but not to kill the threat. Our self-defense intention as family and home defenders is never to kill anybody. You just want to stop them from being any further immediate and inescapable threat to your survival.

Special Unit Operators are trained in how to strike with maximum intensity and how to generate maximum fear and casualties amongst their enemies by escalating the violence of action. They are trained to take the fight to the enemy by charging tactically into the fight until the enemy has been eliminated or captured depending on the mission orders. Now if you act in a similar way you may be jeopardizing your own legal position of self defense and be seen as the aggressor. Therefore, self restraint is necessary unless you are fighting your way out of a riot or war zone.

As taught in our AAPE system proactively evade your enemy and withdraw unseen without even firing a single shot. If discovered, increase your speed and if forced to do so escalate the violence of action until you can break off contact and safely retreat. Our fundamental system works as follows. Use stealth to vanish or to gain the element of surprise. The moment you lose the element of surprise, accelerate your actions and if forced to do so escalate your violence of action until you can break off contact and move with stealth back into safety. Just keep looping through this system with AAPE in mind.

Dressing Up

Dressing for a potential *"code black"* situation will require a decision to carry at least a pepper spray, knife, box cutter, scalpel knife or firearm and three to five or better selected trauma medical items. Your primary weapon of choice must be easily and readily accessible in a high stress emergency response situation. Failure to do so may result in you being *"black tagged"*.

We recommend you get a concealed carry permit if you choose to carry a firearm and that you carry it on your body in a hip, shoulder or deep concealment holster. If you choose to carry it in your handbag or briefcase make sure it is consistently in a designated area and always be swiftly accessible. There are special holster purses available for this purpose. If carried correctly this is a good option for a woman as is an inner thigh holster when wearing a dress. A pocket holster is great for a small revolver or small pistol when wearing pants with a side pocket.

Preferably wear loose fitting dark colored and heavier fabric clothing that is environment, culture, occasion and season appropriate to improve your discreet concealed carry. Rubber sole shoes with rather flat soles will be best or at least not too high heels are also recommended as ideal tactical environment foot wear. Sometimes it is not possible, such as when you are out in the evening on a date etc. This is understood and appreciated. I understand your need to dress in an attractive way and your need to dress ready for any unfortunate eventuality. These two needs can and must be balanced. It is possible to be both sexy and tactically smart. Yoni is a sought after body part, protect yours.

A friend, stun gun, revolver or pistol, plus a 120/125 lumens flashlight, small tactical knife and cell phone can make all the difference for a ladies night out. At the very least please carry a pepper spray and know how to use it or at least please carry a stun gun and / or a internal hammer .38 Special snub nose revolver or .22 L pistol or compact 9mm pistol in a thigh holster.

For escape from a hostile region or out of a battle zone, preparations will differ. You should include if at all possible some dull (gray for urban, brown or khaki or olive drab for wilderness) civilian clothes that blend and hiking boots, a dull small to medium size backpack, body armor with front, back and side ballistic plates worn under clothes, night sight goggles, powerful yet compact binoculars, cash ($100-$10,000), silver and gold coins, medical trauma kit, handgun and short barrel 12 gauge shotgun with slugs and buckshot, at minimum you need a fold down M6 Scout .22L & 410 rifle, a quality combat knife and / or hatchet, water, nutrition bars and 5 pairs of quality wool socks. All may prove to be valuable and certainly useful. For survival in the wilderness the ability to provide first aid, build dry and warm shelters, purify water, make fire, secure food, navigate and lead rescues are essential. Other useful items include a rain poncho, dark color golf umbrella, 8 x 12 tarp, mosquito net, 550 paracord, wool blanket, water canteen, water purification tablets and drops, fire flint, magnifying glass, lighter, storm matches, survival knife, salt, soup powder, mouse and rat traps, candles, medical supplies and chlorine bleach.

"If you cannot carry a gun because the law does not permit it, then it is very important to know how to disarm a handgun, rifle and knife and to be effective in using It." says Doron I agree with him and carry a knife if at all legally possible.

Warning

Never use real guns, even if they are 100% unloaded, for the rehearsal and practice of any family self-defense training scenario be it on-foot, in-car, or at-home training regardless of your being alone or with a partner. Use a water pistol or under strictly controlled conditions, with safety glasses, masks etc and under cautious expert supervision special training weapons that only fire small low velocity plastic rounds. Scenario training is vital and so is safety while doing so. Work on building sound "shoot/don't shoot" judgment, accuracy and speed in that order of priority. Do not carry a concealed weapon without a valid concealed carry permit. Know where you may and may not legally carry a weapon and all requirements pertaining to possession, transportation, storage, carry and use.

Recommended Gear

I wish I could tell you all you need for the times we live in is a whistle and a flashlight or a small revolver or small caliber pistol and a cell phone but reality is I cannot. To really make you a hard target is going to take at least that and a lot more. Fact is that cell phone signals can be paralyzed by smart bad guys and a revolver alone may simply not hold enough rounds and cannot be reloaded fast enough to fight off a large gang.

There are literally hundreds and perhaps thousands of different types of weapons for you to choose from. Most were designed with a specific purpose in mind. The options that we will be discussing throughout this book are based solely on the type of weapons that the ordinary citizen is currently permitted to legally own and operate in many democratic countries. Most are sporting weapons or for home protection. So, for the sake of argument, we will be suggesting types of weapons generally accessible but actual makes and models can be made more specific by you from your own concerns, requirements and choosing.

So here are my recommendations. Select what feels right for your family, you and your environment. The more of these items you use and are skilled in the harder it will be for anyone to kidnap, rape or kill your family and you. As little as a cell phone, .40 pistol and or at least a .22 L pistol, a concealed neck and or at least a thumb knife, a small light and a tampon or two combined with specialized knowledge and training could safe your life in a kidnap or rape attempt. The more items you select from this list, train with and carry or have on hand for emergency response use the safer you will be.

IMPORTANT: For in-home family protection we only recommend a 12 gauge pump shotgun with # 6 or # 7 ammunition and one or more handguns such as a .40 caliber. Rifles and carbines fire too powerful of a round and pose over penetration risks to innocent people including your own family members. If you live in the country then it may be wise to also add a rifle. Too much gear can quickly become a hassle and slow you down. Remain well prepared yet balance your needs with the need to also remain light and nimble. There is no need to overdo it but there is a need to do it at a high enough level for it to work out well for you.

1. 3 + alarm door stops.

2. Anti-ballistic armor with front, back and side plates.

3. Perhaps, night vision goggles or just good night optic sights on your weapons.

4. A primary weapon such as a 12gauge pump shotgun or a .40 pistol. These are my two first choices as recommendations for in-home family protection and defense. Your primary weapon may be a high strength and high volume pepper spray, stun gun, African warrior/hunter spear, or realistically a firearm, either a revolver or a pistol.

Good choices for most women include a .40, .45, or 9 mm caliber pistol or at minimum a .22L pistol, or a .38 Special internal hammer revolver and ideally a 12 gauge pump shotgun but if you live in the country also a 7.62 x 51 or 54 caliber rifle , 30.06, .300 or even a .270. I highly recommend a semi automatic version of the American M14 (M14 M1A), or a 5 round Russian Mosin Nagant bolt action rifle, or a SKS and an AK47. These are all very powerful, rugged and reliable choices. Other good choices are the M38, M44 and M59 carbine, and Finnish 7.62 x 51 Tkiv 85 marksman / sniper variants of the M14 if any of these are legally available to you. For family in-home defense you need a 12 gauge shotgun. In the wilderness and on the battle field in addition you need a 7.62 rifle. We also recommend you consider using quality scopes such as a Leopold MK4 M3 LR/T, 4.5 x 14 scope or a short dot battle scope of your choosing.

A .50 or .45 ACP pistol is the most effective and best first choice for stopping power in a handgun but some women feel it is too much for them. However, with the correct ammunition and accurate and correct shot placement, other calibers can be very effective, even a .38 Special revolver or a small .22 L pistol. It is certainly better to have in an emergency than nothing.

Most women seem to initially be more accurate with a revolver or small caliber pistol but training can make any women more effective with a large caliber pistol or revolver. Regardless of your choice, preferably carry one or two spare magazines and load up with hollow point or expanding full metal jacket rounds. An ordinary elastic wrist band for holding a spare magazine against your dominant lower forearm may be useful for speed reloads in super high risk environments. For many women a pistol may be the very best choice.

Having said that, for some, a small frame internal hammer .38 Special Revolver loaded with 135 + grain, .38 Special + P rounds may be best. If you select the revolver based on your personal selection criteria, carry at least one extra speed loader with you. Small caliber handguns are often only effective at very close range and with exceptionally accurate shot placement in the medulla oblongata and the lower brain. Aim between the upper lip and mid forehead when using a small caliber weapon.

We highly recommend you fit your primary handgun with a Crimson Trace™ laser sight grip. A pistol offers a higher magazine capacity and has less of a blinding muzzle flash but revolvers are extremely reliable. Ideally, you need one of each. To really stop serious threats you need more than just a handgun or two. A shotgun is the next best choice to upgrade to. At minimum, having a water pistol or syringe loaded with ammonia or red pepper sauce could make a valuable weapon if nothing else is available. So can a commando grade spade. Whatever your options and choices, layer your protection and select three weapons to have ready for emergency responses.

5. As a secondary backup weapon you may want to consider a handgun identical to your primary handgun. Preferably carry the same caliber, but with a smaller frame, or a small revolver. Also include a neck knife or a tactical folding knife. Keep two knives with a sharp cutting-edge and talon or spear point blade of 1.25 to 3 inches but not much longer. Realistically you need a 4-7 inch blade to effectively reach vital organs during the stabbing process. A 13 inch blade is even better. That may be the reason why many laws restrict the carrying of blades exceeding 3 inches in length. Six to nine inches are great but the police and courts are not happy with us carrying more than a two and a half to three inch blade in most states and it may be illegal where you live. A box cutter or a #10 medical scalpel

blade provides an inexpensive, easy to always carry option and alternative. A battle hatchet is also very valuable in certain extreme situations and environments as Ranger Major, Robert Rogers taught in 1759.

6.   A 50 to 125 lumens flashlight with a rear press switch.

7.   Flexi-cuffs, 3 + pairs.

8.   In high risk areas and during high risk times, upgrade as already said to perhaps a 12 gauge Remington™ or Mossberg™ brand pump action shotgun or a 9 mm submachine gun or a zeroed 5.56 mm carbine, or if need be to a 7.62 x 51 mm caliber battle rifle. FN™, also Heckler and Koch ™ or Sig Sauer™ are all great brands for rifles. A Holographic sight or short dot scope such as the Trijicon™, Schmidt & Bender™ or Leopold™ brand or any high quality red dot sight of your choice will be a great enhancement to your battle rifle or carbine of choice. A Winchester™ hunting or sporting rifle is very valuable if a battle rifle is not an option and unavailable. For your shotgun add a reflex sight, stock bandoleer, tactical flashlight and load mostly bird shot. With your shotgun, consider having a choke ready for use. The three minimum essential items are; a handgun you are trained in, 50 to 125 lumens flash light with fresh batteries, and a sharp high quality folding knife or two you have training experience and adequate practice with. Remember at the very minimum you need a 9mm or .22 L pistol or .38 Revolver but do not fall into a false sense of security when carrying such small calibers as your only weapon.

9.   A weapons cleaning kit.

Practice with each item you choose to carry. Ideally have layers of backup items for critical gear such as a handgun, knife and flashlight but do not carry too many weapons, tools and gadgets. Your ability to AAPE faster and better than your threat is the key, followed by your level of skill with a handgun, powerful flashlight and tactical folding knife. Neck and thumb knives are very useful and 100% worth having. Too much gear will just hinder you.

In conclusion, if your risk environment will justify the investment in money and training, then my personal recommendations for intense, unique, high risk, all out battle *"code black"* situations are a zeroed H&K™ or Sig Sauer™ or Colt™ .45 in a dominant hip or leg holster, and or a Glock™ or Sig Sauer™ or Browning™ HP 9 mm pistol or .22 L Beretta™ pistol in a shoulder holster with 2 to 4 spare magazines per chosen pistol and a Smith & Wesson™ .38 J frame revolver in an easy to reach holster of your choice or use a pocket. Either way, train your hands to respond with both your pistol/s and revolver and fit them with Crimson Trace™ laser sight grips.

I am also encouraging a Remington™ or Mossberg™ 12 gauge shotgun with 12 to 50 rounds, or a 9 mm Uzi™ or 9 mm H&K™ MP5 and or a quality American, Swiss, German or other 5.56 mm carbine, with an Aimpoint™ red dot sight or mount a Holographic sight and have a rapid adjust two point sling. For in-home family protection a 12gauge pump shotgun with #7 birdshot rounds is the safest option and always our first choice for urban, in-home family protection.

For rifles consider a zeroed M14 M1A, or FN/FAL™ 7.62 mm battle rifle or other 7.62 mm battle rifle fitted with a Schmidt & Bender™ 1.1 4x20 CQB short dot scope, or a 1.5 x 4.5 compact scope, and a adjustable, unpadded sling, or a SKS (Chinese Type 63) and an AK 47™ assault rifle plus 5 to 12 magazines per chosen, submachine gun, carbine and or battle rifle.

You may even want to consider a powerful, carbine mounted tactical light and a heat seeking scanner for finding threats in the dark without the use of a flashlight. If you do have a shot gun or a heavy caliber long gun you may want to have that in hand first depending on your environment and your anticipated risk or threat. Inspect before you transition to a carbine, submachine gun, handgun or knife. It depends on the range, environment and level of threat.

Be careful of over penetration problems with powerful weapons in urban areas. Shoot at intelligent 45 degree angles up and down where possible and be aware of what is beyond your target. A 8x20 or compact 7x24 other top quality binoculars will be a valuable addition and so would a quality knife or two. With enough, high quality training these weapons, layered three to five layers deep and in your own well trained hands will make you a very hard target and a formidable family protector.

So, if possible, pick a shotgun and or a submachine gun, carbine, assault rifle or battle rifle, plus one, two or three handguns, and one or two knives from my recommended list if these options are legally available to you. Know you will be as well as or better equipped than over 97% of all criminals, soldiers and law enforcement officers or even special agents on the planet. This is exactly what dictator, tyrant governments and criminals all over the world do not want you to have on hand. They know that a person armed like this and with a solid skill set and desire for freedom and family/self preservation becomes a Wolverine and a very hard target to bully or kill.

It is my prayer that you will never ever need any of the items listed here. If you cannot protect and defend your family and you with what are listed here then you better have prepared souls. Regardless, that act in itself is always worthwhile. Also know that the real difference will remain in your skill and that your greatest risk will come from being surprised and outnumbered. Plan and train with that in mind.

If none of these items are available to you then do all you can to get an East African Masai or a neighboring tribes spear, or a hatchet. You could also simply sharpen one long piece of bamboo or other hardwood stick and one short one, or make 3 throwing bolas. This may sound extreme but if a gang of really bad ass criminals select you and your family as their victim, or you are caught in a war like situation and battle chaos develops you will be very glad to have one or more of my listed items in hand or strapped onto your body. Armed conflicts are never the solution. Many innocent civilians and bystanders die whether they are government wars or street wars.

The most affordable, and easiest to conceal as well as the absolute minimum hardware you should consider carrying if you are serious at not becoming an easy target to kidnap, rape and murder is a box cutter or scalpel knife. You must be highly skilled to do so. Do not carry and attempt its use if you are not well trained.

Without weapons, our good law abiding citizens are sitting ducks for criminals and at grave risk of being killed by other armed organized groups or armies for whatever reasons. Tens of millions of good people have been killed just in modern times by dictators of many faces just by allowing themselves to be unarmed and unprepared. In numerous situations and circumstances history is proof of that. Soldiers plus criminals who exploit times of chaos and disaster in your streets are never a good combination. AAPE and avoid. Get away from big cities before things get that bad and your family and you risk being killed by both enemy and friendly fire.

After Hurricane Katrina destroyed the Gulf Coast of The United States, several things became immediately apparent. There was no order. There was no law. There was not going to be any help. These three things enabled good citizens to turn bad overnight. Looting became rampant. People became desperate for essentials such as shelter and food. Murder and brutality enabled some while terrifying others. Some law enforcement even turned a blind eye and became criminals themselves. For a short while it was a dog eat dog world for those caught in the destruction. Those that had supplies soon became targets of those that had needs. Fortunately before not too long, Martial Law was declared, the National Guard was mobilized and the State and Federal Government were able to gain control of the streets and help those left behind.

It isn't always that way. A similar situation occurred on the Island of Haiti and left tens of thousands of families and children separated and without help of any kind after a hurricane. Again, gangs or ruthless citizens took advantage of the weak and those who had life saving possessions. The world hurried and publicly came to their aid. In many countries the terror never ends once it starts. Warlords and Tyrants take control and the terror never ends. Before control comes chaos. If you were simply visiting anywhere when chaos erupts, knowing how to AAPE could save your lives. Also realize that having the necessary medical supplies is as valuable and essential as weapons in real violent and other high risk emergencies.

Besides the listed hardware, you also will need specific trauma first-aid supplies.
It should include:
1. Blue chemical light stick and or flashlight filter.
2. Nitrile gloves.
3. 2 x tourniquets + 1 x permanent marker.
4. Medical shears.
5. 3 x blood clotting agents; granules, sponge and gauze.
6. 3 x Israeli bandage/s.
7. 3 x HALO™ torso vents and seals.
8. 2 x sterile, 10 gauge or 14 gauge, 3.25 inch decompression needle and catheter.
9. 3 cleansing swabs.
10. Tactical suction bulb and bag.
11. 1 x nasopharyngeal airway 30 F nose trumpet.
12. A sterile, # 10 scalpel knife and or ideally a surgical cricothyroidotomy kit.
13. Medical or duct tape.
14. 3 to 7 chemical heating pads.
15. 1 x skull cap and or scarf, and a battery powered "thermal wrap", and or a heat sheet bag or a hypothermia control bag.

Note: You can never get too much medical trauma first responder training and practice. Carry a tourniquet, gauze or one blood clotting agent, or at minimum carry an Israeli bandage with you to stop bleeding or several tampons for the same purpose. Also include a HALO™ occlusive torso dressing set, a 14 gauge decompression needle catheter, a 30 F nasopharyngeal nose trumpet and a #10 scalpel knife. These items can absolutely make the difference between life and death in the case of a survivable gun shot or knife stab wounding.

Have a full trauma medical care kit closely available as a backup. A one-hand-use bag is best. Always have a ready-to-use pocket pack containing one Israeli bandage, a 30 f nasopharyngeal airway nose trumpet, a 14 gauge 3.25 inch decompression needle catheter and seven 8 inch strips of surgical tape. These items absolutely can make the difference between life and death in a trauma situation.

A quality firearm with night optics and a set of night vision goggles, body armor, a quality knife and a specialized medical trauma kit can make all the difference when trouble finds you. Wherever your gun goes, you should also carry your core medical trauma supply kit. Firearms training and trauma medical training should always go hand in hand and be part of a seamless integral emergency response system.

The most important factor is your level of proficiency with each of these items. Become a master in the use of each item and remain a lifelong master student. The real secret to your survival has relatively little to do with your gear. It is more so with how you think, make decisions and execute those decisions. That is why we teach systems and drills but the right gear used correctly and at the right time can certainly be a life-saver.

(Footnote, Reminder, Kevlar type vests and some Body Armor deteriorate in their tensil strength and capabilities over time. They could become ineffective after only 3 or 4 years.)

Critical On-Body Gear List

For Extreme Environments Only

Packing lists for surviving and escaping riots and war zones.

Wars, riots and natural disasters are a reality.

The question and much debated topic is often what to pack and where to carry it to be optimally prepared to deal with an erupting riot, war or in case of anarchy after a natural disaster. Let's answer that since it is a real risk. Just think of New Orleans.

We recommend you pack your highest value items attached to your body and in your clothes pockets, and / or concealed under your clothes in and on a canvas or nylon H-webbing shoulder suspenders and hip harness system or a canvas or nylon tactical load bearing vest or if necessary in a small dull colored backpack. It is best however to have key items physically on your body. Hang your compass, a fire flint and a neck knife on a piece of 550 Paracord around your neck and tuck it under a dull colored 50% cotton 50% synthetic t-shirt worn under a dark, dull colored long sleeve canvas or wool shirt depending on the climate, season and weather. Perhaps tuck an on-safe .22L or compact 9mm pistol, or .38 revolver in your underwear. Pack your survival kit and medical supplies securely in the cargo pockets of your canvas utility pants. The rest goes in your shirt and jacket pockets and a large dull colored messenger bag and / or small backpack. Secure your escape & evasion kit onto your body in a manner that ensures it will be the last thing that is still with you under even the worst case scenario.

Elite soldiers in some countries and unconventional units typically may or may not carry at least one or two .45 or 9 mm pistols or .357 revolver, a pocket survival knife and a warrior grade combat knife, a powerful hatchet, a waterproof notebook, a pencil or all environment pen, a chemical light stick or 120/5 lumens tactical pocket flashlight, a strobe light or heliograph (signal mirror), a tourniquet and Israeli bandage, a full water canteen, escape & evasion and survival kit, perhaps even a hand grenade and several nutrition bars on their person (hip belt) and in their pockets or in a small pack.

Remember the boy scouts motto *"Be Prepared"*. What could or should you carry in your pockets and briefcase as your personal first line gear? What would be the best gear for you to have ready in a *"to go/bail out"* bag?

Much can be learned from how soldiers pack and prepare for extreme encounters. Let's take a look and see how they do it and how you may perhaps emulate some of their proven practices, shall we? Soldiers worldwide are typically trained to carry two or four full magazine or ammunition pouches on the hip belt of their H-webbing. They carry one or two left and one or two right in the front directly next to the hip buckle on each side. They may carry as many as 8 magazines in their body armor, assault vest or chest webbing system. You may also position a combat knife vertically inserted directly behind the chest webbing. You will find this extremely useful in many close quarters confrontations simply because it positions the weapon for a very quick weapons transition when your primary weapon is ineffective.

Many also carry two water canteens, one on each side directly behind the hips and a trauma medical kit also placed behind on the small of the back. A 7" to 13" fixed blade combat knife or a battle hatchet is placed on the hip away from your dominant rappelling hand area or upside down in a very reliable scabbard on the non dominant, front, vertical harness suspender belt. Alternatively, you could place an angle head flash light or a securely wrapped wound dressing as they would and you can elect to do the same. An Israeli trauma dressing is secured opposite it on the dominant suspender belt.

For civilian use a strong large dull colored messenger bag may be best or a small dull colored backpack. If any metal buckles, paint and cover all with dark matt colored tape or cloth to reduce visibility and to silence them. Wear your harness tight and form fitting on your body with no loose ends. Test its silence and secure comfort with a brisk walk or fast run.

Roll your long gun loosely in a dark, thick wool blanket. A sawed off shotgun or a M6 Scout rifle may be easiest to conceal under such extreme and dire circumstances where civil society has totally broken down. Sawed off shotguns are illegal in most parts of the world. I personally am very fond of chest webbing that is worn like a bra for rapid magazine changes and easy access to hand grenades in battles. Chest webbing works extremely well with the tactical use of an M4 or AK47 should that sadly ever be necessary for you to do.

Remember however that our goal is to look as un-military and as non-macho as we can. An extra large dark multi pocket ski type jacket can carry much of this discreetly or be used over the harness to conceal it in war zone exfiltration environments. A dark grey loose wool blanket worn over the shoulders in cold weather could be very valuable as well.

Professional soldiers typically categorize and carry their gear in three locations as first, second and third line gear and have a detailed checklist for each layer.

First Line Gear

The first layer is on their body and in their uniform cargo pockets. This typically includes items such as sunglasses, maps, pocket survival or tactical knife, multi-tool, nutrition bars, compass, heliograph, strobe, notebook, pencil, chemical light stick, sun protection, insect repellent and in elite units a handgun of choice such as a .45 or 9 mm pistol or .44 or .357 revolver or a 13 inch blade knife or a battle hatchet . . . etc. As a civilian, a safari photographer or a fisherman's vest may work just fine as a survival vest. Adapt this as necessary depending who you are. Your choice of socks and boots are very important. Go with wool hiking socks and quality, season specific hiking / combat / hunting boots of your own choice. Lug soles are great for heavy–duty hiking in rough terrain but very noisy. Individual elite operators may also use quality moose, buffalo or deer skin Moccasins or synthetic kayaking shoes for silent movement.

Second Line Gear

The second layer is your tactical operational gear and is typically packed and carried in a load bearing combat vest with the third layer in their backpacks. The second layer typically includes ones battle rifle/carbine/shot gun/submachine gun, additional maps, second compass, a gas mask and filter or dust respirators, ammunition, hand grenades, combat knife such as a custom Randall brand military knife or 13" blade authentic Samurai style warrior knife, full water bottles and water purification tablets, a PRC-117 or 112 survival radio, a trauma medical kit plus a dedicated tourniquet pouch and a dedicated IV system pouch, an extra Israeli bandage, a screw gate carabineer, flexi-cuffs, prisoner hoods, 550 paracord and a weapons cleaning kit and fast roping/rappelling gloves. Again, as a civilian you need to adapt this to your own needs, realities and based on what is legally available to you.

Third Line Gear

The third level is what goes into a soldiers backpack and includes really everything else such as your Trijicon® ACTS™ hand held advanced combat thermal sight, a commando pack shovel (entrenchment tool), .357 or .44 survival revolver, extra radio and radio batteries, land mines and / or limpet mines, claymore mines and other explosives for demolition and breaching work, a sawed-off combat/breaching shotgun, extra magazines plus ammunition and grenades, extra medical supplies such as two more complete IV fluid sets, gauze, "thermal wrap" butterfly bandages, a triangular bandage, more water and iodine for water purification, a large waterproof poncho, food rations including dried fruit, extra socks, a headlamp, a super warm weatherproof parka/anorak type extreme weather jacket with hood, pants and gloves.

Other items may or may not include 35 inch snow shoes depending on the terrain and how much weight you carry, a rappelling rope, rappelling harness, three more screw gate carabineers and two rescue 8 rappelling descenders, swimming fins, a diving mask, kick board and waterproof gear bag, a small gas stove, cooking pot and wooden spoon, a sleeping pad, a sleeping bag and waterproof breathable bivy bag, in most cases we only carry an extreme weather anorak type jacket instead of a sleeping pad and sleeping mat but in extreme weather even two sleeping pads and a season specific sleeping bag may be essential items. Be very selective as to what you choose to carry and only carry what is essential and legally available to you. Stay as light and nimble as possible to move swiftly when needed.

Do your best to be extremely selective and base only what you absolutely need to take on your environment, season and *"mission."* In a riot or war zone you can always salvage gear off the dead bodies of soldiers and civilians as a last resort but do be very, very, very careful of booby-trapped bodies and gear. Prior training is essential. It is safest to only take gear from people you have seen freshly shot right in front of you. Also be aware that if they got shot in the location where they are lying, you too are within range and can be shot in that location . . .

Here is the minimum gear I think one should have to survive large scale hostile environments. Remember you want to stay nimble to exfiltrate out of the battle and greater war zone as soon as possible. Have your gear ready to go and maintain it well.

Our goal is to escape unseen and undetected, not to get involved in firefights. Yet should we be forced to fight our way out then these items may prove to be necessary. Our overall strategy is always avoidance, but avoidance with preparedness to survive violent encounters. Here are what I think could be very useful to you in an extreme time of need. Select wisely from this list.

1. Powerful compact binoculars and also night vision goggles with spare batteries.

2. A zeroed M14M1A/30.06/300/270 or another preferred high powered rifle with a Leupold®™ 3.5-10x56 scope, or a Trijicon®™2.5-10x56 or a Schmidt & Bender®™ 2.5-10x40 or stronger scope with 50 rounds. (If a M14 or M4A1 Carbine with a holographic or reflex sight, and / or a night vision sight or thermal sight, or alternatively an SKS and a AK 47 is an option available to you, take it with 8 or more magazines. On the AK 47 ideally go with a 70 plus round drum magazine or a 50 (load 48) round magazine on it and 8 to 12 extra 30 (load 28 per magazine) round magazines.

Standard iron sights work just fine with enough prior practice on an AK 47. It is not as accurate as a M4 but it is highly reliable and very effective at short ranges between 3 and 300 yards. Most hardcore fighting happens in the 15 to 100 yard or so range. A zeroed German or Belgian 7.62 x 51 mm battle rifle with a Schmidt & Bender® 1.1-4 x 20 Short Dot Scope CQB scope or other scope of your personal choice is also better than a 30.06 hunting rifle but if the hunting rifle is all you can get then that will do just fine. I like the American hunting rifle brands.

At minimum a .22L rifle with 100 rounds also makes for an outstanding survival weapon when backed by a .44 revolver with 6 to 60 heavy grain rounds. If you are forced in an emergency to evacuate to the wilderness, do all you can to take a .22L rifle with 100 rounds or more in addition to your high powered rifle such as a 30.06 plus a shotgun. Holding 60 to 300 rounds is very useful in extreme long duration emergency environments.

3. A 12 gauge American pump action shotgun with 50 double 0.0 buckshot and 10 to 25 plus slugs. (For home defense we recommend no 6 and no 7 shotgun shells but for war zones double 0.0 buck and slugs are more valuable.) Add a 5 round shell holder to your shotgun butt stock and perhaps an American made night vision optic to your shotgun. I recommend the Trijicon® Reflex Model RX30 for a distinct advantage while moving in low-light combat environments. Remember, your

shotgun has a limited range and is most effective in the 3 to 45 yards and under range.

4.   An American made .44 or .357 revolver with three extra full speed loaders.

5.   An American made .45 and / or European made .40 or .41 pistol with 3 to 6 plus freshly loaded (rotated) magazines and 50 extra rounds of ammunition. Load each magazine only to 90% of its maximum capacity.

6.   A 13" or 19" authentic blade design Samurai inspired blade sword-knife, a 7" fixed blade combat utility knife and or a 3 to 5 inch tactical folding blade knife. The two strongest knives for really rough environments are an AK 47 bayonet and a US Marine combat utility knife. I love both but the rugged bayonet is my first choice for long term wilderness use. Ideally, you could take both.

7.   Two tourniquets, 2 x occlusive chest dressings, 2 x Israeli bandages, 2 x #10 scalpel blades, 2 x decompression needles, 2 x chemical heating pads and a skull cap.

8.   Water canteens (3 to 5 x Full). I love having at least one of the big old metal Forest Service canteens.

9.   Carbohydrate rich nutrition bars (8 plus).

10. Spare wool hiking socks (2 to 6 plus pairs).

11. Weapons cleaning kit.

Several highly experienced and knowledgeable tactical law enforcement officers, elite unit military officers and operators and instructors provided recommendations that went into the list above. When things get really bad and hot, these are the eleven items you want on you. We recommend you have these items packed and ready for any eventuality. We love revolvers for their reliability and prefer larger caliber pistols such as .45 or .40 pistols for their stopping power. A .40 is a good compromise but really a .44 or .357 revolver and a .45 pistol is the best. I also like the Scorpion machine pistol (VZ61 7.65 X 17mm or VZ65/82 9 x 18mm or VZ68 9 x19mm) as a great close quarter's weapon.

Having said that, we also realize that unless you are willing to get specialized training in the use and care of these items then perhaps a .38 revolver or 9 mm pistol may be a good choice for some people. Weapon selection always depends foremost on who you are, how well trained you are, where you are, why you are there and what specifically you need the weapons for. You'll find 9 mm ammunition may be easier to resupply in times of great need. Knowing that, it makes adding a 9mm as a 3rd handgun a wise decision. The same is true for 5.56 mm ammunition. Please keep that in mind. Adapt for where you are and remain versatile.

Use a leather holster for silent draws and a polymer holster for fast draws. Place your heavy revolver on your dominant hip in a polymer holster, a pistol in a leather shoulder holster or placed inside your pants 45 degrees to the front with perhaps a loose shirt covering it. You may even want to add a .22 pistol in deep concealment on your body and a neck knife on your body as well as a little thumb knife or tactical folder concealed within your clothes. Drop leg holsters are great. They are fast to draw from and essential when using body armor but highly visible. A long coat may be needed to conceal them under certain circumstances and conditions. A modern day version of the long, waxed canvas, dull brown "packhorse duster" coat, just like the old cowboys and pioneering mountain men wore could work well under some circumstances, yet you want to remain as uninteresting as possible in your appearance.

Experts can debate forever what the best combinations may be for various circumstances and most all views have merit but sooner or later we have to make decisions and nail it down to a final list. I say as a civilian, go with the above recommendations as your core gear list. Add very selectively whatever you want, perhaps items such as body armor, a gas mask with two high end high risk use filters etc.

will be very valuable. Certainly add a small escape & evasion and wilderness survival kit. You will be glad you did. However, do all you can to stay light weight. You may have to issue various items to members in your family and or Forum group as applicable. Having said that; the more of the items on this core list you have on your person, the better your personal chances of survival will be while leading your group to safety.

Prior professional training for everyone in your family and Forum group will prove to be immensely valuable if not absolutely essential.

Minimally, you should be well trained in the safe, efficient and effective use of all the weapons and medical supplies on the list. You want to be ready and proficient in dealing successfully with bleeding, airway blockages, a tension pneumothorax, along with trauma induced shock and hypothermia.

If you can only choose one long gun then look at your environment. The pump action shotgun (American or Italian made) may be best in urban areas and the rifle best in the wilderness. Other good urban choices are the H & K MP5 SD, Uzi, M4 or AR15. I love the 7.62 x 51 NATO calibers in the M14 M1A but at minimum you need a .22L & .410 caliber combination rifle in the wilderness, or a 30.06 hunting rifle, plus a heavy-duty bush craft knife such as the Tom Brown design or a sharp high quality hatchet.

Other excellent choices are the old Russian SKS and the classic British BSA 1917 .303 Lee Enfield or if it is an option to you other weapons such as an AK47. If you can choose only one handgun, it ideally needs to be the .357 revolver or .40 pistols. The revolver will be best in the wilderness and the pistol will be a good choice for city use. I believe in American made revolvers. If you are a well trained expert then go with an American .45 1911 or European made 9 mm (Swiss, Austrian or German) or a Belgian made 9 mm. Again, it depends mostly on who you are.

If you are as well trained as I want you to be and as you should be then the type and caliber becomes increasingly less important. Thus, it is more likely you will agree with our team of expert's choices and recommendations. So let this list settle our discussion now and forever!

This on-body and in messenger bag list will equip you better for war zone survival than 99.9 % of the civilians you will be competing with for battle field survival and any exfiltration out of a riot or war zone. Place all the rest of your gear that you cannot hang on your body, carry in your clothes pockets or in a messenger bag into a super strong but dull colored backpack. Do all you can to keep the weight below 45 pounds. Soldiers often carry 65 to 165 pounds or more but even the toughest and best will tell you 45 lbs. of total weight is the ideal maximum if you are to be nimble enough to survive any war zones. Be as light on your feet as possible. Slow moving targets die quickly on battle fields.

Train for worst-case scenarios and train carrying as much weight as you expect to carry in a real emergency. Regular hiking, running, plyometrics and kettle bell drills will prepare you well. Change your socks often and keep them as clean and dry as you can. In really intense battle field environments never take your boot off and always rest in a tight 360 or loose diamond formation, with scouts at least 25 yards out on all sides depending on the terrain. Once you are out of the high risk area and if forced to hike very long distances, let your group rest for 3 to 5 minutes every hour to elevate their feet, or if safe to do so massage their feet and change socks. It has been said many times, "Take good care of your feet for without them you are not going anywhere." Half of your team must keep their boots on, while the other half change socks, work in buddy pairs.

As the leader, carry some foot powder, foot cream, antiseptic ointment, aspirins™ and large *"band-aids™"* for taking care of their feet. Foot hygiene and care is very important. Be careful not to spill foot powder. Let them apply it themselves while you or designated guards provide 360-degree security. You personally should have well conditioned feet and be able to hike 6 to 20 plus hours without needing any or much foot care. During your conditioning phase use Epson salts to soak your feet before and after long hard hikes. Please see all the other checklists for ideas that you may want to consider but again and again let this be your primary and foundational list if we are talking war zone survival for civilians.

As the leader, you must also be spiritually, emotionally and physically prepared. Be well trained, knowledgeable, wise and sharp. Demonstrate foresight, a pragmatic approach and stay calm under pressure. You should guide and train those who are with you by your example. Say *"Follow Me and do as i do"* and be worthy of those words. Be a subject-matter expert in leadership, small team tactics, weapon handling, combat and wilderness survival and trauma medicine. Be a highly competent, caring and humble leader with a small i. Be highly capable and tactically proficient. Be in integrity, courageous and caring.

Master the basics in this book and the fundamentals of leadership and always strive for outstanding excellence. At minimum, after studying these recommendations, pack a messenger bag today even if it only contains one or two revolvers (.44 or .357) or pistols (.45, .40, 9mm, .22L), compact binoculars, one full water bottle, one tourniquet, an Israeli bandage, several tampons, a survival knife, a wool cap, a 120/5 lumens flashlight, 6 nutrition bars and $100 to $10,000 in cash or a couple of gold and silver coins. Ultimately, you need to *"Man-Up"* to master our list above.

The bottom line is this. When you are confronted by violent armed assaulters you are in the best position if you are on high ground, behind solid cover against fire, in a dark area and have a minimum of three to five weapons, one of which is in your own trained hands. (Have a zeroed 7.62 x 51 battle rifle or .308, 30.06, 300, 270 or an effective high powered hunting rifle or a 12 gauge pump action shotgun with ideally 3" 1 oz slugs and double 0.0 buck rounds plus a .44 or .357 revolver on your hip and a .45 or .40 or if you insist a 9 mm pistol in a shoulder holster on your well conditioned body. Hide an Italian .22L pistol or American .38 snub nose J-frame revolver with an internal hammer in your underwear and back it up with a quality tactical knife with specialized medical trauma supplies.) Body armor is also very valuable.

Start out with the rifle in your hands and the shotgun close at hand. AAPE and scan from left to right, close to far, low to high for threats. Retreat and escape without engaging if you can. Crawl, pray, run, talk or buy your way out if that is at all an option. Escape in an unexpected direction sideways and away from the crowd and perhaps even dogleg in behind the assaulting force. If necessary, simply play dead.

As a last resort and if you are forced to engage then begin by using and if necessary eventually emptying the rifle and as they close in on you transition to the shotgun. Once you have run out of shotgun rounds, transition to your largest caliber pistol, then to your revolver and finally if necessary to your .22L pistol or .357 or .38 revolver and eventually your knife.

The real intention of advising you to carry a legally concealed .22L pistol or .38 snub nose revolver and neck knife or tactical folder or thumb knife is to provide you with potential escape tools in case of a kidnapping or prisoner situation or for their use in the case of a rape attempt. If you had to make a last stand then ideally add supporting shooters from your family, circle of friends and or Forum group and your chances of survival will improve exponentially. Above all, we suggest you have a prepared soul and stay out of fights. Choose non-violence and peace. Be a peacemaker.

Use this checklist to prepare your own *"tactical vest"*, *"messenger bag"* and *"evacuation & survival backpack"*. Checklists are where it is at! All true professionals use checklists. In the world of nuclear power they use a 70 plus page checklist with two experts co–signing their initials all the way down all 70 plus pages. There is a checker and a backup checking the checker to ensure and verify everything has been professionally checked. I want you to be that professional because that is what is necessary.

If all that is just to overwhelming for you then just have and take the 12 gauge American made pump action shotgun, and if available to you M14 M1A or SKS or AK 47 or 30.06 hunting rifle, depending who you are and where you are, and perhaps either just the American .44 or .357 revolver and or also the American 45 or .40 pistol, as well as the James Williams warrior and Tom Brown survival knives, and a U. S Army Airborne Ranger style hatchet. When well trained in these tactics and with these items, you will be more than adequate for most civilian applications. End of discussion. Take care of yourself and of all those with you. GOD Bless.

Lessons from Mogadishu

Operation *"Gothic Serpent"* Mogadishu, Somalia October 3, 1993

After clan warlords repeatedly ambushed relief convoys and stole the humanitarian relief food supplies brought in as part of Operation Restore Hope that started in the spring of 1992 on August 28 1993, Task Force Ranger arrived on the "Horn of Africa" in Mogadishu, Somalia.

Task Force Ranger commanded by General William F. Garrison was on a mission to capture General Mohammed Farad Aideed, the war lord ordering the food raids that was causing hundreds of Somalis to starve each day.

Task Force Ranger was a formidable group which consisted of some of Americas very best warriors. Delta Force C Squadron operators, (4) U.S. Navy Seals from Team Six, U.S. Army Rangers predominately from the 3rd battalion 75th Ranger Regiment, U.S. Air Force Special Tasks Team members from USAF 24th Special Tactics Squadron including Combat Search and Rescue (CSAR soldiers) and 160th SOAR (A) *"Night Stalker"* pilots. This battle group was supported by 19 aircraft and a dozen ground transports of which nine were Humvees and the balance were trucks.

The call sign was Irene.

At 1542 hours the spear head Delta *"snatch-and-grab"* team landed in MH-6 *"Little Bird"* Helicopters at the Olympic hotel in the Bakara gun market area. It was the largest small arms market in East Africa and a hornet and vipers nest of danger. It was exactly the kind of area where one would expect Delta and the Rangers to lead the way. Their mission was to capture two of Aideed's lieutenants that according to intelligence sources had been spotted in a building one block from their hotel and on their way to a meeting. A total of

163 highly motivated, superbly trained and equipped elite American warriors participated in operation *"Gothic Serpents"* assault force mission launch.

Delta was supported by eight MH-60 Black Hawks carrying chalks of Rangers from the 75th Ranger battalion and additional Delta operators. A 12 vehicle ground convoy (heavily armed with M-2 .50 caliber machine guns and MK-19 40 mm grenade launchers) was also heading towards the target building to serve as the exfiltration convoy.

As the spear tip of Delta went in, Rangers were fast roping down at the four intersections on each corner of the target building to secure Delta's area of operation. Their mission was to ensure that nobody entered or left Delta's area of operation. Delta swiftly, effectively and efficiently seized their targets. They captured the two wanted lieutenants and along with them another high value individual plus 20 of their bodyguards. Delta's mission was successfully accomplished in under 15 minutes and they radioed command for extraction in the 5 ton trucks and Humvees.

While loading the captured prisoners, a Black Hawk (Super 61) helicopter piloted by Cliff Wolcott and carrying Delta operators, was shot down by a Somali with an RPG (rocket-propelled grenade). It crashed three blocks from the target building. One of the Delta snipers who were in the crashed Black Hawk was defending the downed crew, in spite of his being severely injured, until reinforcements arrived.

A *"Little Bird"* assault helicopter carrying the Delta squadron commander and other Delta operators along with a Black Hawk carrying a 15 man Combat Search & Rescue (CSAR) team plus a 6 man team from the Ranger blocking chalks rushed towards the crash site to rescue the survivors or at least to recover the bodies. The Somalis had a fearsome reputation of mutilating enemy bodies. The Delta squadron leader, a calm, pragmatic and competent man and his crew got their fast; and with a team growing to roughly 20 men on the ground and in the heat of an intense firefight exhibited outstanding and selfless courage worthy of medals for valor while they evacuated two wounded soldiers and the remaining bodies.

The CSAR team secured two defensive positions, providing cover for the men pulling the crew from the wreck and during treatment of the injured Delta sniper. The fighting was fierce and while the medics worked on stabilizing those that they could, the security perimeter of Rangers was rapidly running low on ammunition. Some apparently had already used up the 8 magazines they were carrying. They were at great risk of being pinned down and the rescue force began to take casualties. The battle field was loud, chaotic and desperate while the communication nets were jammed with activity. The combat controller was doing his best to call in air support while Somali RPG and AK 47 ammunition rained in like a hail storm. With cover from pairs of low and fast flying Little Bird gunships coming in repeatedly for hours, the men on the ground eventually managed to move into and secure a compound close by that at the time was housing a group of Somali women and children. (A detailed account of this incident can be read in the book, "The Battle of Mogadishu", Edited by Matt Eversmann and Dan Schilling.)

Soon after the Super 61 was downed by an RPG, another Black Hawk, piloted by Michael Durant was also shot down by another RPG and crashed just less than a mile to the south of the first crash site. Delta snipers, MSG Gary I. Gordon and SFC Randall D. Shughart repeatedly volunteered to go in and secure the perimeter for protection of the survivor/s and bodies until more help could arrive. After their third insistent request, they were granted permission and they performed one of the most heroic known last stand defenses of the surviving pilot Michael Durant. For almost an hour the two of them fought off hundreds of swarming, blood thirsty and hyper aggressive Somali gunmen to the point where the last surviving Delta sniper ran out of ammunition and apparently used enemy AK 47's he recovered from dead bodies until he was eventually shot dead. The two Delta snipers were each only armed with a 7.62 x 51 rifle and a .45 pistol. MSG Gary Gordon eventually fought on armed only with a .45 pistol until he too was fatally wounded.

What inspiring and exemplary valor. They both were posthumously awarded the Congressional Medal of Honor for their selfless service and bravery in the face of overwhelming danger. We can never bestow enough honor and praise upon the memory of these two fine men. We are forever richer by their example and poorer for their departure to eternal life.

In the meantime, all the members of Task Force Ranger (Delta Force, SEAL Team Six members, Rangers, the 160th Special Ops pilots and other Air Force specialists including combat controllers and pararescue men (PJ's) were locked into one of the most intense and chaotic asymmetrical warfare street battles since Vietnam. Records may vary but we showed eighteen (18) killed, seventy-three (73) of our men were reported wounded and one (1) captured from a force of one-hundred sixty-three (163). It became an all out fight for survival. The fighting was so intense that even men who carried as many as thirteen loaded rifle magazines were running out of ammunition.

Roadblocks of the many streets along with initially hundreds and later thousands of armed Somalis made Mogadishu a giant deathtrap for our guy's. The Somalis high on Khat (an aggression inducing amphetamine plant) would charge down the sides of the streets and line the streets continually firing at the occupants of the Humvees while hundreds more would fire at them from the roof tops.

A quick reaction force consisting of a company of the 10th Mountain Division troops was eventually launched but they also rapidly became trapped by more very heavy Somali gunfire. Only well after 0100 hours on October 4, 1993 did a support force consisting of more Rangers, a few SEALs, 10th Mountain Division soldiers and Malaysian APCs eventually arrive at the second helicopter crash site and while under heavy AK 47 and RPG fire this combined team struggled until dawn to retrieve the dead pilot's body.

At around sunrise this same main body of soldiers arrived at the Pakistani controlled stadium but pilot Michael Durant was still being held as a prisoner by the Somalis. Additionally, several other men were also still out there after more than 18 hours of intense fighting.

The capture of the twenty-three (23) prisoners and especially the two Aideed lieutenants along with an additional high value individual made the mission a success. Our soldiers fought exceedingly well against overwhelming odds. We lost a total of 19 soldiers before we withdrew. Six (6) of which were Delta operators, two (2) of which died in the first helicopter crash while one additional soldier, SFC Matt Rierson, was killed Oct. 6th, 1993 by a mortar attack that fell on the base the following day. According to some sources, it was reported that TFR killed hundreds of Somalis and wounded hundreds or perhaps even thousands more in what the Somalis remember as *"The Day of the Rangers"*.

(All loss of human life in war is sad, no matter which side they are on. It is especially sad in this case as our efforts were for well intended humanitarian aid and as a mission to remove a leader who was starving his countries fellow citizens to death. What will it take for us humans to eventually choose non-violence and a more caring way of living in harmony across the planet and to create a better world for all?)

Lessons Learned: Many of the key lessons learned on the streets of Mogadishu are best confined to Delta, SEAL and Ranger training classes but what we as civilians can take from this may be relevant to us as well. We learn of the importance of dominating the high ground, the importance of quality body armor, the value of specialized training. We need to have three to five layers of firearms with more magazines, ammunition and medical supplies than most people think is necessary. All the while, you want to still remain nimble enough to fight your way out of a riot or war zone battle if ever forced into a fight. Our goal is not to be or train commandoes but to learn what is useful and how to stay alive in places when trouble suddenly erupts all around us in an urban area.

My view of this type of situation is that if I can give you the mindset, skills and a system to forecast, avoid and survive a chaotic asymmetrical and long duration large scale battle such as the October 3, 1993 street battle in Mogadishu; you will be more than well equipped to deal with rapists, drug fueled gangs of criminals or even professional kidnappers if sadly you are ever forced to do so. The Battle in Mogadishu is also the most interesting known modern day case study on urban war fighting and makes for an outstanding lesson in our combat history.

Note: Delta Force (1st Special Forces Operational Detachment DELTA) is said to be Americas "fabled", "secret", "tier one", "best-of-the-best" counterterrorism unit specializing in hostage release operations and tier one high value target capture (man hunting). Although some historic operations such as Operation Eagle Claw in 1980, Operation "Just Cause", Operation "Acid Gambit" and Operation "Nifty Package" in Panama in 1998, "Operation Gothic Serpent—The Battle of the Black Sea" in Mogadishu in 1993 and the more recent hunt for Bin Laden in the Tora Bora mountains of Afghanistan has brought publicity to DELTA, the unit remains cloaked in secrecy, and rightfully so.

These are the men who are said to operate in the most hostile enemy territories and the deepest penetrations behind enemy lines while in the very heart of enemy occupied territories. Thank heavens for men like these who are both willing and highly capable of tracking down evil and bring primary evil doers to justice. In conclusion and through glimpses into their world, I feel that it is perhaps best to respect their privacy and we will continue to honor that here. Let our prayers be with them and their families and let's financially support foundations that take care of the widows and orphans of fallen Delta, SEAL, Green Beret, Ranger and other elite operators. That is the least we can do in return and as a thank you to them for their brave and selfless service. Let us remember MSG Gary Gordon, SFC Randy Shugart, MSG Tim "Griz" Martin, SSG Daniel Busch, SFC Earl Fillmore, and SFC Matt Rierson.

Historical Note:
TF Ranger (Task Force)

In studying the on the ground history of what happened in Mogadishu in Oct 1993, we quickly see that there are many misperceptions about the incident. A little background: the US had twice committed forces to Somalia to alleviate the widespread starvation, which was being used as a weapon in the Somali civil war; once under president George H.W. Bush, and again under President Bill Clinton. A major difference was that the first deployment was under US command and control, while the second was under UN command and control. During the second deployment, the Habir Gedr clan militia under the command of Mohammed Farah Aideed ambushed and killed several Pakistani peacekeepers. This action ultimately led the US to form and deploy TF Ranger in August, completely separate from the UN forces, with the mission of killing or capturing Aideed.

TF Ranger was comprised primarily of members of the 1st SFOD-D (Delta Force), 160th SOAR, and 75th Ranger Regiment. Several other units rounded out the Task Force. Aideed had not been seen since the June massacre of the Pakistanis, and the US intelligence apparatus was unable to provide the TF with any information concerning his whereabouts. As such, TFR adopted the plan to take out his support, and embarked on 6 successful missions to capture his key supporters and eliminate his physical infrastructure. On the 7th mission, TFR received information about 2 of Aideed's key lieutenants, and quickly deployed to capture them. The mission was executed flawlessly, despite the heavy fire received within the pro-Aideed Bakara Market section of Mogadishu. Before the exfil was completed, one of the TF Blackhawk helos was shot down. TF Ranger had planned for this contingency, but this changed the entire flow of the battle. Instead of quickly returning to the base, the TF now focused on rescuing the pilot, co-pilot, crew chiefs, and Delta snipers who were providing support from the back of the helo.

The militia understood the PR importance of capturing or killing US Soldiers to show their strength, and TFR was determined to save their downed comrades. A race was on to the downed helo, with the CSAR and Ranger chalk arriving just ahead of the Somalis. While this action raged, a second Blackhawk was shot down, piloted by Mike Durant, who subsequently wrote of his experience, "In the Company of Heroes." Since the CSAR was already employed, TFR put together another element, which was repeatedly turned back by heavy fire. Aboard another Blackhawk circling the battlefield, Delta snipers Gary Gordon and Randy Shughart volunteered repeatedly to assist any possible survivors at the Durant crash site, and were finally given permission. Their selfless actions saved Mike Durant's life at the cost of their own, for which they were awarded the Congressional Medal of Honor.

After a long night of fighting, the crew chiefs and snipers aboard the first helo were brought out safely, but the pilot and copilot were both killed on impact. Their cool headed actions on first being hit undoubtedly saved the lives of their passengers when the aircraft hit the ground several seconds later. Their bodies were recovered by TFR, denying the Somalis an opportunity to defile them. Durant's copilot and crew didn't fare as well; they were all killed on impact or by the Somalis on the ground, along with Shughart and Gordon. Their bodies were all recovered several days later.

Now let's address some of the misperceptions:

The so-called Mogadishu Mile, as immortalized in the movie, was actually a planned dismount from the vehicles of the relief force—made up of TFR personnel, US Army 10th Mountain Div, Malaysian APCs, and Pakistani tanks—to dismantle a road block, and then proceed from the dismount point to the first crash site with dismounted troops and APCs providing mutual support. (A similar force—a handful of Delta Operators, 10th Mtn. Rifle Company, and APCs, went to the second crash site, found no one there, and returned to the dismount point). The distance was almost exactly 1/2 mile. After the WIAs were loaded aboard the APCs and the pilot and copilot recovered, the force then returned to the dismount point, where a reaction force had remained in place throughout the night. When the movement started the APCs gradually pulled away from the dismounted troops, due primarily to the language barrier. Fortunately, the Somalis seemed to have lost their stomach for the fight by this time, having suffered tremendous casualties, and the firing at the dismounted element on the way out was sporadic and ineffective. At the dismount point the dismounted troop's boarded vehicles and the entire force returned to the base. The movie, in an effort to dramatize, gave the impression that a small group was abandoned by the vehicles and ran back to the base one step ahead of the militia. Although dramatic, it is historically inaccurate.

The first media reports after the battle (no American journalists were in Mogadishu at the time) referred to a failed mission, botched mission, debacle, etc. etc. This group think was based only on reports of American Soldiers being killed in a combat action. If this is the metric for success or failure in combat, how would we characterize the Normandy invasion? The fact is that the mission of apprehending two of Aideed's LTs was accomplished in text book fashion. However, the old saying that no battle plan survives the first shot held true in Somalia, and the downed Blackhawk changed the entire mission. When it was all over, a tragic loss of life did not equate to a failed or botched mission.

The battle of Mogadishu provides us with an outstanding example of the chaos found in asymmetrical warfare and how specialized training in close quarter battle (CQB) tactics and advanced medical trauma drills can help you and others survive such encounters in more predictable ways.

Our AAPE System and first contact drills show you how to out-think the bad guys so that you do not have to out fight them during a slaughter or be slaughtered situation.

I want to add massive value to your life. My goal is to help you to be so proficient and so well trained and equipped that even if you were suddenly and unexpectedly to find your family and self in a kidnapping attempt or wake up to a violent home intrusion or find yourself in battle chaos such as that seen in the movie *"Black Hawk Down"*; you will have a better than average chance of surviving due to your tactical and medical trauma knowledge gained here. I want those who are with you to look up to you for leadership and to feel confident that if they follow you and do as you do by example they will have a real chance to survive.

Civilians in war zones across the world, historically and increasingly get in the way of soldiers locked into fierce urban battles and many get killed as a result. It is a reality and one I hope you and your family will never face but I might as well prepare you on how to survive such a zone as we may all sooner or later end up in such a terrible place. I also feel if I can train you to have a chance to survive full scale battle chaos you should have a better than average chance against small time criminals. Yet let's not underestimate the criminal threat and become arrogant. It is wise and prudent to always remain humble and better prepared than you think is necessary and better prepared than your attackers expect.

There are many more misconceptions regarding the Battle of Mogadishu.

In studying the history of what happened in Mogadishu we can easily conclude how the young Rangers due to their *"Ranger Indoctrination Program"* (RIP) and extensive training were eager and keen young warriors. They reported in their own words afterwards how they felt invincible in the spirit of *"Invictus."* We can see how their intense and extensive Ranger training, their Ranger creed, and their highly qualified leaders made them believe they could not fail or even take casualties on their side. Their weaponry consisted of the modern M-2 .50 caliber Humvee machine guns and MK-19 mounted 40 mm grenade launchers, SAW machine guns, M16 and CAR-15 rifles with advanced combat accessories such as "TacLights" and M-203 40 mm grenade launchers plus a minimum of 210 rounds, their body armor, and sawed-off Remington 870 shotguns and the presence of the Delta Men and four (4) DevGru *"SEAL Team Six"* Men as well as some Air force combat controllers and combat search and rescue CSAR PJ Para jumpers/rescue team and the awesome black MH-6 Little Birds and MH-60 Black Hawk helicopter of *"Task Force Ranger"*. They were certainly one impressive, capable and formidable force that somewhat reminded me of the 300 Spartans of old. This Task Force Ranger represented some of America's best men and equipment at the time both in the command post and on the streets of Mogadishu.

My initial perspective and the story as told in the media is mostly the story as told from the perspective of the young Rangers. Let it be known that these are very capable men and that the Rangers represent only 1% of the entire US Army. They are truly worthy of respect as specialized soldiers.

Here is a valuable comment in the words of a man that was there;
"While the story of BHD is told primarily by Rangers . . . RIP, eager, etc., the fact is that the bulk of the force was experienced Delta Operators in the assault element, and equally experienced TF pilots providing air support. The Rangers provided security positions for the assault force."

To me these battle groups and their final battles are some of the most interesting, inspiring and fascinating battles ever. It also brings the core of Shakespeare's Classic *Henry V*, St. Crispin's day speech to mind, does it not? Those warrior spirited men amongst us who by destiny missed the last great Samurai battle, the Battle of Agincourt in 1495, The famous *"300"* Battle of Thermopylae (The Hot/Fire Gates) at the Malian Gulf in ancient Greece of the Spartans in 480 BC and the famous Mogadishu *"Battle of the Black Sea"* on October 3 and 4, 1993 have missed some of histories greatest battles indeed. We were both very lucky and very, very unlucky at the same time.

What a guy the Spartan king Leonidas was who defiantly said *"Come and get them"* when Xerxes with his army of two million soldiers demanded the Spartans surrender their weapons. Likewise what valiant men the members of *"Task Force Ranger"* were and how brave even the Somali men, women and children were. Let's be big enough to give credit and honor where it is due.

The Rangers of Task Force Ranger were entering a city with a million or more people in it and heading for the area of the *"Black Sea"* district very close to and actually right in the *"Bakara Market"* which was one of the largest small arms markets in Africa. We read and get the impression that some of the young Rangers felt overconfident and relaxed as a result of six previously successful missions out from the base. A few did not take their night sight goggles or even much water with them thinking they would be back shortly. They never expected to become part of one of the most intense, if not the most intense and chaotic modern day urban battles on record. After all, they were only going after two of a warlord (Mohammed Aidid) officer's. We also read about communication problems.

Again, to set the record straight, here are the words of a very experienced man who was in the actual battle;
"I didn't take NVGs when I went in, and never needed them. There was plenty of ambient light. I only would have needed them if I was room clearing in a dark building, which I didn't. Every element of TFR had the same communications systems. In an environment like Mogadishu, you can't carry enough water or ammo for an 18 hour battle. Resupply was required regardless of how much each Soldier carried. It's always a fine line between what and how much to carry versus staying light enough to be able to move quickly and not wear out.

The Somalis did not have body armor or nearly the U.S. forces level of training, personal combat gear or super cool helicopters flown expertly by the competent and brave 160th Special Operations Aviation Regiment (SOAR) *"Night Stalkers"*. The Somalis wore cotton shirts, old worn out non-combat shoes or sandals and most carried AK-47's and RPG-7 rocket launchers. The Rangers in comparison had M-60 machine guns, M249 SAW, M-16 rifles and CAR-15-203 rifles, some 870 shotguns and .45 cal pistols, at least two fragmentation grenades each, flash-bang and perhaps rubber ball grenades, trauma first aid kits, two–quart water canteens, UHF and other radios with spare batteries and some night vision goggles (NVG) although some Rangers left theirs at the base. The Somalis did have RPG-7 Russian rocket propelled grenades highly capable of taking down helicopters or stopping Humvee vehicles and killing men clustered together. Also what the Somalis had were large numbers and great local support with even women and children actively helping them during the battle. They also had remarkable "*gutzpah*" aggression, audacity and courage in battle. They were playing on their home field in front of their home crowd in protection of their own families and friends. That alone is a powerful motivation. We heard and read how shocked and surprised the Rangers were to see both Delta Men and fellow Rangers being shot and killed. The younger Rangers went from being keen on battle in the beginning to in minutes learning how sudden and destructive war is and certainly not fun or glamorous as it is often portrayed.

It is likely and reported that the average Somali in the fight had a lot more real world urban combat experience than most of the younger Rangers of Task Force Ranger men. Street fighting was part of their lifestyle in Mogadishu, Somalia. It was a war torn city without electricity, or sewer services but an abundance of weapons, drugs and firefights.

More words from another senior SF operator on the ground;
"*Fortunately for TF Ranger, while the Somalis—particularly the Habir Gedr militia—had extensive street fighting experience, what they didn't possess was a training base, to include fundamental marksmanship. While the movements of the Somalis suggested an obvious command and control in effect, their marksmanship was abysmal, and many of the hand grenades they threw at TFR laid on the ground with the pins still in. (Lesson learned—bravery isn't enough; you need training)*

Of interest, an AC-130 was part of the rehearsal package, and TF Ranger expected it to deploy. It was cancelled without notifying TFR due to political, vice operational, considerations. TF Ranger's size was also capped due to political considerations."

Just like the Somali fighters were under the influence of narcotics, experienced, tough and crazy brave, the same will most likely be true of the hardcore criminals that may find you, your family and assets of interest. Expect them to be more experienced, prison and street hardened and more ruthless fighters than you at this point much like those Somali's who were on "*Khat*". (Amphetamine plant) Life on the Horn of Africa is exceedingly tough and breeds tough people. The same is true for the backstreets of any major city. Your criminal assaulters will probably be on drugs. You will also most likely be outnumbered. To wake up at 2 or 3 a.m. and attempt to escape and evade with your entire family requires some form of an early warning. To successfully engage them coming from a deepened sleep state requires serious preparation and training. Never underestimate and never quit your plan.

To ensure your family has a fair chance of survival you will need great leadership skills, proven tactical skills and time tested medical trauma care skills. Nothing less, other than just G-D's grace, will save your family and you. The police and paramedics may get there in 5 minutes to help but a lot can and will happen in those first minutes. It may just be 5 minutes too late for your child, spouse and self. If leadership is of interest to you then you may also enjoy the recommended book "Heart of a Leader".

The mindset, the foundational gear and core tactical and trauma medical skills needed in war zones are exactly the same that you will need in a criminal gunfight or shooting. A major difference is the scale is much greater in war and the slaughter can be much more rapid and intense. Both situations can be horrible. Combat in any form is dangerous, super stressful, exhausting, and dirty and it stinks. Both require specialized training and preparation.

You are lucky that destiny placed this book in your hands. "**Fear Not**" is here and this is it for you! Here is where you will gain the professional mindset and the skill set you need to stand a reasonable chance to protect your family and lead them to safety. Even better would be to avoid them getting into a nasty dangerous situation in the fist place. If an evil did come after good people, I want to know I did what I could to help them be prepared and ready spiritually, tactically and medically.

Are you ready to begin your training? Study and master my AAPE system which is similar to the well known *"OODA"* system. Master the Task, Conditions & Standards skill requirements, all of them. Emphasize the shooting, the unarmed combat non-lethal response options and especially the trauma medical protocols and procedures. Study and take to heart our counter-kidnap recommendations. That is how you need to prepare to be ready for any eventuality. Strategic big picture wisdom and micro tactical knowledge and skills are both needed. You must pre event learn how to deal with everything from a natural disaster, to a criminal home invasion to surviving war conditions. The philosophy and principles in our AAPE system apply everywhere as an overall Meta framework.

For the record, Delta did a great job and succeeded in securing the building and capturing the wanted personnel they went after and brought them in. In spite of all the chaos, the loss of a total of nineteen American soldiers on October 3, 4, 5 and 6th of 1993 and the loss of hardware and assets such as two Black Hawk Helicopters and other vehicles, the mission was tactically a success.

The Somalis and many others think that the Somalis won this battle. They think that our American soldiers were literally forced to run away and the media perpetuated this misconception. (*"The Mogadishu Mile"*) However, America did withdraw from Somalia shortly after and never did succeed in concluding their core mission which was to capture the warlord General Muhammad Farrah Aideed. Ironically, a lesser known fact is that Aideed was later followed as leader by one of his sons who had studied in America and was once a US Marine. It is an interesting world, is it not?

The *"Battle of the Black Sea"* will unfortunately always be remembered for the images of American soldiers being dragged through the streets of Mogadishu that so shocked the American public and later changed American war policy. Now, how about you? How ready will you be for your night of destiny should it take the form of a fire fight? How will it go down in your family history? What can you do proactively to be not just better prepared but be the best prepared for a violent eventuality?

The following are recommended references and excellent further reading on "The Battle of the Black Sea".

BLACK HAWK DOWN Mark Bowen
IN THE COMPANY OF HEROES Michael J. Durant with Steve Hartov
THE BATTLE OF MOGADISHU Matt Eversmann and Dan Schilling
LEADERSHIP AND TRAINING FOR THE FIGHT MSG Paul R. Howe

Escaping a Riot/ War Zone/ Natural Disaster

Since wars are raging around the world and far too many innocent civilians get killed, here is some life preserving ideas for you. Please realize that there is very little good, fun or anything nice about war. It is horrific, destructive and far too often greed based. It is tough and it will always smell bad. It is a place of brutal slaughter and carnage and one you are best advised to avoid if you can.

Modern day battles typically begin with a series of surgical missiles and cluster bombs from aircraft, including bunker bombs followed by heavy artillery from ships and or tanks. That is followed up with the light infantry artillery such as mortars, which may include lots of air burst and incendiary and armor piercing ammunition. Follow this up with special operations assaults with hand held rockets, 60 or 82 mm commando mortars, sniper fire, small arms fire, hand grenades and possibly even bio/chemical agents. Everything is reduced to burning rubble filled with toxic smoke from burning vehicles, buildings and other combustibles as well as a giant matrix of other dangers. These are very, very nasty environments. Never be so certain that you may not end up experiencing such an environment. Wars and armed conflicts happen to many good people who never imagined it would happen to them. You could just be in the wrong place at the wrong time.

In the event of a natural disaster much of this may not be your first course of action. As a good citizen, your first response should be to help others and those less fortunate that have been affected. In such cases as these, perhaps a chain saw, an axe, a first aid kit and water purification tablets etc. will be of more value. But, in the event there is a break down in the societal order, we suggest you follow our S.O.P. and our primary recommendations.

Without getting too much in detail, here are some guidelines for surviving a war zone and escaping that battle zone as a civilian if you ever get trapped in such dangerous chaos. It is best to AAPE the world's macro and micro political situation and to get out of or avoid potential war and battle zones through a high level of awareness and proactive avoidance. However, I understand that war or battles can and will sometimes suddenly erupt without any warning to the civilian population. Be sharp, observant and be proactively responsive. Get and stay ahead in the loop with our AAPE system.

Please also realize that my goal is not to hype this stuff up or to train you to be the "ultimate commando". My goal is simply to create awareness of how dangerous things can suddenly become and what it realistically takes to survive such an unfortunate and extreme situation. It unfortunately does require some "commando" type mindset and skills in my opinion. Please forgive me if all of this looks just way too over the top. I really just want to educate and serve good people at the highest possible level that I know how to. My motivation is one of caring!

The best initial action is to get down low behind good cover if there are sudden shootings or bombings. Get behind solid cover and AAPE the situation and as necessary follow our various tactical drills and medical protocols and procedures to survive. Keep the 2.2 concept and system explained in this book in mind and act accordingly.

If you can, wear dull uninteresting clothes that do not make noise. Avoid cotton if there is a risk of getting wet to avoid hypothermia. Also avoid synthetic fabric that could burn easily. Wool and the color gray are both excellent choices. Exit with a mass of people, stick to the center of the mass and eventually move to the edge. From the edge of that mass vanish unnoticed sideways and away from the shepherded masses or based on your AAPE immediately go a different direction from the masses. Follow your instincts. Use deception, distraction and disguise if you must to survive and escape. Be unconventional with daring, bold and audacious guile. Lead those with you by example, coach them, guide them and direct them.

Utilize your utmost skill and whatever technology is available to you. Focus on what you can control and do as you evolve the situation to reach safety. Be physically fit so that you can endure and persevere against great odds and in the face of enormous challenges. The intensity of war is way beyond anything most civilians have ever experienced and 99.99 % are totally underprepared for it. (Emotionally, physically, spiritually and in terms of gear and supplies) Look civilian rather than military and not too macho. Move at a steady and medium pace. Go to a pre planned place in nature. Use a dull civilian messenger bag for emergency supplies and keep your ten most necessary items for survival in your clothes pockets. Hang your two or three most valued items on Para cord around your neck and concealed under your clothing. This may at minimum be a small neck knife, a mini compass and a fire flint.

Observe, AAPE, scan left to right, close to far, low to high and 360 degrees around. Use darkness and shadows. In cities get real good at noticing surveillance cameras and avoiding high surveillance areas. Avoid making eye contact with people. Get away from the hot zone. Get off the roads and away from people. Selectively use the high ground. Be silent. Constantly observe with super high situational awareness. Be decisive. Lead those with you with confidence and certainty. Act dead if necessary if discovered in a hide. If fighting may be unavoidable adopt a *"combat mindset"* of *"controlled aggression"*. If you cannot reach or cannot trust the official gathering points then you'd better go your own way. Be skilled, fit, prepared and self-reliant enough to make your way out of the city with your family, friends, forum buddies or alone as applicable.

Get into a non-active, isolated area in nature. Go for the high ground or cave or tunnel areas where there is drinking water and natural foods and lots of cover against sight in dense natural areas and ideally a vast area to search. Disappear into it and only move at night if you must. Cut the sole edges of your boots or shoes a little rounder and smoother and cover it with smooth soft fabric or smooth rubber to reduce your traceable foot print tracks *"spoor."* If you think you are being followed *"dogleg"* back and observe from high ground in good cover and shade or darkness and apply the AAPE system taught in this book. Walk as if you are stalking a deer if you must be silent.

Take an entrenchment tool (small spade) and a dozen or so empty sand bags with you if you can. Also two knives, a hatchet, water purification tablets, nutrition bars, waterproofed matches, a metal cup, a wooden spoon, salt, soup powder, survival candles in cans, 100 ft of 550 Para cord, 125 grain and 165 grain broad head arrows, as well as bird snare style arrow tips, fishing hooks, snare wire, mosquito netting, a wool blanket and large plastic sheet and other essential and handy survival supplies, medical supplies and various carefully selected gear. Have that ready to go as of tonight and within a minutes notice.

If you can take a .357 revolver and a .45 pistol with 60 extra rounds for both those handguns along with a .22 L survival rifle with 50 to 500, 40 grain rounds. Perhaps, depending on many factors, conceal the .22 L & 410 M6 scout rifle in a dull colored and loosely rolled blanket if you consider it wise and smart or appropriately legal to do so. The M6 survival rifle can fold down and pack into a small backpack.

Here is a short checklist of some very valuable urban war zone escape and long term wilderness survival items.
1.   Small powerful binoculars (8 x 20, 8 x 40, 8 x 42)
2.   Night vision goggles with spare batteries
3.   Body armor (*worn under clothes*)
4.   Multi-threat mask and respirators
5.   Entrenchment spade
6.   Machete, and a all steel axe.
7.   Commando wire saw and or a 12 inch folding saw
8.   Water bottles (Full)
9.   Water purification tablets
10. Metal canteen or cup
11. Wooden spoon
12. Small tomahawk style battle axe or a second 29" all steel utility axe
13. Knives (2 or 3)

14. Salt, Spirulina, & Vitamin C, Ginger and multi-vitamins
15. Snare wire and a small pair of pliers or multi-tool
16. Hand disinfectant
17. Toilet paper
18. Fire flint, lighter, storm matches, magnifying glass, and survival candles
19. Poncho, mosquito net, micro fleece jacket, tarp and wool blanket/s
20. 300 ft 550 Para cord
21. 12 empty sandbags
22. Dental floss, additional dental health and care supplies
23. Wool skull/commando cap and a warm, weather proof dull color parka with a hood and with matching pants
24. Heavy leather gloves
25. 6 pairs of wool hiking socks
26. Foot powder
27. Rice, raisins, soup powder, nutrition bars, protein powder, mouse and rat traps
28. Vegetable seeds (organic)
29. Advanced and specialized combat trauma and wilderness survival medical kit/s
30. Arrow tips 125g and 165g, arrow fletchers, arrow nocks, super glue and a survival fishing kit or at least fishing hook and some fishing line
31. Duct tape
32. Religious wisdom literature, survival manual, wilderness first aid manual.
33. Hunting rifle, shotgun and two or three handguns and ammunition plus cleaning kit.
34. Camping sleep mat
35. Kick Board and a large, high quality professional grade waterproof bag.

Having more of the above items the greater your chances of success. These items will give you hope and a chance to survive. However, you must balance this against the need to be nimble of foot. A 30 to 60 lb or heavier pack gets heavy after some walking in arduous terrain and severe weather. Condition your mind, back, legs and feet to be able to handle that. You life will depend on it. With what is on the list, the right mindset, prior training and a good woman or man, you can start a new life, community or even civilization again if you were forced to do so. Do your own research. Add to the list at least five more items of your own choice but do keep the weight in mind. Make two packs. One can be a vehicle pack and one being an on-body pack with your highest value items carried on you.

If forced to walk, ideally you want to set out wearing high quality hiking socks and quality hiking boots. Change your socks frequently if you can. The health of your feet is vital. Select and locate a safe hideout place on high ground with extensive cover against sight. Construct a deep concealed underground hide and maintain strict self discipline while there. Be still and quiet. Alternatively find a safe, deep cave and deeper inside quietly construct a low thick stacked stone wall to shelter behind. Watch out for snakes and predatory animals. From here AAPE / AAPPEE and consider your next step options. Always plan and aim to retreat and escape unseen.

Advance study and practice wilderness survival and wilderness first aid skills. You will be glad you did. Be prepared. If trouble is highly likely and expected in your part of the world responsibly pre cache useful supplies i.e. (tools, food, blankets, medical supplies etc) in three different secret locations just in case. You need supplies and tools for shelter, purifying water, making fire, getting food, treating medical challenges, navigation and self-rescue. If you are stuck without any weapons, at minimum make for yourself at least one stick spear and a stone or sand *"bola"*. Pre study how to prevent and deal with heat diseases, with hypothermia and other cold injuries as those are two grim killers of humans in nature. Please realize that for soft untrained city people the wilderness can hold even greater hardship than a prison camp or urban war zone. You will have to become part Coyote and part Wolverine in your behavior to stand a chance of survival. You must be elusive, aware, cunning, adaptive, tough and fierce.

Your education, training and preparation should be as rigorous as the ancient *"Agoge"* warrior training of Spartan males from the age of seven until the age of 29 in ancient Greece. The Romans also had their own version of the *"Agoge"*. In Sparta gaining full citizenship depended on making the grade in the selection, training and assessment process.

Sadly, wé lack this kind of authentic, undiluted, raw masculine education and rite-of-passage. Men who seek it out for themselves stand head and shoulders above the rest as outstanding leaders with authentic, merit based confidence and skill. Be that person. That is what my leadership and Forum retreats are for. If that interests you then let us have that conversation. I also offer advanced escape, spiritual guidance and survival training to select small groups and individuals.

Reading and studying this book FEAR NOT, plus HEART OF THE LEADER and also THE VITAL SEVEN and by joining my team, and I, in a wilderness "Crucible" and "Vision Quest" and "Wisdom Circle Forum" retreat and by taking my world renowned "Test of Steel and Fire" will give you, your sons and forum buddies a unique and concentrated modern day "Agoge" education and experience. It is a powerful experience with immediately usable take home value to last a lifetime and one that will transform you deeply on a personal and professional level—guaranteed.

It will show you how to be a leader who attracts the best people in your industry and with them the best clients and customers. You will learn how to plant your business flag on higher ground without destroying and losing your family, health and soul in the process. It will equip you with new confidence and certainty, unstoppable momentum and what you need to bring more professional breakthroughs, life balance, relationship happiness, personal health, spiritual growth and financial prosperity into your life. It will fuel you with authentic masculinity and it will even make you a very hard target to kidnap, rape or murder. It is something every man should engage in at least once in their life. It will make you a better leader, better spouse and lover, better parent and provider, formidable family protector, better

entrepreneur, more loved forum member, friend and a better national and global citizen.

That is my mission that I offer to you. It will give you an edge and a better, more rewarding and fulfilling life. If it does not overwhelm you it will leave you a better and more capable person (man/woman) for a better world. (Guaranteed) Come and discover how "rich" and "secure" life can be. www.menofthecode.com Note: The Agoge is not about combat training, it is all about being a more capable, more peaceful and conscious person. It is about a new paradigm for healthy, authentic, mature masculinity and co-creating a safer, better, more sustainable world. It is about being a better man in a better world for all.

Prepare a personal emergency evacuation survival test and sling bag or backpack today and always keep it close on hand as much as possible. Set a high standard for yourself. The information here is the critical few basics. Get yourself relevant training. If that interests you we could have that conversation as well. Think and plan ahead. Be a leader. If a threat finds you then enter the tactical drills learned as necessary. Remember AAPE is always your master framework for any response.

It is good to know what the most likely worst case may be to expect in a riot and unfolding war zone, from a professional kidnapping or during an emergency common criminal attack should you ever have the experience. It is also necessary to know how to equip and prepare yourself for such a sad eventuality and how best to respond.

Your assaulters may be common gang thugs armed with hunting and battle rifles, shotguns, .45 and 9 mm pistols, .38 revolvers, knives, machetes, axes, baseball bats, knuckle irons, chains, sticks and even stones. Worse than that and especially if you are working on projects or vacationing in foreign countries such as Africa, Central or South America or even Eastern Europe, you may find your assaulters even more heavily armed with RPG-7 rocket launchers, RPD's, zeroed Draganov (SVD) 7.62 x 54R snipers rifles, SKS and AK 47 7.62

x 39 assault rifles and AKS-74U Krinkov 5.56 x 39 assault rifles and Mokarov 9 x 18 mm and Tokarev T-33 7.62 x 25 mm pistols. In other parts of the world including Mexico, depending on who they are, where and who you are and why they have an interest in you may dictate why they may be armed with rifles such as a M14 or Remington® 700 bolt action rifles with a Leupold® Mark IV 10 x M3A scope firing heavy .300 Winshester® Magnum rounds or even carrying highly sophisticated American, Italian and German military weapons. As always, again it depends on who they are, who you are, where you are and why they are interested in you.

The absolute worst case scenario outside of such extremes such as nuclear and biological or other chemical type attacks or just being severely outnumbered may be to be trapped in an operational zone where tier one type shooters are active and especially if they are not friendlies. Typically, where these types operate, the area gets sealed off watertight and nobody gets out or in. If they are truly sophisticated and top tier professional shooters such as world class mercenaries or other high end direct action assaulter or kidnappers or saboteurs or assassins or elite soldiers, then you are in very big trouble unless they are friendlies. Their gear may or may not include:

8x 42 or 8 x 20 or 8 x 35 binoculars, zeroed .50 caliber semi-automatic snipers rifles, 7.62 x 51 mm caliber battle rifles with holographic or with 1.1–4 x 20 CQB short dot scopes and / or personal carbines . They may also have Remington® M-870 12-gauge combat shotguns (or Mossberg® 500 shotguns) loaded with # 6, #7, double 0.0 buck, slugs or some kind of specially loaded rounds, or MP5SD3 sub machine guns and Colt 1911 .45 ACP, 9 mm Browning® HP / Glock® / Sig Sauer® or HK 45 pistols with sound suppressors and perhaps a 7.125" black blade James Williams designed, classic Samurai inspired 7" Hissatsu® operators combat knife or 13" blade Hisshou® short tactical *"sword-knife"* or Marine combat utility knives or classic World War II Sykes Fairbairn or the modern day Fairbairn Applegate® version of the double-edged commando daggers, and sharp combat hatchets, or other quality and exotic weapons.

The 13" blade Hisshou®™ is a formidable weapon and so is a *"Gurka Kukri"*. Both are very intimidating and difficult edged weapons to disarm. Most men are more prone to slashing then actual stabbing and it is very powerful and effective. Having said that, the most dangerous men are the 1% who are 100% willing to shoot humans at close ranges of 3 to 15 yards and out to 75 yards. They are emotionally able and willing to stab into vital organs, are trained to do so, and have had experience in doing so, with a bayonet or double edged commando dagger, or old timer frontier hunting knife without much remorse.

When you see men with lean hard faces, some of them tall, wearing a variety of military and civilian hiking boots and who have a confident and athletic walk, dressed with gear like this you are either very lucky because the most lethally capable and best-of-the-best good guy's just showed up or you are in very big trouble depending who you are, where you are and why you are there. Can you see why I want you to be better equipped than just having one .38 revolver or 9 mm pistol?

The best scenario is when you are the highly skilled guy dressed like this and are with other super competent men dressed the same way. If not, then act dead, hide in the darkest area, crawl or run away or if forced to do so fight bravely from behind solid cover in the darkest area and from the highest tactically advantageous area available because you are at very, very high risk of imminent death—guaranteed. Equipped like this, chances are high that they are *"friendlies"* but they may not be! The best thing to do is to stay well out of their way. Hide, stay low and be soundless and motionless. If forced to do so, you may have to run, talk, buy or fight your way out.

Fighting is always our very last resort. As an individual you hardly stand a chance against a team of highly skilled, aggressive, determined and well equipped killers. Avoidance is crucial. Luckily, very few men are this well equipped and very few others are highly skilled. Even less have that cold blooded ability to be ruthless in killing another human being up close and personal. Yet, there are enough of them both on the good and bad side to always make the situation a real risk during a crime or erupting street battle in times of post disaster, societal breakdown or during war.

Real "badass" professionals may even be equipped with 7.62 M60A3™ or 5.56 M249 SAW™ light machine guns with a collapsible commando stock, M14 battle rifles and fully customized M4 commando version carbines, XM84™ flash bang stun grenades, rubber ball grenades, M18™ smoke grenades, M26™fragmentation grenades, 13" blade knives, commando helmets, tactical goggles, knee and elbow pads and both body armor and assault vest filled with extra magazines. They may have a .357 handgun, one or two battle hatchets, compact 8 x 20 binoculars, mini tactical flashlight (Surefire® E2D LED Defender™ or a X200™ or X300™), mini strobe, chemical light sticks, a variety of tactical folding knives, a multi-tool, 3 x carabiners, fire resistant knuckle gloves, PRC-117/19™ or PRC-137™ HF or other radios and wear push-to-talk / throat microphone systems. They'll carry commando grade medical trauma kits in their assault rucksacks filled with among other items—(tourniquets, tracheotomy kit, chest occlusive dressings, chest decompression needles, wound gauge and dressing, 500 ml IV set, chemical heating pads, "thermal wraps" and morphine and other trauma medications), a hydration system and even perhaps use PVS-7/9 NVG™ (Night Vision Goggles) or AN/PVS-21™ low profile NVG or the latest technology innovation night vision equipment. Having some of these items where it is legal and situation specific and knowing how to use them well could be a great advantage in an all out battlefield.

Do you realize why you may need to be well trained and equipped? Most or some of these items are not available or legal for civilian possession in most civilized parts of the Western World but they may be picked up in the midst of a battle zone in extreme environments and during a society breakdown. When the really *"bad"* guy's are at work, bodies and equipment are typically booby trapped with grenades and are therefore best left untouched.

Disease will also quickly spread during such conditions. Avoid all contact if possible. Retreat rapidly; always choose non-violence and peace as your first, most urgent and highest choice. Have your own shot gun or battle rifle or both, 1 to 3 handguns, a warrior knife, a sharp combat hatchet, water supply, gas mask with fresh filters, and a comprehensive trauma medical kit and get out of there, as soon as possible. Go live in a quiet area very far from all that and maintain a quiet and low profile.

If suddenly caught in an unfolding riot or even worse a war zone battle, you are likely to encounter at least some friendly or enemy warriors equipped with this level of weaponry and tactical gear. That means big trouble for somebody and hopefully that is not your family, buddies and you. Can you see why I am so adamant and insistent that you also are exceptionally well equipped and well trained?

I keep telling you these extreme things and I keep showing you list after list of what may look to you completely over the top because I care and I need you to get it just how serious things can get in the real world and how totally under equipped and under prepared 99 % of all people are. You as an individual will potentially be fighting against prison-hardened individuals and perhaps even gangs of ruthless, well equipped thugs or even ruthless military type professionals. That requires serious preparation. So with that in mind i am going to be redundant in telling you core information over and over and over.

Remember to stay light enough to remain nimble. For intense and large scale riot and war zones, one long gun with 3 to 8 magazines or 20 to 60 plus extra rounds if it is a shotgun, one handgun with 2 to 6 magazines and one 7" or 13" fixed blade or at minimum a 3" to 4" folding blade tactical knife and a quality hatchet should be your minimum personal family protection and personal defense system. Weight is always a concern and even more so when you need to tactically move silently or swiftly around, over and / or under obstacles during a shootout.

Please be even better prepared than that. Be ready to go into action with quality body armor on and with a zeroed 7.62 x 51 mm battle rifle with a holographic or short dot scope or a zeroed 30.06, 300, 270 or other high powered hunting rifle in hand or a 12 gauge semi-automatic shotgun with a reflex sight as a back up weapon intelligently and tightly strapped to your body. Carry at least one but ideally two, three or even four handguns of the same caliber or mixed as per your own choice (.44 / .357 revolver, and / or .45 ACP and / or .40 or .41 or 9 mm pistol/s with a 4, 5 or 6 pound trigger pull), also a .22 L deep concealment pistol) along with a quality short sword or tactical knife or bayonet of your own choice.

I like the AK 47 bayonet and I also love the Samurai style 7.125" or 8.75" black blade Hissatsu™ knife and / or heavier 13" blade Samurai style sword knife made by CRKT®. The Tom Brown wilderness survival knife is also great and worth considering as a survival tool for when you need to evacuate into the wilderness. I also like hatchets. The choice is yours.

For fighting though you need a narrow long, authentic Samurai style blade. Armed like this and if properly trained; you will at least have a chance of survival if and when serious trouble ever finds you. If you are well trained and armed with at least three of these listed items, the average criminal thug or gang is going to be in for a big surprise and shock when they violently assault your family and / or you. Having said that, it will be a very horrific, sad and best to be avoided day or night and situation when you actually need to use some or all this gear out of forced necessity. It is my prayer and hope you will never face such a need.

At the very least *i* believe humbly that when mayhem breaks out you need to wear quality body armor and have a 12 gauge pump action shotgun with a reflex sight and loaded with # 6 or 7 bird shot, double 0.0 buck and slugs in your own well trained hands and a reliable heavy caliber handgun (.44, .357, .45 ACP or .40) or perhaps a quality 9 mm pistol of your choice in a dominant hip holster or dominant leg holster and a second handgun, in a body-fitting concealment shirt if you are not wearing body armor, or shoulder holster, and a third more compact frame handgun of your informed choice in deep concealment. Now that was a sentence to remember. Your minimum medical bag with you should have a tourniquet, wound gauze, Israeli wound dressing, occlusive chest dressing, chest decompression needle, tracheotomy kit and chemical heat pad or "thermal wrap".

This is what it will take to stand a chance of surviving a chaotic modern day war street battle, a hardcore kidnap attempt or a violent large gang home invasion. I consider these suggestions to be wise and prudent. I also understand that many may think it is just too much. You decide; no worries. Your choices and those outcomes are yours and yours alone.

To be *"Mogadishu ready"* and survive that kind of long duration battle chaos you need also to plan and prepare by having night vision goggles or some form of night vision optics. Have also a gas mask with filters or at least a dust mask, chemical blood clotting powder, at least one hydration bladder, one canteen full of water, two to 14 nutrition bars or gels and a weapons cleaning kit. If you have access to a battle rifle, try to have at least 3 to 8 loaded magazines if possible. *i* prefer 6 to 12.

That makes for a very heavy load and requires you to be very fit, tough and determined. If not, you need to have a rather static, tactically superior cover on high ground and in optimum darkness to fight from. To ensure magazine reliability we recommend you under load each magazine by two rounds of its maximum capacity. You have to balance taking enough weapons, ammunition and water to be able to be self reliant without resupplies for at least 72 hours. In fact, you need to be able to take the lead and have enough weapons, ammunition, water and food to also issue others and possibly take care of those around you who are less prepared.

It is very difficult to operate independent from a support chain and to carry all you need on your body. Carry what is most essential in your clothing pockets and in some form of H-webbing or load bearing / assault vest. The less immediately necessary gear goes into a messenger bag and the least essential, back up and extra items in a backpack. When you hit intense contact be willing to drop your heavy backpack, in order to be more nimble and understand that you may or often may not be able to recover it later. Zeroed and functionally clean weapons three to five layers deep with full and extra magazines, full water bladders and canteens and a good supply of carefully selected premium quality trauma medical supplies are absolutely the most important items to have on you.

Carry only what you will be able to hike 40 miles and more with. Ideally you should be able to run 1 to 5 miles at a fast pace with all your most essential gear without it falling from where you carry it and without dying with exhaustion. May *i* recommend you run a mile with all your most essential gear on you (rifle / shotgun, revolver / pistol, combat knife, combat hatchet, water bladder / canteen and medical trauma kit) while wearing boots and then immediately at the end of the run firing 3 to 9 accurate shots with each weapon from 25 yards at 3 or more separate targets hitting a 6" x 12" area around the heart and / or the spinal cord and / or the area between the upper lip and one inch above the eyebrows on each target.

If war zone survival and escape is a concern for you then practice hiking and condition yourself through gradual increments to be able to go 40 miles with a 45 to 65 pound backpack in 24 to 72 hours. One of your many problems may be the fact that you do not have an equally well trained and armed team supporting you.

If kidnapping is your primary concern, focus on preventive actions such as constantly changing your routes and departure times. Change the vehicles you drive in and if possible change your position in the vehicles. Be less predictable. Definitely carry three layers of handguns and a sharp tactical neck knife. Become really skilled at being an alert observer and highly skilled at *"Krav-Haganah"* and *"Jiu-jitsu."* At minimum, master the drills on the FEAR NOT DVD. I can also introduce to you my own Kusemono-Do system. Interpreted, it means "The Way of The Reliable Man".

If rape is your greatest concern, avoid being alone as much as you can. Become masterful at a front kick to the groin as well as the palm thrust to the lower jaw, the thumbs in eye's technique and the lethal neck jerk technique. Become effective with both while standing and when on your back. Carry at least a powerful pepper spray and know how to use it. Even better would be to carry at least a loaded .38 internal hammer snub nose J-frame revolver where you can rapidly, smoothly and easily access it in an emergency and then have in addition a sharp tactical neck knife or a tactical folder and be highly skilled with both your handgun and knife of personal choice.

If criminal home invasion is your greatest fear, get two to four alert and capable of defending you dogs. Get battery operated doorstop alarms and door and window slider stop rods, a 12 gauge pump action shotgun with #6 and # 7 ammunition as well as a .45 or .40 or 9 mm caliber pistol with hollow point ammunition or a .357 or .38 Special revolver.

In your training, practice and rehearse smooth magazine changes and tactical reloading. Practice rapid weapons transfers at least three layers deep. For example transferring from a 7.62 x 51 mm M14 M1A, or FN/FAL® battle rifle, or the 7.62 X 39mm SKS or AK47 or Remington® 870 12 gauge pump action shotgun to a M-1911 Colt® .45 ACP or HK45 pistol or Glock® 17, 9 mm pistol or Smith & Wesson ® 357 revolver to a more compact handgun or a 13" blade Samurai sword knife or a 7" to 10" blade combat knife or battle hatchet of your choice. These are very serious, lethal and under certain circumstances very valuable weapons to have and be trained in. Very few criminals would want to face a man or women or family team armed like this, guaranteed.

Practice doing the following drill. Fire your rifle or shotgun in a tactical standing position, change magazine / reload and empty it again from a tactical kneeling or prone position. Then transition to your heaviest caliber handgun and do the same, now transfer to your second handgun or your knife or hatchet. You should practice shooting accurately at a reasonably fast pace. Train until all magazine changes or reload transfers are smooth, seamless and fast. Then train shooting accurately with your 7.62 x 51 or 39 rifle from the prone position at 100 and at 75 yards. Now transfer to your shotgun for shooting at the 50 and 25 yard distances from a kneeling position and transfer to a handgun next but shoot standing from 25, 15, 7 and 3 yard distances with a magazine change at 25, 15 and 7 yards. Lastly, transfer to your short modern day (13 to 18.5/21") Samurai sword knife or 7" to 9" blade combat knife and action direct vital organ stabs, or two intense slashes and 3 direct vital organ stabs on each of three separate targets. Then switch over to a powerful hatchet action on three separate targets, and finally a threat-stopping head twist on a training dummy.

Now, immediately retreat to a dark area behind solid cover ideally located on high ground, scan for more threats and then ASAP take a long deep breath and immediately begin your medical self-check. Rehearse dealing with massive bleeding in the arms and legs, a blocked airway, multiple torso wounds, tension in the chest along with shock and trauma induced hypothermia. Always practice integrating your tactical and medical trauma care drills seamlessly as a whole and as a complete self sustaining loop. Be tactical, accurate and swift—in that order. Use the FEAR NOT *"Tasks, Conditions & Standards"* as your foundation. It will not make you the "ultimate commando" and that is not my intention but it will make you better prepared than most criminals will expect you to be. It will also give you a level of surprise in your favor and that also is very important.

AAPE and if forced to engage you want to dominate as best you can the high ground, use the best cover with the best escape route options with the darkest shadows and continually scan left to right, close to far, low to high and 360 degrees around. Look through cover; not at it. Look at people at high chest level and notice both the whole person and more closely notice their hands. You want to practice seeing people before they see you. Notice shadows or movement and get into the habit of scanning doorways, windows and rooflines. Notice cars and people in cars. Get really good at being aware and observant. Have a prepared soul, sharp mind and well conditioned body. Nobody can really ever carry enough water and ammunition for battles like the *"Day of the Rangers"* as the Somali's refer to

"Operation Gothic Serpent" / "The Battle of the Black Sea" and still be swift, energetic and nimble. Essentially, you want the use of speed, surprise and violence of action in combat. These are important lessons learned from battles such as Mogadishu and others. Your personal level of skill is more important then the type of weapons you have available to you. Skill plus great equipment is the ultimate advantage. AAPE / AAPPEE

Take a quality training program that professionally teaches weapon safety, legal essentials, gear selection, weapons handling and emphasizes accurate shooting, target discrimination, tactical first contact response drills, the tactical use of cover, medical trauma protocols and procedures and how to deal both with prisoners and the police.

With the AAPE system, with our second-by-second and minute-by-minute in-home, in-car and various on-foot immediate action drills, medical trauma kit, protocols and procedures along with these weapons and *"Tasks, Conditions & Standards"* training and testing drills; *i* feel you have the best possible chance as a civilian to respond to and escape and survive anything from a solo amateur criminal threat, to a large gang assault, a professional kidnap attempt or even perhaps an unfolding urban war zone battle. It will make you a hard target to rape, kidnap or kill—guaranteed.

Without any of this or similar training and weapons you may find yourself in grave danger as an easy target. The choice is yours. When you are up against hard core gang thugs and outnumbered or amongst battle hardened professional soldiers or mercenaries you will wish for what *my expert advisors and i* recommend here in **FEAR NOT** and be very glad to have a little bit more rather than less. Yet, always stay nimble and be both well conditioned and well trained by the best trainers you can access and afford.

Soldiers are familiar with the old truth that very few battle plans survive the first contact with enemy shooters. It exists because it is true but with adequate training and self disciplines our first contact on-foot, in-home and in-car drills could save your life and that of those you care about. Be highly skilled in the drills and willing to be an independent thinking and flexible in action individual. Foresight, preparation, a pragmatic approach and calmness born in professional training and competence are worth gold in emergencies.

I have unreasonable standards and expectations because *i* know just how professional, equipped and capable real world bad guy's can be. To tell you all you ever need is a .38 Special internal hammer J-frame snub nose revolver and one day of training will be irresponsible and a lie. It is a worthy start but please hold yourselves to a higher standard. If you do that, then you will be in the best position possible to **FEAR NOT**. May God have mercy on us all if we are ever in the epicenter of an erupting battle? Please take care and be prepared. AAPE and avoid all of this the best you can. If you are not there in the first place, then you are not at risk so by being aware you avoid being involved at all.

Study this book, commit its core relevance to you and its content to memory and then perhaps you should burn it as it really contains very dangerous information if it falls into the hands of bad people and if the information is misused. Possession of such a highly specialized book may perhaps just count against you in a court of law even if you were 100% right, legal and taking appropriate action in a family-protection and self-defense situation. As always remember our goal is not to engage but rather to remain undetected and to retreat and withdraw from all potentially high risk and violent situations. If forced to engage we only want to stop the threat not slaughter the threat/s. We are the good guys, not thugs. However, we also do not want our families or self to be the victims of gang thugs or professional bad guy's. If forced to, be as intense as may be necessary to stop the threat. You are going to find your own balance and peace in all of this. In this work my primary objective is to prepare you to protect your family and survive extreme crime and combat dangers. The FEAR NOT System can absolutely make you an effective, lethal and formidable threat-stopping family protector if taken serious enough. The choice, responsibility and yes even the consequences are entirely yours. Please be careful, avoid all violence and take care. AAPE

Footnote: Violence, aggression and anger all most often relates to unresolved father or mother issues. Also, the inability to resolve conflicts through communication leave one feeling disempowered. Violent behavior can also be rooted or derived from unhealed, unloved, neglected or abused second energy center also known as a chakra. Sexual pain, inappropriate behavior, anger, frustration, dysfunction, neglect, abuse or some form of misuse of sexual energy are all integral parts of the bigger problem. Violent people often grew up with inadequate fathering and / or inappropriate or misinterpreted love and have deep rooted parent and / or sexual problems and challenges including repression and misuse of their sexual desires. This may then manifest in rape and other utterly destructive violent criminal behaviors. Violence can be expected from uninitiated men who have not done enough inner / soul work as yet. In Africa there is an old saying, "If we do not initiate the young men, they will burn the village down". How true is that in today's world? That is why I created the Agoge. **www.menofthecoode.com**

A Greater Responsibility

Beyond your escaping out of the pending or unfolding battle zone and beyond the war itself we all have a responsibility in making a contribution to bring wholeness to the world. Globally we men have especially disappointed women. First our mothers, then our wives and then our daughters and in many cases our sons as well. We mistrust, exploit and kill one another and we pollute and poison the earth with our greed, arrogance and ignorance. This need not be so. There is a better way to live. We are smarter than that, are we not? We need to seek and apply more wisdom, don't you think?

Our world needs better leaders and more conscious, awakened, wiser and more caring men and women if we are to prevent a breakdown and facilitate a breakthrough. It is really as simple as that. The difference between what we actually do and what we are potentially able to do is all that is needed to make the difference and that will make all the difference. We cannot think it is other people's responsibility or that we are so weak, un-resourceful and non influential that what we can do does not matter. It matters! Every person's daily choices and actions matter very much. Alone we may be weak but 10, then 100 then 1000 then 1 million of us together are very powerful. When two people gather and pray together there is power. When 10 good men or men and women or women meet in a sacred wisdom circle with good intent there is power.

Together we can find solutions for restoring things to wholeness. We can educate and inspire people. Together we can plant a food garden, build a shelter, a library, a hospital, a place of worship, create a protected water source, plant a food forest, create natural energy systems and so much more to make our world a better, happier and safer place for all. We can no longer just take, and take and take and exploit or waste resources. We need to restore balance and the harmony with wisdom only and just take what we really need. We need to take prayer with more respect and gratitude and share with more love in our hearts. We need to give more back because if we do not then wars will continue to devour our lives and lands. A more gentle and more spiritual path is important and the best way.

Helping Orphans and Widows

The Special Operations Warrior Foundation (SOWF)

If you are captivated and as touched as I am with the "Battle of the Black Sea" and believe as much as I do in the value of special operations warriors that help keep our world a safer and better place, then let us together support foundations such as The Special Operations Warrior Foundation (SOWF). This 501 © (3) nonprofit tax-exempt foundation was originally founded as the legendary US Army Green Beret Colonel Arthur D. "Bull" Simons Scholarship Fund to provide college educations for the seventeen children surviving the nine soldiers killed or severely crippled at the Desert One, Delta Force Iranian hostage rescue attempt.

This fund purpose is so that no child should be left behind if one of their parents is killed on a mission or during a training accident. (SOWF) provides college scholarship grants that include tuition, room and board, books and more. In addition, family and financial counseling and life coaching is made available to children of hundreds of fallen special operations soldiers.

We are committed to contributing to this foundation from the profits of **"FEAR NOT"**. Helping widows and orphans is a noble obligation as was written in God's word. We want to thank you for your purchase and further support to the Special Operations Warrior Foundation. **www.specialops.org** P.O. Box 14385 Tampa, FL 33690 **warrior@specialops.org** 1-866-600-SOWF

Your Foundation

If you have limited or no military, police and civilian gun or self defense training, I suggest you first study the appendices in the back of this book please. Developing a solid foundation will be essential.

Build your foundation on the AAPE system, kidnap prevention, fundamental firing positions and on-foot, in-car, and in-home first contact action drills, the bodyguard technique, the prisoner management and the war zone survival and escape strategy along with the medical trauma protocols and procedures taught in Fear Not. You should become masterfully proficient at all the *"Task, Conditions and Standards"* tests.

Get real good at taking a training dummy down with a palm thrust and also with a lethal head twist using *"surprise"*, *"speed"* and *"controlled aggression."*

Next, master the use of both a handgun and a shotgun and then become really comfortable and confident with one and two knives in your hand/s.

Study Appendix A. Weapon & Personal Safety and Appendix B. Weapon and
Shooting Fundamentals in great detail.

Experiment with the Israeli handgun combat shooting stance, the Isosceles stance and the Weaver stance. Next, get really good at instinctively using an aggressive modified Isosceles stance. The modified Isosceles and the Israeli shooting stance are in my view the two very best standing shooting stances for real world high intensity gunfights. Do your own research and decide for yourself.

Here is how real pro's do it in life and death situations:

1. Step forward with a short slide as you begin to draw or even better yet have your handgun already in both your hands with the barrel two inches below your eyes in a ready position.
2. Set yourself a solid stance.
3. Bend your knees slightly with feet shoulder width apart.
4. Lean slightly forward at the waist and be ready to rotate 45 degrees in either direction and if necessary shuffle and slide your feet to adjust to new threats.
5. Hold and keep your shoulders and hips facing squarely forward towards the target.
6. Shoulders relaxed, rolled forward, arms forward and elbows tucked in tight.
7. Arms up and almost fully extended with only one or both elbows slightly bent.
8. Hold the handgun with a firm grip in both hands with your palms together. Grip high and firm with your thumbs aligned. Hold your firing hand slightly relaxed with a relaxed trigger finger and with a firmer grip with your supporting hand.
9. Head up and both eyes open.
10. Take aim on your target/threat with your handgun front sight centered and
    100% level with the rear sight and the top edge of the front sight accurately aimed at the heart, lower brain, pelvis, spine or upper thigh of your threat.
11. Use only the front pad of your trigger finger when you shoot. When you fire, press the trigger straight back in one smooth motion. To become proficient you can practice with special dry fire ammunition. Take up your trigger slack and press the trigger straight back while experiencing resetting the trigger. With effective training and use of an appropriate stance, grip, breathing and trigger control you can and will improve your accuracy dramatically.
12. Fire two accurate and fast shots at the heart and one more accurate shot into the lower brain as a standard foundational drill. Mix it up with firing 3 to 7 shots at one target. Place your

rounds three to four inches apart and not in a tight shooting competition grouping. This will help stop your threat more effectively. Get a lot of practices doing this entire drill on a random number of multiple targets. Use three to thirteen or more targets at a time.

Work on safety, stance and accuracy first and gradually increase your speed until you can perform this drill consistently in a smooth and accurate manner in fewer than two seconds from a safe and legal concealed draw. Study and practice doing a smooth, fast and accurate magazine transfer. Get consistently and outstandingly good at this drill in low light conditions, under induced stress conditions and in confined spaces. Let this become your core default foundation for handgun use. Also use this stance as a foundation for handgun and other weapon shooting and for knife fighting and unarmed combat. (The exception is for the Samurai sword where you want to keep more weight on your front foot, about 60-70%) It is the classic warrior stance. Remember to practice changing magazines in static positions and while on the move while using this stance as your foundation. Use this stance philosophy with your shotgun, handguns, hatchet, and knife.

Remember to constantly scan left to right, close to far, low to high and 360 degrees around. Watch and notice people's hands. Do all you can to avoid engaging in fights of any kind. Calm and deescalate the situation. Talk, buy or run your way out of there if you can. If that is not possible, utilize a non-lethal option and retreat ASAP. If forced to do so, you want to be willing to dynamically engage with a lethal threat stopping option while using the foundational principles and practices in the 2.2 System.

Fundamental Firing Positions

If armed, and forced to do so after a less lethal option will not stop your unlawful violent assaulters; draw and present your firearm. Take one of the following three foundational defensive firing positions and reassess the threat while you do so. If the threat froze at the sight of your gun do not fire. If the threat persists and increases, then fire immediately if that is your only option and last resort for survival. Use the best cover available against their threat to you. Do not rest your firearm against or on cover. Be sure that your weapons muzzle is clear from the cover and far enough away to prevent the fired shells from hitting or entering the ejection port. It is a good habit to develop.

Master these three fundamental firing positions and be open when necessary to being unorthodox in your adaption of each. Instinctively adapt according to your unique threat encounter. Be intelligent and understand the use of safe angles and safe distances when needed which are taught in our practical hands-on classes.

Notice the detail in each position. For example sitting back onto your foot in the kneeling position with your back foot pointing forward and ready to propel upward and or forward if need be.

Frequently practice the following three firing positions:

1. A chest forward, lowered, standing position out of a sideways slide or the high ready position as demonstrated in the picture here.

2. A low, reversing, tactical kneeling position.

3. A rear, prone position. Our focus at this foundational level is on positions and tactics complementing legally justified and safe family protection and self-defense.

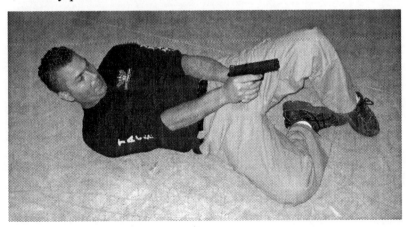

Remember, a fast hand thrust under the jaw can be very powerful and give you a brief chance for retreat to safety. As a surprise, thrust upwards hard and fast. Use your legs, hips and body weight while exhaling. Follow through energetically with focus and or follow up with two more strikes. Swiftly pull your hand back. Avoid getting into a ground fight wrestling or grappling situation unless you are a master at it or if you are physically much heavier and stronger than your opponent and only if you are not outnumbered. Ideally stay on your feet, strike and run. If the threat persists and justifies such a response, rapidly draw your weapon and if needed as a last resort fire two quick rounds into the threats torso and re-assess with a quick AAPE check what to do next. Before actually shooting first rapidly reassess the evolution of the imminent threat but do not hesitate. Be wise, just and intelligently decisive. Sadly, if need be, fire 2, 3 or more man stopping shots. Fire 2 in the heart/ lung area and if necessary to stop the threat one in the face/lower brain area between the upper lip and mid forehead per imminent threat as a last resort shot placement. (One shot per threat, if there are many of them and they are closer than 30 feet from you and especially if you only have a revolver with a limited number of rounds.) Observe your threat target's response and fire as many additional rounds as needed to stop the threat. Shoot until the threat goes down and stays down.

In body-to-body situations a revolver, 13" Samurai style fixed blade knife or a quality talon blade knife or hatchet may be best. There are situations where a pepper spray or stun gun simply will not be sufficient for dealing with a violent real-world threat and sadly a handgun will be the minimum self-defense requirement. Be mindful that even after receiving several fatal shots, a person typically has enough life left to remain a threat for another 15 to 30 plus seconds. So do the best you can to watch them very carefully and scan for further threats?

If attacked by multiple assaulters you may have to limit your initial shots to one or two well placed shots per threat. This depends on how close they are, how many there are, what they are armed with and what the ammunition capacity of your chosen firearm is. As a general guideline shoot the one that is either the closest or the greatest threat first. If your time-distance-opportunity allows, shoot the assault leader first. Remember, our key targets for stopping a violent, lethal threat are situated along the midline of the body from the pelvis up and mostly in the upper 30% of the torso or above the upper lip. Directly behind the nose is where the brain stem is situated at the lower end of the brain.

As soon as you can safely improve your cover and or retreat immediately call 911 when it is safe to do so. Legally it is best not to leave the scene of the shooting unless there is further imminent danger. If you do leave, go directly to the nearest police station. Call 911 as you leave the scene of a shooting. The law requires you to remain at the scene of the shooting. Do not go home and do not shower or change clothing, especially if you are covered in blood. This is all vital evidence and may not be tampered with. Doing so could and most likely will be used against you in court. Sadly, it is best to not talk with the police and not to provide a statement without legal council being present. At most simply say, **"That you feared for your life, that you are currently overwhelmed and you would like to see your lawyer please"**.

Be especially careful when sitting in a public toilet with an open door/stall design. Be careful where you put your handbag/briefcase and avoid being grabbed and pulled by the ankles thus causing your head to hit the floor. This leaves your exposed body trapped midway under the locked door while one or two people assault or shoot you from one or both sides or over the top.

For men standing at a urinal, it is wise to be intuitively aware, engage your periphery and use the tile wall to watch your back as well as you can, depending on the light. Should someone grab your concealed weapon, immediately clamp down with your elbow and while feeling their body in close, spin around and hit the attacker on the temple with your other elbow. Use your hips, breathing and weight to add power to your strike. Sharply exhale through your nose as you strike.

The best preventive strategy is to position your handgun directly into your pants and 45 degrees to the front when in crowded areas. In fact, if you have a concealed carry permit it is very effective to carry it without a holster like this most of the time. Simply conceal it with a longer, loose, not tucked in item of clothing.

On The Shooting Range

It is important that you invest enough days and hours on the shooting range to become really competent. Professional instruction is essential. Here are a few pointers.

Pack the weapons of your own choice based on what you have and plan to become truly proficient in. Here are my recommendations.

First, please avoid or at least minimize the wearing of camouflage clothing at all public shooting ranges and please avoid all hyper aggressive and macho stuff. A more discreet approach is best. One or so moral patches are okay and a little bit of merit based and authentic masculine or feminine style and attitude is just fine.

Unless you are going to a private shooting range do not carry or use large knives, smoke grenades etcetera. It is however important to train and practice wearing and carrying exactly what you plan to wear and use in a real world emergency zone situation.

Remember your training and practice drills must always, as much as possible, resemble exactly what you intend to do in real world, high risk and fast paced violent encounters. However, not all shooting ranges will welcome that style of training. In fact, very few will. Find a shooting range that understands your needs and can offer realistic tactical practice.

Be always mindful of our overall understanding; "What you do or fail to do tactically in the first 2 to 3 seconds of a violent encounter and do or fail to do medically in the first two to five minutes of a wounding can make a more than 90% difference between life and death." Please train with that in mind. Also, train seamlessly to integrate shooting and medical drills. Make a pre-practice request that everyone wear their blood group identification on them and make a pre-practice list of their blood group by name. Have the list on you and preferably in your top left chest pocket.

Begin each range session by recapping the most important safety rules and by ensuring everyone knows where the master medical trauma kit is. Have it on you or close to you. Insist (or issue) that everyone present also has Nitrile® gloves, blood clotting agents, gauze, wound dressing bandage or two tampons or sanitary pads, a tourniquet, a Asherman®/ Hyfin® or similar occlusive one way valve wound dressing, a chest decompression needle, an airway trumpet and two mini chemical heating pads on their person and know exactly how to use each. Keep a "thermal wrap" ready in your rucksack. Train / Re-train everyone in the use of each item prior to the first shot being fired. It is the wise, responsible and right thing to do. You must as often as possible train with the following in mind:

Always remember to AAPE. Wear body armor. Be professionally trained by the best. Carry quality weapons. Scan systematically from left to right, close to far, high to low, deep through cover and 360 degrees around. Look at the edges of alleys, scan roof top lines, shadows, doorways, windows and look in and low around vehicles. Notice peoples hands, shadows and muzzle flashes.

If forced to do so, maintain;
1.   Surprise
2.   Speed
3.   Violence-of-action

As you lose the element of surprise, increase your speed and as the situation gets more intense, proportionately increase your violence-of-action until you stop the threat and dominate the territory from behind the best cover on the highest ground and in the darkest concealment. Always know where your best retreat and escape routes are.

While you dominate the high ground, again I want to remind you to use the best cover and concealment including the darkest areas. Shoot 2 accurate shots at each threats chest (heart) and your time and opportunity permitting add one or two shots as necessary into the brain of each threat. Depending on how the threat responds, you may want to add one or two extra shots if necessary into the threats pelvis. The foundational principle is to shoot as many rounds per target as is necessary to stop the threat. Do not waste ammunition. Use a heavy enough caliber (7.62 x 51 or 7.62 x 39, or .45, .44, .357, .41, .40 or if you insist a 9 mm or .38 Special) to stop most threats with a maximum of two well placed (accurate) rounds. A .41 or .40 pistol may be the best overall compromise for most non career shooters. A slightly larger grouping, practiced on the range, will do this better in most cases and so will wounding the face and side torso.

Please be highly skilled in safe weapons handling, marksmanship and medical trauma first-aid as relating to gun and knife wounds. You need to train and practice all of this to be effective and accomplished. The previous recommendations are simply the core fundamentals of becoming an effective warrior when forced to be one. By mastering this, you will become a formidable family protector and a very hard target to kidnap, rape or murder.

Packing List for a Day on the Shooting Range

1. Binoculars (8 x 20)

2. Body armor. (Level IV)

3. Ballistic safety glasses, electronic ear protectors, sunscreen, sun hat / cap and a foul weather parka or anorak with a hood as well as shooting gloves if the season or weather requires it. (Wear season specific range wear)

4. Targets. Lot's of targets and bullet hole stickers to refresh your targets.

5. Shot timer + spare batteries.

6. Water (4 quarts) and food. (Absolutely no alcohol, never)

7. A zeroed battle rifle, hunting rifle or carbine of your choice—30.08 or 30.06 hunting rifle with a Leupold® or Trijicon® scope of your own choice, or a 7.62 x 51 mm M14 M1A, FN®/FAL® or similar quality battle rifle with a second generation Schmidt & Bender© CQB 1.1–4 x 20 short dot scope and an unpadded V-Tec® rifle sling, or a 7.62 X 39 mm SKS and/or AK 47, or 5.56 carbine if you insist. Pack 5 + (6–8) magazines and 50 to 1000 + rounds. Include chest webbing and a Samurai knife discreetly hidden behind it, if on a private range.

8. 12 gauge Remington® or Mossberg® pump action shotgun with Trijicon© reflex sights and 25 to 50 + rounds. (No 6, double buck and slugs)

9. Colt® 1911 .45 ACP, or .357 Smith & Wesson® revolver with 2 speed loaders / .40 Smith & Wesson® or Heckler &

Koch® pistol / 9 mm Glock® 17 or 19 / 9 mm Sig Sauer® or Browning® HP with 4 + magazines and 50 to 500 + rounds. Perhaps also a .38 Special snub nose, internal hammer J-frame Smith & Wesson® with a laser sight and / or a .22L Beretta® or a subcompact 9 mm pistol of your own choice with ammunition. Take one or two Safariland® 6004 ALS drop leg holster if you have body armor, one leather or polymer hip or pocket or purse holster and one leather or polymer shoulder holster with you. Also at least two pistol magazine pouches.

10. Surefire® E 2 LED Defender™ flashlight. (Frequent night training is essential. Train to use your light very briefly and sparingly, if at all. Rather use night vision goggles or quality night optics and get used to shooting accurately in low light conditions.)

11. CRKT® Hissatsu™ 13 inch blade Samurai style sword blade.

12. Viking Tactics® knife (3.75" fixed blade) or a commando dagger or combat utility knife of your choice or simply a box cutter knife. Again, please be private, discreet and careful with knifes and hatches. Especially on public ranges.

13. Comprehensive personal medical trauma kit.

14. Weapons cleaning kit.

15. A charged cell phone, conformed as switched off.

16. Range chair.

This is a fantastic list of high quality hardware to own, train and practice with.

Begin your collection with the shotgun and one quality handgun, a medical trauma kit, safety gear and a cleaning kit and add to it as you can. Use a dedicated gear bag for all your equipment.

Shooting Range Safety Rules

Observe all known safety rules and regulations as listed in the appendices section of this book. Make this your minimum standard. Research all relevant safety rules and regulations and observe them diligently. Please study Appendix A before going to the range. Here are 15 key reminders. (These recommendations are not intended to replace Appendix A, but to support the measures indicated there. It is always your responsibility to familiarize yourself with any range and legal rules regarding firearms.)

1. Share all responsibility for the range safety and safety of everyone present and around the area. Everyone's safety is your direct responsibility.
2. Immediately report all observed risks. Call CEASE FIRE the moment you witness any unsafe behavior.
3. Keep all your weapons holstered or in a weapons case until ready to use. Re-holster and encase any weapon after your range use.
4. Maintain strict and wise safety device discipline. This pertains to your weapon, your place on the range and your handling of any other weapon or ammunition.
5. Maintain strict and intelligent gun muzzle discipline.
6. Maintain responsible trigger finger and appropriate trigger discipline.
7. Demonstrate an uncommonly high level of personal good conduct discipline, I.e. Playing around, yelling and cheering, careless lack of mutual consideration. Be respectful of all range personnel and guests. Be professional yet you do not have to take yourself so serious that you appear as a grumpy old goat.
8. Do not take any shooting practice with over talkative, egotistical, bragging, loud mouth men or women who lack wisdom and respect for the range rules. Avoid them in all areas of life as well. Seek out wise, mature, experienced, confident and respectful trainers who are not bullies but who are also skilled trainers who will educate you in the hardened old school ways that come without being pampered.

9. Have only one appropriately qualified person provide range orders at any given time.
10. Wear your body armor, safety glasses and ear protectors on the range.
11. Always shoot only in a forward direction and below the level of the safety walls. Know what is behind each target before you engage and start shooting.
12. Stay well behind any active shooter.
13. Keep yourself well hydrated because even slight dehydration can cause a headache, reduce your good judgment and reduce your performance capabilities. It can also lead to accidents. If nothing more, dehydration can also cause personality mood swings. You could become an old grump who can cause even more problems.
14. Have a comprehensive gun wound medical trauma kit on hand and know exactly how to use every item in it.
15. Contact the Range Supervisor or even 911 Emergency for any serious irregularity or emergency.

Managed public shooting ranges typically require the following or similar additional safety and general order and conduct rules.

1. All shooters must receive a thorough safety orientation before each practice.

2. Everyone present in the shooting areas must wear ear and eye protection. During more tactical drills everyone must wear body armor with front, rear and side plates of an appropriate level to weapons in use.

3. Shooting is only allowed in designated, marked and approved areas and only at approved, non-human image targets with only lawful firearms.

4. Asymmetrical warfare type drills are frowned upon and only allowed with explicit prior permission. Even then, all bullets must hit the front backstops and no tracer or armor piercing rounds are allowed on public recreation ranges.

5. Alcohol and drugs are prohibited on all ranges as are all persons under the influence of said chemicals.

6. No fires are allowed.

7. No excessively loud music is allowed.

8. Smoking on the range is prohibited.

9. Minors must be accompanied and supervised by a parent or designated adult supervisor.

10. All pets must be leashed and under the owners control. Owners are responsible to remove all pet waste.

11. All driving and parking signage must be obeyed as posted.

12. Obey all shooting range staff requests and decisions as the highest level of authority.

13. One person present must be a certified and designated medical first aid responder with at minimum a charged cell phone and wound dressing on his/her person.

14. Do not bring big knives and battle hatchets or hunting bows onto the range without special permission, and even then be discreet.

We cannot emphasize it enough that you need hard, realistic, professional training. Get trained by the best people you can access. Come and train with our team. To train in and practice the official **"FEAR NOT"** system you will need training directly with me or one of my certified professional trainers.

Our ultimate goal for you is that you become masterful at out Tasks, Conditions & Standards (TCS) drills and immediate first contact on-foot, in-car and in-home action drills. To become outstanding at this, you need dry fire and live fire practice in those exact drills under expert professional supervision.

To develop a solid foundation for your warm up and each time you go to the range I recommend you practice the following drills. These are great range drills for at home and in between training sessions with my team and *i*.

Shooting Drills

Once you have a good basic level of broad spectrum skill, use each training or practice session to work on improving a specific skill or competency such as dry fire skill drills, shooting positions / stances, zeroing, *"bullseye"* marksmanship from a specific distance, tactical magazine changes and reloads, weapon transfers, weak hand shooting, hand gun draw and presentation, fundamental, intermediate or advanced first contact combat drills with or without a partner. Especially practice solid in-home, in-car, on-foot and medical trauma drills. Always include drills where you integrate tactical shooting, unarmed combat and medical trauma drill skills all in one seamless and compounded drill.

Make sure you get a lot of *"bullseye"* marksmanship shooting practice for accuracy as well as lots of handgun draw with fast accurate shooting practice. Again, I stress extensive and highly detailed trauma medical treatment practice drills as well as unarmed combat drills. This is the inner core of our system.

Do you initial warm up by doing several dry practice drills. Correct mistakes safely with empty weapons training first. It is advisable to precede each drill with a dry run using an unloaded and safe weapon first.

1. Now begin your live fire with 5 to 20 + slow, accurate rounds at 25 + yards (up to 100 yards, your choice) with your rifle in any firing position of your own choice, 15 + yards with your shotgun and 7 + yards with your handguns. Repeat several times and zero your weapons as necessary and to your preference.

2. Next, at 15 to 100 yards empty a rifle or shotgun magazine in the standing position, tactically reload and repeat in the kneeling position and then reload and repeat in a prone position. Now transition tactically to your primary handgun and empty one magazine from prone at 25 yards, the next magazine from

15 yards in the kneeling position and finish as you empty a third magazine while you tactically walk forward and shoot from the 7 yard position. Walk with short fast paced yet secure and determined steps. Make accuracy your priority and as you close in on your target accelerate your shooting speed to optimum-maximum speed. This is your highest possible shooting speed with control and accuracy. Shoot at the heart, spinal cord, lower brain and pelvis and even the upper thighs. By doing this your intention is to overload the threats with chaos induced by you. If forced to do so, I want you to respond in such a powerful, precise and dynamic way that your threats will retreat or drop down and crawl up in a fetal position and surrender completely.

3. In this session, I want you to set up 5 staggered targets and shoot each with two heart and one or two head shots with first your rifle at 25 + yards or shotgun at 15 yards from a standing or kneeling position then transition to your primary handgun and shoot closing in on the target one to four magazines or speed loaders full of ammunition. Close in to about 7 yards. Never go closer then 7 yards if you have the choice. Even that is tight. Staying 25 plus yards is a much safer distance to be from any threat. In fact, *i* believe the further the better. You should be so far from them that no shooting is necessary or could be effective. Distances of a mere 3 yards down to 1 yard are very dangerous in the real world. This is the domain of snub nose, internal hammer revolvers and tactical swords and knives. This is a very dangerous zone. After the above drills are completed, move forward to the 3 or less yard distance and do a quick revolver and sword/knife/box cutter drill for practice. It may one day be exactly the distance your threats may be to you. Be prepared for this eventuality.

4. During this exercise set up 3 to 7 staggered targets (your choice) at 7 to 15 + yards and shoot each target with your primary handgun. Shoot 2 rounds in the heart, then 1 or 2 rounds in the brain and occasionally a third round in the heart and one additional round in the pelvis. Also, practice counting

your rounds along with performing smooth tactical magazine changes and practice transferring to a second and even third handgun in a tactical manner. Use standing, kneeling and prone firing positions and practice shooting while moving forward, sideways and backwards in a safe and tactical manner. Remember to breathe. In a real world situation your adrenalin and breathing play an important part in your ability to be accurate. Learning to control your excitement here will work well for you later.

5. The course now gets even more difficult as I am asking you to set up 3 to 5 random targets staggered at between 7 and 35 yards and fire two accurate chest (6" x 8" zone) rounds with your rifle or shotgun into each in less than 3.5 seconds. Now transition (remember to engage your safety selector) to your primary handgun and repeat this in under 3 seconds and transition to a second handgun or do a tactical reload and repeat the process in ideally as little as 2.5 seconds. You should train to always hit your first 3 targets accurately in the chest in well under 2 seconds. You want to alternate at times while shooting each target at will and impacting into the heart or brain and pelvis and upper thighs. Occasionally it is a good thing to mix up your pattern and expand your capabilities. Having said all that and in the final analysis, at your core you should have one fundamental system you are a master in. Develop one system that will serve you well under all conditions and circumstances. May *i* recommend two heart/lung shots, one or more brain / face shot/s and if necessary as many pelvis and upper thigh or additional brain and heart shots as it takes to stop the threat. Always begin with two accurate heart / lung shots followed by a headshot. Elite soldiers specializing in hostage rescue train in delivering one or two super accurate head shots to begin with. Practice eliminating the closest threat first and then move on to the next.

The above drills on their own make for either a solid training and practice session or a great warm up for our FEAR NOT Tasks, Conditions & Standards drills and tests. Use only 100%

safe, plastic training guns for your disarming and unarmed combat drills. Use as necessary only safe 6 mm plastic or paint bullet training weapons for all force-on-force training and practice scenarios. Use the necessary safety gear and always put safety first. Again, be aware that most managed shooting ranges will not allow this kind of training without a prior formal written request and a written approval. Please respect that. The same goes for knife throwing and edged weapons training and practice.

6.   Your practice day on the shooting range should include some slow and highly accurate *"bullseye"* rifle shots from somewhere between 100 to 500 yards. (Range Limits Permitting) Then select random distances such as 75, 63, 50, 29 and 25 yards. Practice also some slow accurate shotgun effectiveness from 25, 15 and 7 yards and again work in some slow, accurate handgun rounds from 50, 35, 21, 9 and 4 yards.

7.   Frequently work at our bodyguard drill with a dummy. Remember to use very controlled and safe conditions when working with a partner. Grab the dummy by the neck and complete all of the drills with the utmost attention to safety.

8.   Now, run a 5 to 7 round speed drill from between 18 and 3 yards where you will draw and as soon as you have your handgun muzzle pointing on target at hip level begin to shoot. Follow the spine as your guide and place rounds spread out and upwards like a ladder from the pelvis upwards into the stomach, heart, upper chest, face and mid to high brain. Do this as fast as you possibly can while maintaining the highest safety standards. Immediately after each shooting drill scan from left to right, close to far, low to high and 360 degrees around. Remember to keep your muzzle pointed safely down range. Also practice dropping safely into a rear prone position and repeat the exact previous shot placement pattern from bottom up.

9.   If you have access to the right and a 100% safe environment, you may also want to occasionally do a *"jungle lane"* / *"man-hunt"* drill just for fun. Let a buddy set up several targets along a deep, isolated and dry riverbed or some other 100% safe checked perimeter secured area. Secure all access roads with guards in safe positions and with tested working radios that are within range and all on the same frequency and with spare fresh batteries. Use 3 to 15 + targets. You can randomly place each target partially hidden away at varying heights along a 25 to 100 yard lane. If you are in a 100 % safe and secured area use a random number of rifle and / or pistol rounds (2 to 7) per target. For safety purposes we recommend you use a shotgun with #7 or lighter bird shot and only fire one shot per target. Super high safety standards are 100% critical in this drill. Know what is behind each target or do not shoot. This is a proven military drill but requires a 100% controlled and very large training area and secured shooting range with massive safety margins. It is a real treat with pop up targets, smoke and flash-bang grenade trip wires all over the route and with several safe smoke only land mines designed specifically for training purposes. Do not even think of setting this up at a normal shooting range. Shooting only in a forward direction is allowed on shooting ranges. This is a potentially very dangerous commando drill and requires very experienced and responsible supervision and a 100% safe environment. If in doubt, please do not attempt to run this drill. I overstate things in **FEAR NOT** because our world is full of distractions, full of Hyper Attention Deficit people and because on occasion it is necessary.

Here is a superb alternative or additional real world preparation
drill. Use a blindfold or a totally dark training area and / or
place a black heavy hood with a string or large paper shopping
bag with a pull string glued under strong paper at the top
(ex–bottom) with the paracord or other string running through
a small pulley above. A full length, four sided wall made out
of black cloth or heavy canvas can also effectively be used.
The choice is yours. Be innovative. Place one or more new
targets to shoot at random distances and unannounced pull the
cover off of the persons head. The shooter needs to draw and
respond ASAP. You can also randomly use blue sprayed targets
as *"friendlies"* amongst bad guy targets and let the shooter
make shoot/non-shoot decisions. This is an outstanding tactical

drill that speeds up threat recognition and reduces shooter response time after having had thorough practice. It really sharpens one up. This drill is also great for weapon disarming drills and unarmed combat drills. You can silently position one, two, three or four real person practice partners *"assaulters"* in random and alternating positions around the hooded defender for unarmed combat training drills. As the light goes on and the bag comes off, he or she must immediately AAPE and deal with the attacking *"assaulters."* You can also place one or more wounded and down *"friendlies"* in the area for him or her to deal with after the assaulting threats have been stopped. Do this drill like all the others while wearing your full *"battle gear"* and with other protective training gear as necessary. This exercise could be carried out in as little as just sleep wear and barefoot depending on who and where you are. Also do this drill starting from a lying down / sleeping position. Use whatever safety precautions and protective body pads, helmets, mouth piece, knee and elbow guard's etcetera you may find necessary to avoid any serious injury to anyone. The defender must rapidly gain control and both stop the threat and dominate the *"combat zone."* This drill, *i* can tell you from experience, is easier said than done. It remains a worthy and very valuable exercise regardless of the outcome. This drill will make you super sharp and prepare you well for real world violent assault responses. Practice it often. All these drills are somewhat similar to Special Forces type drills. Elite Special Operations units demand the highest possible levels of safety, unbelievable accuracy and incredible speed in each of their drills. There are men who can shoot more than 1000 rounds per man per week with weapons and practice tactical drills as a focused unit to become extraordinarily good as a unit and with their weapons. Some operators in "Tier One" units develop a hard callus in the web of their shooting hand and consider 5000 attempts as the minimum number of times a drill needs to be repeated to develop a high level of skill. That certainly puts things into perspective, does it not?

11. For a Close Contact Drill, position two targets, one at 1.5 yards and the other at 3 yards from you. On the go, raise your non-shooting elbow vertically up in a rapid elbow strike position and keep it up at face level as a sharp shield against an attacker. You are holding it well above where you would usually be positioning it at your heart level when you normally prepare to shoot. This will depend on who you are. It may be safer to just place your non shooting hand on your chest. Simultaneously draw your cocked handgun from your holster, align it with your target while still holding it at a low level close to your body. Disengage the safety and fire one shot to the chest of the closest target. Take a short shuffle step backward, fire rapidly one accurate shot now using both hands at the 2nd target. Then fire one more round each at the face of the first target and the second target.

Next kneel down in a tactical rear kneeling position with your handgun on safe and concealed down low. Scan left to right, close to far, low to high, and 360 degrees around. Prioritize what you look at. Where can another shooter be? Check doorways, windows . . . Always notice people's hands. Who represents a threat? Who is the highest risk right now? AAPE! Also, with suitably qualified professional supervision on a proper shooting range, practice dropping into a rear prone position on the draw and fire accurately and rapidly on each target. Again, when you've completed shooting, scan 360 degrees around. Always maintain outstanding safety discipline and continue the exercise by taking cover.

You may want to rehearse by also carrying a tactical fixed blade knife at chest level affording immediate access. Imagine now that target one is attempting to grab your pistol or carbine and with your non-shooting hand you must stab the target in the heart with your knife. Now pull the knife back while stepping to the rear and follow the previous described drill exactly to its completion. Please be careful. Replace the knife at the earliest convenience. Adding the knife drill is valuable for when you are in very close quarters and there is the risk that shooting may result in your hitting a "buddy", other "friendly's" or anyone or anything else you do not intend to shoot. This will also apply to any situation where there is the risk of over penetration or when excessive noise could be a factor. Get in the habit of intelligently and with wisdom adjusting your shooting angles up or down as may be necessary to ensure maximum safety for all concerned.

Note: At times, in very close quarter situations, especially when you may be using a shotgun, battle rifle, carbine and even a handgun; it may be grabbed by your attacker. In such a case it may be faster and safer to simply transition to a well placed and ready for use fixed blade tactical knife rather than transitioning to a second firearm. After one fast lethal stab as may be necessary, transition back to a firearm ASAP. Ideally, make it your primary firearm.

If this type of training is of interest and could be useful to you; I can potentially introduce you to a master instructor in these techniques. He also offers the best knife designed for this application. From learning these drills and having the right equipment, you will literally have the "edge".

12. Partner Drill (Advanced Combat Shooting Drill)

Although I personally prefer the military commando style "Buddy-Buddy" (leap frog) system of tactically moving forward onto a target, team size may also allow peeling off with an integrated flanking attack. The following drill is also worth practicing when there is more than one of you. There are and may be times under special circumstances where a partner and you want to or need to move in unison.
Try dry practicing this first and only do this drill under qualified and responsible supervision. It is a dangerous, high risk drill for most people and is best only considered for use by carefully selected and highly trained SWAT members and specialized militarily trained personnel. Having said that, if this exercise is done with care and wisdom, it can also be very valuable for couples in a family defense situation. Practice it over and over

with water pistols first, then perhaps 6mm plastic round firing training guns. Finally, while under expert supervision and with all relevant safety measures being considered, first run through the exercise very slowly now using the real deal.

Above all, it is essential to maintain a high level of situational awareness, partner awareness and always conscious of the muzzle and trigger and any safety device. Walk with short, fluid and secure steps. Shuffle if you have to. Do not run. Stay 3 to 9 yards apart. (When there are no more targets and you are still in a high risk zone, go 45 degrees shoulder to shoulder. In this way you cannot shoot each other. Otherwise, stay at least 3 yards apart, space permitting, with the target line halfway between the two of you.) Stay perfectly aligned, side by side. Move in perfect unison as a team. This tactical drill can be very effective when done right.

Start out with your handguns on safe in your holsters. If applicable, you may be using "carbines" on safe. On the "go!" draw your firearm in a safe, smooth professional manner and deliver your first shot each in less than one second but definitely well under two seconds. You both fire virtually at the same time and at a 35 to 45 degree angle from each other and slightly downward to ensure your round will not hit anything it should not be reaching beyond the target. Know exactly what is beyond each target before firing. Be safe. Know at all times exactly where your partner is and do not shoot unless you are certain of his position. Stay aligned side by side and one person can verbally lead as well. When you cannot see your partner, kneel and remain still. You may want to transition to your fixed blade knife at this point if you are forced into an assault, but this should really never happen if you know where your partner is and what his or her status is at all times.

Next, set up 3 to 15 paper targets. (Not steel) Spray paint one target "blue" for a "friendly" no-shoot decision and place it deeper into the target line to force yourself to watch your shooting angles intelligently and responsibly. "Battle Talk" as is necessary to reload, transition weapons, moves forward in unison etc . . .

This is a fantastic drill for conditioning yourself to operate in close proximity to another shooter. You also need to safely and responsibly practice this drill at night. As a night drill, use tops a 50 to 125 lumens tactical flashlight. Illuminate the target, move and shoot only while remaining 100% committed to your partners safety and the overall safety of all concerned. Again, it is recommended repeated dry runs in this exercise before going hot with weapons. At the end of your drill include prisoner management drills, and detailed medical trauma drills.

At the end of the target line, scan tactically 360 degrees around with total partner, muzzle and trigger finger safety. Immediately place your firearm on safe and re-holster as soon as possible and always before turning back to your starting point. Remain aware and AAPE.

Note: Remember our mantras: Always remain ready to bring order to where there is chaos and if forced to do so, to bring chaos to your threat so as to interrupt his or their AAPE with surprise, speed and appropriate violence of action. As you lose the element of surprise, increase your speed and if need be your intensity. Be ready to act in a calm, systematic and methodical manner. Use the shadows, the best cover, and the high ground while staying low and on your feet but be able to escape unseen and prepared to talk, buy or run your way out of trouble if you can. If forced to engage as a last resort; engage only very briefly and only to stop the threat so you can break contact. Now find safe cover in the darkest area on the highest ground. Remain ever alert. AAPE! Scan 360 degrees around, left to right, close to far, low to high. Prioritize what you are looking at. Notice peoples hands first. Call 911 ASAP.

Do what is right and responsible. Be safe during the process. Be ready for change. Always have another layer of weapons to transition to, three to five layers deep. In all of your drills, remain mindful of these life saving fundamentals. Let all of it always be totally integrated. Avoidance remains our master key. It is the awareness that makes all the difference.

In some of our advanced training sessions with some of my expert friends you may even be expected to shoot through car windows from the inside or into car doors from the outside. We do not encourage you to do that at *"home"* but in the real world this happens with regularity.

Clean and maintain your weapons and other gear well and store it responsibly.

With the aforementioned recommended list of gear, quality professional training and frequent practice under the watchful eye and coaching of a world class professional you will be better prepared for a real world violent encounter than most people on the planet. Many career soldiers and police officers in non-specialized units do not have such training. Provided that you have had enough training and practiced often in the above shooting drills and mastered my Task, Conditions & Standards Tests plus have your equipment on you; *i* am very confident that you will take heroic care of your family and self in almost any violent emergency. It may be a home invasion, in-vehicle assault, rape or kidnap attempt or even an unfolding war battle zone but with these tactics and exercises you will certainly gain the edge you need to prevail.

Those are all extremely dangerous situations and the risk must not be underestimated. Prepare your mind, body and most importantly your soul. Study this book diligently and practice on a disciplined schedule. If you will do all of that then you have done your part exceedingly well.

In all of this, please realize that with this level of highly specialized training and being equipped or even just in possession of some of the gear I have recommended you could potentially be seen by lawyers and others as a lethal warrior rather than a helpless and soft sheep of a citizen. Many would prefer you to be just that. Be warned, remain discreet and be careful to always be a responsible gun owner.

Many police officers and paramedics want you to leave it all up to them the *"real professionals"* to take care of crimes on your behalf. It is a nice thought and we love and respect them for that. We have already established it is certainly not realistic since in 99% of recorded assault cases they cannot or will not be able to reach you in time to prevent the crime against your family and their trauma or death.

Do you remember the kidnapping, rape, strangulation and arson case where the police sat right outside the house observing the home of the victims while the mother got raped and strangled? The father was able to escape and crawl to the neighbors but the criminals later set fire to the family home and their two daughters were burned to death? That happened in a quiet, low crime, upscale neighborhood near New Haven, Connecticut. Your family depends on you and your ability to protect, feed, house, love and defend them. You need to stay alive so you can do that and be trained well enough and equipped well enough to really be able to do so.

Train yourself in an ethos of being willing to defend your loved ones regarding what is good and right. Legally, we are required to always break contact and to retreat as soon as possible. Respect that but also cultivate the attributes of what it takes to endure a sustained all out nothing barred *"kill–or–be–killed"* fight for that instance when you are forced to defend. Train yourself for having courage, determination and fortitude, yet also embrace and train yourself for being a person of self-restraint, mercy and compassion.

On-Foot,
First Contact Action Drill

When out and about on the streets, consciously choose to be more aware and alert. Do not attract risky and unwanted attention to yourself by your way of dress or behavior. Walk with confidence. Be mindful of being observed, of the approach of strangers and use your intuition to notice suspicious and abnormal behavior. Avoid dark isolated places. Be very aware of panel vans, and slow moving cars with multiple men in them, especially if they have a gangster style about them.

Also be very aware of men with an uncommonly clean cut, conservative yet very handsome look to them that wear suits or khaki chinos with black shoes and black shirts or black jackets. Notice their footwear, especially specialized high performance shoes and military type boots, belts and watches along with other items. Also, be cautious of guy's wearing all black and especially so if it includes an untucked black t-shit or sweater, black leather jacket or even more so black synthetic pants. Also watch out for two or more men dressed in blue jeans, dark polo shirts and sun glasses If he/they have a well developed butt, powerful, sexy, confident way of walking he may just be a high testosterone tough guy, avoid all eye contact. If they give you an intense 1000 yard, hawk eye stare, AAPE him/them and the situation. You should always be AAPE and be ready to really go AAPE if need be.

In parking lots, ideally try to stay 20 to 40 plus feet away from anyone and anything that looks like potential trouble and danger. Always do what you can to keep a safe distance. Avoid being out alone as that almost certainly makes you a softer target and inviting prey for predators. Always scan for potential dangers, for potential cover and for the best escape routes. With multiple threats, avoid getting distracted by any one and avoid being open to a side or rear attack. Get your back into a corner or against a very high wall or high vehicle. Do your best to line them up so that they get into each others way if you can. Escape rapidly if possible. If not then flank them if that is a workable option.

If after going through our AAPE loop you clearly recognize that your only resort and last action is without a doubt to engage due to the imminent threat your assaulters have created then act decisively, methodically and systematically. (Please be sure to first study all the listed safety and legal requirements in the appendices of this document and get adequate professional training before you ever handle any firearm or tactical item of any kind.)

If you are not armed and depending on your unique situation, you're three best possible last resort responses may be to:

Perform a weapon/ rifle, handgun or knife disarming with intelligent and daring guile as taught in our hands-on class and as instructed in the CRI Counter Terrorism School training DVD's. Disarming are very dangerous maneuvers and extensive training is vital. If need be, in a simple yet very dangerous grab situation, kick with one or more fast, low and powerful front kicks to the groin and add roundhouse or side kicks to the knees or use several powerful knee strikes to the groin, specifically the testicles, or a block kick to the shin. If necessary, with arms length contacts, thrust your non shooting hand into your imminent threats face and instinctively draw and fire your weapon from your hip. Practice this. Have a laser sight fitted because a laser sight will improve your confidence and ability for all unconventional instinctive shooting requirements.

Depending on the situation, palm thrust your assaulter under the chin with one or both hands simultaneously, or press your thumbs forcefully into your primary assaulter's eyes. If you are being grabbed then twist his/her head violently up, back and sideways or you can twist the head as your primary response. This can be lethal! Follow up with a knee or elbow strike or kick and run away.

Hit with a fast, hard knife blade hand or forearm strike on the windpipe and/or with an upward palm strike under the chin or nose. Follow this immediately with a knee strike to the groin and an elbow strike or punch to the temple of the head and run as fast as you can to call and get help and or to escape. Your objective should be to survive the imminent attack, respond with a swift, surprising, non-lethal but man-stopping counter attack, and to retreat to safety at the earliest opportunity. You have to be both mentally and physically prepared. Your mind is the key. Professional training and frequent practice is essential if you are to stand a real chance in a violent home intrusion, kidnapping attempt or to escape and survive an unfolding riot or war zone battles.

I urge you to practice and perform a variety of fast, powerful combinations of three strikes at a time. The eyes, temple of the head, jaw, trachea, groin and knees are the primary targets in your emergency counter attack defense response. Practice violent head twists on a rubber training dummy. **Head twists are lethal and can paralyze. Do not practice this on friends, family, training partners or other non-threat people.**

Do not be slack. Practice both disarming and counter disarming drills. Practice key unarmed combat drills and practice your medical trauma drills. To build skill requires lots of practice. 5000 repetitions are what you should consider lots of practice, not 10 times. Also do not be fooled. It does require some inner and outer body strength so do be diligent in maintaining a regular body conditioning program for functional fitness. I think kettle bell training is the way to go, as well as plyometrics and running. Strength, power, speed and endurance are all needed in hand-to-hand defense. Train with that in mind. Train both with just your clothes on your body and also train fully geared up with all the weapons and supporting gear you expect to wear in real world home invasion, kidnapping and unfolding war zone battle situations. We always train as close as possible to the way we expect to really fight.

Technique is the key but will only work well in a real world encounter if executed with a strong mind and strong body. Surprise, speed and violence of action are all keys to your success.

You are most vulnerable when you are in the shower or bathtub or on the toilet. I want to repeat again, should you ever be attacked while unarmed remember to strike the assaulters windpipe with your hands edge. If grabbed, strike fast and hard with your forearm to the windpipe, press your thumbs forcefully into the assaulters eyes, or violently grab and forcefully twist the threats head upwards and sideways. Follow up with an elbow strike or punch to the temple of the head and a swift powerful kick in the groin. Now run and get a gun, stun gun, pepper spray or knife and help.

Do not be fooled by self-defense marketing statements. It is not all that easy to survive an intense assault unarmed, especially not when unarmed. Try hiding a well oiled blade box cutter or Japanese carpenter's cutter or a hatchet high up in your shower within your bathroom or wear a synthetic / hard plastic or stainless steel neck knife while you shower if in high risk times or places. It may be a smart thing to do. At minimum, simply lock your bathroom door and have a handgun concealed within easy reach under a towel if necessary.

The Bodyguard Technique

When walking with a beloved, always be ready to pull that person behind you, **(ideally push her/him down and out of the line of fire)** and to shield her/him/them behind your body and family defense weapon in case of an imminent life endangering threat. When walking you should keep yourself on their right hand side and just behind them if you are right handed. Pull the person behind your body while you simultaneously swiftly draw and present your weapon in one smooth thrust forward using controlled aggression. This is a classic body guard technique for providing cover and evacuating a VIP. Shield the person with your body. Move backwards and at your earliest opportunity, go rapidly sideways out of the incoming line of fire. Get behind cover; get behind the engine block and front wheel of a car or into a get away car or a building. Go for the high ground . . . and if need be shooting back rapidly to suppress them. A wider grouping than target practice is good in this case. Shoot for their heart, pelvis, thighs and brain. Remember to move rapidly sideways out of the line of fire yet into and behind solid cover. Seek better cover and new escape routes as you move.

Once in a vehicle or building, enter our in-car or in-home/building tactical contact drills as and when needed. If forced back out onto a street, reenter our on foot drill. If wounded, hide in the darkest areas and keep our battle principles outlined in appendix D in mind and enter our trauma medical care first responder loop. Constantly apply our AAPE System. Be systematic, methodical, proactive, decisive and unorthodox, intelligently flexible, bold, audacious and adaptive. This is the best pathway out of danger.

This requires a legal concealed carry for this application and ideally as my personal first choice I would choose a revolver placed on your dominant hand hip, in your dominant hand pocket or in a cross shoulder holster. If you choose to carry a pistol as your primary weapon it has to be ready to use and on safe if the weapon has a safety selector. It is vital that it must be ready for one handed use. **("Cocked and Locked" as some say)** As taught in class, place your cell phone, an extra spare magazine, a tactical folding knife or a roll of wrapped quarters for weight in your dominant side coat pocket. This will help you draw better as demonstrated and practiced in our class.

If forced to do so by the perpetrators assaulting your family and self, fight as fiercely as a Wolverine and as effectively as you possibly can. Anticipate danger, be trained in effective drills, be armed and choose to become and be a hard target. Actively defend your family by creating total sensory overload and battle chaos for your assaulters in a full on *"code black"* encounter. Follow our drills methodically, systematically, precisely, smoothly, surgically and efficiently within the legal parameters of appropriate force and with cautious target discrimination. Do not target fixate. Constantly scan from left to right while you scan 360 degrees around. Fight from out of the darkest areas. Look low to high, close to far, multi-dimensional to observe the whole picture with an uncommonly high level of situational awareness. Do not underestimate your threat. Ideally, if forced to fight, generate massive fear in your threat. Be flexible, unorthodox, elusive, and ferocious. If attacked from two sides and you have an armed partner be ready to go back to back. Prior training, rehearsal and repetitive drills remain vital.

"If you never fired a real gun before, you must go to a shooting range and fire a weapon several times. Also practice in low light conditions. You must get used to the sound, muzzle flash, smell and feeling. It is always better to experience this for the first time in a safe, controlled and supervised environment rather than in a real life deadly encounter. This is a critical component in the emotional and mental side of crime survivability"—Doron Benbenisty.

Note: If you and your partner are both highly skilled and armed, you may preplan a response in a high/low tactical position whereas one will stand while the other kneels or one can kneel and the other takes a rear prone position. Decide in advance who will be doing what. After a shooting, if you are 2, 3 or more people in defense, you may assume a back to back tight 360 degree battle formation from which you can observe and further defend before you decide (AAPE) to tactically retreat. If forced to resume fighting, you can dynamically move into a tactical flare and advance or peel off sideways as taught in our more advanced training classes.

In Car,
First Contact Action Drill

If you come under attack while in your vehicle, speed out of the killing and danger zone. If you must, use your car as a weapon and get distance between you and them ASAP.

Accelerate and speed away, change direction often.

Ram any vehicle out of your way if need be. Use the technique we teach in our class. Place your thumbs over the steering wheel. Hands in the 10 and 2 o'clock positions, accelerate and ram the blocking vehicle behind the rear wheel as trained.

Shoot back if you must to survive a direct imminent attack. Use the principles previously learned along with the specific techniques we teach in our hands-on class and that are covered in the appendix dedicated to **weapon handling**.

Only exit the vehicle if it is on fire or fails to proceed and your risk becomes too high by remaining in it. Burning cars generate lethal, hot, toxic smoke that can kill with as few as two or three inhalations.

If forced to exit the vehicle, crawl out, stay low, go upwind and get away if the car is burning. Move fast, low and in an irregular zigzag manner. If you cannot use the engine block and front wheels as your primary cover, create extra or better cover and concealment using the methods we teach in our class. Military personnel often use smoke grenades to create extra concealment to retreat or reposition during combat. Civilian smoke grenades are available for mountaineering and yacht rescuing purposes. A cloud of red or even white smoke could attract attention and hopefully attract help from law enforcement personnel. At a minimum it could create concealment at a critical moment to enable you to move behind better cover and or to retreat sideways or backwards in a moment of surprise and confusion. Be mindful of the wind direction and strength. Do not turn your back on the danger as you retreat. Optimize your use of cover. Please be sure that if you buy and transport a smoke grenade that it is legal to do so in your jurisdiction

Stay about an arms length from your cover so you can observe a bigger picture and especially at corners. This also reduces the risk of being hit by ricochets unless there is a potential for sniper fire from a higher angle that will force you to stay closer and lower. Retreat to better cover when you can safely do so and escape ASAP. Avoid turning your back on the threat, especially if you are alone and do not have someone providing high volume and accurate fire while you retreat. Walk with a short backward walk with your toes touching the ground first to feel for obstacles. Ideally move sideways with small lateral foot movements towards better cover while utilizing peripheral vision. If there are two or more of you that are armed, then sprint and leap-frog out of the kill zone as taught in our hands-on class? Maintain momentum. Expose as little as possible of your self for the shortest possible time when moving or firing from behind cover. (The Israeli method used by elite soldiers makes an allowance for sprinting or rolling to cover when you have highly trained, trustworthy people providing cover fire during a tactical backward retreat. In testing this, the Israelis found that running with your back briefly turned provided the fastest, safest and most effective option.) However, we still recommend in most cases to never turn your back on a threat.

When the police arrive be very cautious of both police and evil guy gunfire. AAPE continually. Look for shadows, at the edges of alley ways, muzzle flashes and dust clouds caused by shooters. Observe and notice people and specifically notice their hands while constantly looking for more advantageous cover and shooting positions. As you scan left to right, low to high and close to far, do so with your weapon muzzle up two inches below your eyes and follow your eyes as you scan. Continually transform your fear into *"controlled aggression"*. Once you are out of the vehicle, apply the principles learned in the on-foot drill, and once you enter a building apply the principles learned in the following in-home drill. Just keep going AAPE and insert the on-foot, in-vehicle and in-car drills as and when needed. Constantly loop in and out of these drills in the 2.2 Family & Personal Protection System faster and more effectively than your assaulters can adapt to your response and next drill. This is the key to your survival. Our system and drills are designed for realistic worst-case eventualities. They will help you tremendously and give you an advantage once mastered.

Most professional kidnappings occur when one is in or close to ones car. Often used are panel vans, large SUV's or large sedans. Anticipate the situation and intelligently prevent you and or your family from becoming a victim with the AAPE System and our first contact drills. Also prevent from becoming a victim by randomly and always changing your departure times and your routes. Even change cars and your position in the car if possible. Always lock your doors. Be observant—AAPE. Preferably you might "harden/armor" your car. Always have at least a .40 caliber and .22L pistol or .38 Special revolver as well as a neck knife and a concealed thumb knife and two tampons available for a wounding. A hatchet is also great to have in your car. When real trouble shows up a shotgun or submachine gun may be best.

"Get some tactical driving training. Your vehicle is one of the best weapons available to you. If your vehicle is still running and can move, then with proper driving tactics you will have a 90% change to escape. Please view our short video from the CRI Tactical driving course at www.critraining.com/tactical driving." Doron Benbenisty.

Important: Understand the transportation requirements of firearms in your own city and zip code and of the areas you travel in. When stopped by law enforcement officers, get your driver's license and your hands ready on the steering wheel in full visibility and keep them there. Know in that area if you need to declare your weapon. If so, have your permit with your license in hand and expect that the officer may command the surrender of your weapon to his/her control. Do it gently and with caution if you are sure it is a legitimate police officer serving a just system. Avoid having pro-gun association stickers on your windows that will attract unwanted attention to you. If possible, drive a modest yet heavy and solid car. If you fear that you are a potential target for kidnapping than consider two car loads of professional bodyguards if you can afford it. Have such a high profile as to dissuade any attackers if you can justify the investment. This may be necessary if you live in a high risk region or country.

Doron Benbenisty of CRI Counter Terrorism School Inc. is a master at teaching in-car counter kidnapping skills. Here he demonstrates in-vehicle counter kidnapping and car-jacking strategies and tactics.

In-Home,
First Contact Action Drill

Harden your home ASAP against intrusion. At minimum, use several battery operated alarm doorstops and other heavy duty doorstops. Place at least one alarm doorstop under all your perimeter doors and especially positioning one under your bedroom door is highly recommended. It will not stop committed and professional assaulters from breaching your door right out of its frame but it will go a long way in warning you of entry attempts by most criminals. Alarm door stops are great. They are inexpensive, battery operated, portable, and reliable and cannot be disarmed by intruders as with your normal home alarm system.

Also purchase a reliable yet powerful illumination tool such as a 120/5 lumens LED tactical flashlight similar to what law enforcement officers rely on in hostile low light environments. As experienced cave divers and SWAT members know, it is wise to have three sources of light rather than just one. May I recommend one on your rifle, one on your shotgun and one on your primary handgun or at least one backup hand held tactical 120/125 lumens flashlight. Only use a tactical flashlight when absolutely necessary and be brief. Simply flash it on long enough to identify the target and shoot but remember to immediately switch it off while you move to a new location.

If you suddenly become aware of an imminent threat while still in your home, respond using primarily the lessons learned in our on-foot drill. Know that you are most vulnerable when you are asleep, taking a shower or bath or sitting on the toilet. Draw your curtains closed. Lock the doors and be skilled enough to fight back with your bare hands if need be. A regular real world based martial arts practice will be of great benefit to you as part of your personal full spectrum readiness strategy. Krav Maga, Muay Thai, Tae Kwon Do, Jujitsu and Karate or Kung Fu are all great options. Go for a hybrid approach in mixed martial arts designed for real world street defense and survival. The best system in my opinion is Krav-Haganah (Combat Defense) as taught in person and on DVD by its founder Doron Benbenisty of CRI. (**www.critraining.com**) A shotgun, handgun, short sword, hatchet or warrior knife is always more effective than any empty hand technique when real danger shows up.

Even if you are a black belt in one or more martial arts I recommend for your home you obtain a shotgun, a heavy caliber and a small caliber pistol or a heavy caliber revolver and one or even better two tactical knives, a battle hatchet and a tactical flashlight. Also set up your professional quality medical trauma first aid kit. You must learn how to master the use of a shotgun, a handgun, a tactical knife and become masterful with at least a boxing punch, a karate front and side kick, a basic judo throw, a mixed martial arts ground technique or two and also become uncommonly proficient at specialized medical trauma protocols and procedures which will be needed in and after violent fights and in war zone battles.

We insist you harden your home. Emphasize your doors and windows against unauthorized entry. Heavy steel security doors are best. Use super heavy duty locks and large durable hinges and twice as many as normal. Use heavy duty doorstops and or battery operated alarm doorstops as instructed. If climate allows, plant cactus plants in front and around all your windows. If you have children or dogs and not the right climate for that option then be creative and innovate. If the risk in your part of the world becomes very extreme, consider planting several buried planks as a deterrent with upward facing nails just outside your windows. Realize and recognize the risk involved as it will surely be seen as illegal booby traps. Therefore, this is not a legal option in the USA and should be avoided as such. Other practical and useful actions like these may also be considered as illegal and as booby traps in various parts of the world. Please be warned and understand this kind of action may only be appropriate when the world has broken down into anarchy and is used as a desperate last resort measure when there is no electricity and intrusion levels are high.

One or several great guard dogs are a real asset. Put out a sign post "BEWARE OF THE DOG" with polite signs. Get at least one inside dog and do not feed it at night so that it will be more alert. If you have outside dogs, please give them a warm in winter and dry when it rains wooden box. Prepare it with lots of hay flooring and a warm wool blanket for winter. Install powerful external motion detection and normal lights with surveillance cameras. Your two most effective and most reliable measures will be a system of two alert and powerful outside dogs, two inside dogs, plus the use of 9 volt battery operated alarm door stops inside under your bedroom door and all other perimeter doors. Use strong and well fitting "stopper-rods" in all sliding door and sliding window guide grooves. If you do not have a shotgun and / or handgun, we recommend for emergencies you keep in your master bedroom or safe room a large African spear, baseball bat or a water pistol filled with an ammonia and red pepper mix in a plastic bag or container. Store and use it with the same caution and responsibility as a real gun. Test it for functionality. This is a great plan for hotel use when you travel in high risk countries and dangerous cities or towns. As I previously mentioned, be aware that anything other than a real fire arm will be inadequate in most cases. I do not want you to assume a false sense of security.

The sad fact is that police records show that women have been brutally raped and kidnapped in their homes in spite of having big dogs, an alarm system, security lights and even security doors. There are even occurrences while a 911 operator overhears and records the entire traumatic incident after the police have been called and have been dispatched. This simply proves that ultimately a stun gun, hand gun, shotgun or knife and a 120/125 lumens LED flashlight in your own trained hands remains the most important last resort defense tools for surviving a violent criminal home intrusion.

For safe and responsible storage we recommend you install a fingerprint scan safe for your primary handgun at your bedside. This provides nearly instant access even when you are in shock and have lost some of your fine motor skills in your fingers and will work well even in low light conditions. However, be 100% sure it has a backup power source or is battery operated and can be opened manually with a key. Test it frequently and keep the battery fresh and strong. You want to be certain that if the power gets cut you can still swiftly access your weapon for any emergency response.

If you can safely and responsibly do so, you may want to place your shot gun or hand gun under a towel or blanket on the floor lying directly beneath your bed. Remain mindful that it is there and only consider this as a safe option if you can lock your bedroom door and your home is kid free. Be mindful and 100% diligent and lock it away each morning

Here, step-by-step, is what to do when in your home and there is an intrusion.

The moment you hear a suspicious sound, open your mouth a little to improve your hearing. Turn your head slightly towards where you think it is and listen.

1. If you have any reason to feel even the slightest angst, get your primary weapon of choice in your hand in a high ready position and be still and silent. I recommend you get a 12 gauge shotgun loaded with bird and buck shot or a handgun you have trained with in your hands first. Tuck your revolver or pistol of choice into your pants. May I please respectfully recommend a 12 gauge shotgun plus a .40 caliber pistol backed up by a compact or subcompact 9 mm such as a G-19 or a .22L revolver or pistol. If you have body armor and the time to do so, put it on. If nothing else at least get a loaded .40 or .45 or 9 mm pistol or a .44 or .357 or .38 Special revolver or at the absolute minimum a .22 L pistol in your trained hands. If you have a dominant hand, attach an elastic wrist magazine holder with a spare loaded magazine. Slip it on immediately given your time and permitting the safe opportunity to do so. Having a plan such as a first contact immediate action drill that lets you know in advance exactly what you are going to do in a proactive, systematic yet flexible manner will make fear of the unknown a lot less scary. It will give you both confidence and a tactical edge for survival and success.

2. Should your reason for concern increase, take up a low tactical kneeling position behind the best cover available or immediately go back to back as a couple. Watch the two highest risk zones. Call 911 ASAP and keep them on the line.

3. Get your flashlight. Have it on a wrist loop lanyard.

4. Preplan your emergency response cover and prepare it in advance or enter a prone waiting position for them in a blind spot as taught in our class. He watches the most dangerous highest risk area such as the door and she watches another danger zone/ high risk potential entry point like the windows or ceiling. Call 911 immediately.

5a. If you are alone or a couple without kids, you/she can call 911 and stay on the line with them so they can hear what develops. You/She can also activate the external flood lights and monitor the surveillance system. He will remain in a tactically ready defensive position as the principal family protector. Role clarity is absolutely important.

5b. If alone, activate the external lights and with gun in hand kneel behind solid cover in a tactical position and call 911. Remember to keep the 911 operator on the line to hear how things evolve as the situation develops. If you have kids, then move out with tactical intelligence to get to them ASAP. Be proactive and tactful. Again, if you have the luxury of time, quickly fit body armor if you have body armor with ballistic front, back and side plates and if available get an anti-ballistic shield in hand. Do this immediately, prior to taking your defensive position behind cover, in a blind spot if you are alone and especially if proceeding to the children.

5c. If you have children or an elder, you must safely go to get and protect them immediately. Tactically leave the room watching each others backs. Use your flashlight very, very, very sparingly and only if you absolutely must do so to locate and identify the threats. If possible, carefully consider using a red light filter or white light and scan in short, irregular, left to right sweeps when necessary or not at all. Red light may not be best to use if your laser sights are also red and may make blood harder to see. Green laser lights are available. You can also selectively bounce light off large light colored surfaces such as the ceiling to create better overall light conditions if necessary. If you use a powerful white light it may be very effective as a surprise to blind an intruder briefly and gain an advantage. Study and practice the "FBI" method, the "Harriers" method and the "Ice Pick" method as well as others and see what resonates best with you. Keep your weapon close to your body to prevent it from being grabbed as you move forward. Perhaps use a single point sling to secure your weapon to your body if you use a shotgun or rifle.

6. Move tactically through doorways, around corners and into rooms as taught in our hands-on classes. Maintain strict muzzle and trigger discipline. Stay an arms length from walls in hallways. Keep the barrel of your primary weapon (shotgun) or handgun two inches below your eyes in a high ready or with a handgun keep it close to your dominant hip or at high ready. If you find the bad guys and when forced to shoot, use intelligent angles. Use a tactical standing firing position but if you immediately draw fire, perhaps drop rapidly into a rear prone firing position depending on how close they are. If necessary and to stop the threat, shoot 3 to 7 shots or more aiming for the heart, pelvis, thighs and brain.

If at any point you get tangled up in an unarmed combat situation, you should do the hand palm thrust to the jaw or if necessary the violent neck twist. Both these movements can even be done on the ground. If the fight continues beyond that and your assaulter and you are still standing then kick his front leg or testicles violently. Punch him powerfully on the jaw or throat and add one or two more swift kicks to his testicles or leading legs knee or two punches to his temple. Then, if necessary and before he recovers, perform a swift and powerful MMA takedown by hitting him low with a shoulder or head and grabbing his legs while pulling him off balance in a spike attack. As you hit the ground, throw his legs off to the side or out of the way and get behind him and begin a rear strangle choke. Failing to do that, fight dirty with 3 to 7 punches and or powerful elbow strikes to the eyes and temples and when opportune, get him in a strangle lock until he submits or faints in a choke out. A choke hold can take approximately 10 seconds to be effective but death can begin in as little as 20–60 seconds which depends on many variables.

Having suggested this MMA sequence, I suggest it only be attempted if you are very strong, confident and well skilled in those mixed martial arts techniques. For most it is best to stay on your feet. Keep some distance as distance is your friend in a fight. It is best to rely on controlling and dominating the situation and stopping your threat with verbal commands and emphasize your shotgun or handgun. This MMA drill is more intended as a confidence builder only.

7. When you reach the kids or elderly, shield them first with your body and firearm and then evacuate them. Set up a last stand citadel in your safe room or master bedroom as taught in person in our practical class. Your *"safe room"* should be a fortified area with easy access and only one point of entry. Equip it with a strong sealing door, a steel plate ceiling, reinforced walls, telephone, fire extinguisher, water, gas masks, a safely stored shotgun and handgun, medical trauma supplies, food and more if you can afford to do so. If evil doers pursue you into this safe space, be ready to use the secret tactics taught in our life class and spare no effort while keeping with a mindset of *"controlled aggression"*. Take a few deep breaths and take up a kneeling and high ready tactical position or our secret position and location as taught. You must be ready to defend your family in a systematic, methodical, decisive way and as fierce as a Wolverine if that is what it will take to stop the threat. If lethally shot while in a prone position you have at least 15 to 30 seconds of life left to fight back, compared to 3 to 8 seconds if standing. Rehearse going to the safe room with your family.

You could allocate a room as a primary and then an alternative room to retreat to. Have a secret family code word and signal for each. Always call 911 ASAP and keep the phone going so they can hear what is going on and record it as evidence.

8. Only exit the home if it is on fire or if the known risk in the house is greater than the anticipated risk outside. Position at least 2 or 3 strategically placed fire extinguishers in your home and before all emergency exits. If you are forced to exit your home in an emergency try to take a concealed shotgun out with you. Cover it with a towel, sheet or blanket until you can get the lay of the land and safety status outside. AAPE. Watch out for both enemy and friendly fire risks.

9. There will be times for reasons we cannot explain that you may not be able to get your hands on any weapon. If that is the case, then you may have to rely on skills other than guns and knives. There are principles of hand to hand combat well worth remembering and becoming conditioned to.

Here is what Ken Haan, a world class mixed martial arts and close quarters combat coach told me:

a. Know your exits.
b. Decide whether you will fight or flight. This will depend on which one is more acceptable.
c. Understand the ranges of engagement and counter distances—far, mid or close.

"For far distances, if unarmed and you are going proactive, close your distance on their weapon ASAP. Stay focused on the weapon. If you are up against an unarmed person, use kicks or straight punches. Keep all kicks below waist level and linear. Concentrate on groin and knee joint kicks utilizing side or front kicks. Prior training and practice is necessary to develop gross motor skills and muscle memory under stress full conditions."

For mid range we recommend open hand palm strikes or fist strikes. Knees and elbows or head butts are good to. **If necessary, you may**

need to grab onto the persons hair and smash their head against a wall. Continually look for weapons in your immediate environment. Biting is not recommended but can be an effective last resort.

The key to striking hard is having a snap or bounce. It is more important to recover back like a rubber band. Strike only with the two main knuckles. Use your hip, pivot inward, pivot on the balls of the feet or at least by turning with your hips. Punch with one or a series of exhales through the mouth. You will need a strong core to deliver a strong punch and to control the recoil. (A mirror drill or video drill when punching is good to monitor your turning.) Use a heavy bag of 50 to 200 lbs. to practice on. Punch intensely for 3 to 5 minute rounds. Practicing 3 to 7 rounds with a heavy bag is an excellent workout.

Only at close range, MMA style grappling is recommended and only if absolutely necessary and you have no other choice and only if you face a single assaulter. Grab him by the hair as we suggested and throw his head into a wall. The best thing to do is to put your back tight against a wall to prevent or defend against any take down attempt. Push the person away and loop back into fighting from mid then long range again. At longer ranges you have more options. Be careful that your assaulters do not grab your hair/head and smash it into the wall behind you. Be ready to respond or even to fight intelligently into them and savagely if necessary.

If the person tries to grab you, step 45 degrees out to the side and parry/deflect/redirect the punch with your hand at their wrist and by indexing (by pressing) behind the elbow or triceps to limit your attacker's options. Bring your hand up and use your forearm and elbow as a shield and dynamically push them away with your other hand.

If you need to go a little bit more aggressive; you can after the above sequence and while maintaining pressure and contact on their triceps transition to sliding your knife hand onto their throat and lock a naked neck lock choke while kicking behind their knee. You must remember to stay on your feet when they start to go down by turning out of the way and off to the side. Do not go to the ground. There may be other assaulters in the area. Be aware and be ready.

Another alternative could be, after stepping to the side, kick the inner knee with a stomp and aggressively slide the foot edge down the inner lower leg and perform an elbow strike to the side or tip of the front of the jaw. (The elbow is the most durable joint in your body.) Immediately snake your hand around into a guillotine choke and simply step back while taking them to the ground or jump up and wrap yourself onto them. If the choke is aggressively applied and comes as a surprise, it can be used to choke the person out in 3 or so seconds. If you are up against a skilled, strong and aggressive fighter, a choke out may not work. Bite, scream and scratch like a wildcat if you must.

The Dynamic Head Take Down is another method we may want you to use. The principles are as follows:

1. Use surprise and speed from a well balanced position.
2. Step dynamically only a half step in or jump if you are agile enough.
3. Push the assaulters head up and depending how lethal you need to be, turn or powerfully snap his head sideways to take him down while you step out to the side and continue applying force. You want to stay on your feet.

This is a brutal, fast and highly effective but also dangerous method for a take down. A high level of surprise, speed and violence-of-action can result in paralyzing or even killing the person. At the *"Full Spectrum Family Protector"* level this is our core takedown technique. We favor this technique above the MMA style take down for any real world high threat attack. Here is the main drill and test.

(As the person punches at you, immediately slide step 45 degrees to his weak side, kick the back or side of his knee powerfully and only then if necessary, grab his head under the chin and up high behind the head and either gently or dynamically lift and twist as necessary.

It is brutal and potentially lethal. Again, stay on your feet and swiftly and repeatedly scan for additional threats.)

The actual MMA technique as opposed to the commando style take down is a great confidence builder. Here is the technique that I learned from Ken Haan at Ken's professional MMA gym in Las Vegas, NV. while I was sparring with one of his fighters/ instructor, David Derek Hinkey.

Go into a professional boxer or mixed martial arts fighting position with your feet shoulder width apart, fists held high at face level and close to your face with your elbows in covering your ribs. *(If your opponent has a knife, you would turn your wrists in, but only then.)* Be light and nimble on the balls of your feet. Have your chin tucked in and put your tongue on the roof of your mouth behind your front teeth. Breathe through your nose.

When available, jab his face with your leading fist and follow it rapidly with continued fist jabs. Notice his reaction and throw one or two more punches if necessary. *(When you punch, exhale and punch with horizontal knuckles at the end of your punch and make contact with your largest knuckles. Roll the heel of your fist out for a longer and harder punch. Guard your chin with your shoulder and other fist. Practice this under experienced supervision to master the details.)* If your opponent responds with his leading hand punch, drop low and shoulder hit him in the solar plexus while you grab his legs just behind the knees and dynamically lift up and take him down to the ground. Exhale as you make your attack with your shoulder spike while looking up and lift during the take down process. The moment he falls onto his back, immediately and without hesitation get your right arm under his left leg if you are right handed and throw it over as if you are "swimming" under his leg. Rapidly get behind him and apply a "naked choke hold" until he "taps-out" in surrender if you are practicing. In a real life kill or be killed battle fight you want to stay with the hold until he loses consciousness.

When you perform a choke, wrap your back hand as low and tight as possible which makes it difficult for him to grab your hand and break the choke with a reversal technique. If possible, kick him in the testicles with one heel and wrap both legs left and right around his body while placing both heels into his groin. Squeeze tight with your thighs which will help to reduce his ability to get air. Do not cross your ankles as this can set you up for a counter drill. Pull your chin and head in tight against his. (Be aware that this is a dangerous drill and may lead to death or a serious injury.) You may ruin a friendship and create a grudge if you choke a sparring partner too hard and for too long. (More than 2–7 seconds on average) Be very careful and gentle when practicing this and with expert supervision only. I once again recommend working through these drills slowly for safety and suggest you find great in-person coaching to get the details right. It is essential.

Alternatively, as you finish your punching assault and at the most opportune moment, you can also perform a hard inside and / or outside low roundhouse kick on his inner and outer thigh or if necessary to his knee. Perform a Muay Thai or Kung Fu step down kick onto his knee. (Again, please be cautious, controlled, disciplined, responsible and gentle in practice and in the test since knees can dislocate and break easily.) From there you can swiftly and unexpectedly do a takedown. The correct and most effective way is to go in low at about a 35 to 45 degree angle and hit him in the solar plexus with your head while looking up and simultaneously grab him hard and securely behind the legs at the back of the knees with both hands. Powerfully pull and lift him up while continuing to drive forward with your legs and hips and use your body weight and momentum. Let your leg power, speed and leverage be the advantage and knock him over. Again, very rapidly as he is falling, get your right arm under his left leg and throw it powerfully and dynamically up and over putting his back in front of you and you behind him. Put your neck choke on him, roll under him and as before, wrap your legs around him. If necessary, you may need to be on top of him but continue to choke hard enough to cut off his air and choke him out.

Sadly, if this is a real life threat you will want to eliminate them altogether. These MMA drills adapted for the street are not as lethal as our commando style unarmed combat drills but it is certainly one of the most effective mixed martial arts drills available to non-security cleared individuals outside the military and police special tasks units.

Remember; start with a ghost punch simply to distract him, followed up by a low level kick. Control his triceps, spike down and grab the person for a take down. Dump the person and stay on your feet if possible. You only want to go all the way to the ground if you are certain that it is a confirmed single assaulter. You must also be prepared to experience receiving a knee to the face. Going down to the ground is always not recommended and should always be a last resort.

If you have to stop/eliminate/kill the threat in a real life situation; use this option, which is for very fast, highly dangerous environments when there are more enemy fighters nearby. Let your opponent commit with a punch and as he punches, take a 45 degree slide out and away from his power hand and leg and brutally kick him behind the knee with a fast, low and powerful Muay Thai style roundhouse kick. Follow that with a powerful dominant hand punch right on the back of his neck or immediately apply a standing MMA naked rear choke / *"Lion's kill"* hold and hold for 10 to 15 seconds or more as is necessary. **Important! In training and during testing, never choke hard and never for more than 2 seconds for you could accidently break the wind pipe or strangle your partner.)** Stay on your feet during and after the choke by stepping to the side as you choke the person. You can also kick the person behind the knee in the process. Get professional coaching and focus on mastering all of the details of these or any of our drills.

As before, you next want to back up to a wall if necessary, get a weapon in hand and call 911. You must master this drill before attempting to use it. It is very valuable for real world emergency responses. It combines the best MMA and the best of empty hand commando techniques. We do the MMA take down to build fighting spirit, aggression and to provide confidence while having a bit of manly fun but the head take down is the real deal and can be lethal.

If you can consistently shoot accurate head shots at imminent threats from reasonably safe distances with a long gun, take out 3 targets at 7 plus yards in less than 2 seconds with a pistol and master the in-home, in-car, on-foot first contact immediate action drills we stress, know your 2.2 medical trauma system covered in FEAR NOT plus master the dynamic head take down as I have explained it here then you are on your way to becoming a very formidable family protector, self-defender and war zone survivor. Remember to also combine your strength and conditioning exercise with long distance hiking or rout marches, jumping rope, plyometrics and kettle bells. **Conditioning is the key to survival.** You can know all the techniques but without the stamina, power and strength you will most likely not win. You must condition both your mind and body together. I want also to be very clear that the best course of action I can recommend is to be humble and to avoid all fights the best you can.

If you are a hard core operator with gear on, grab the guy by his helmet and twist violently and then use your knife or your knuckle gloves.

In our Family & Personal Protection, hands-on class we teach how to set up an effective last stand defense. This is something every dad, mom, granny, granddad and single mom needs to learn. Due to its highly confidential nature this is not something we can disclose in this book. We only teach this in person to law abiding people with proof of no criminal record.

Note: For further training, special incentive gear and a weapon give away; check out Doron's training programs at critraining. com/antihomeinvasion. Here you can watch some great short video clips of the CRI Anti Home Invasion course.

I say not from a place of ego, but from a position of caring that we trust this to be the very best family protection program offered because we know your family will need and deserve nothing less!

Use of Light

Always use light very sparingly and intelligently. Use it to conduct brief searches that can identify and illuminate threats. When used correctly, a light can effectively blind and disorient intruders and assaulters and is quite useful in preventing you from falling onto things or into a shaft as I once did in a very dark building. Lights will give your position away. Use it very sparingly if at all and remember to always move as you use it or relocate immediately thereafter. The ideal *"home defender"* light should be stronger than 50 lumens. We recommend 100 to 125 lumens 99.9 % of the time. A light of 250 lumens or so may be good in very dark country environments but remain mindful and very careful of the after-burn effect on powerful hot lights stronger than 125 lumens.

There are many excellent flashlights on the market and several ways to use them. The determining factor is primarily the location of the activation switch. At this introductory level we will explore and learn the "Ice Pick", "FBI" and "Harriers" methods as our base line techniques for low light environments. Tactical rear switch activated flashlights used in combination with a handgun can be extremely effective especially with adequate professional training and frequent practice. Professional training and coaching in realistic force-on-force training scenarios are of great value and are highly recommended.

Practice each of these three demonstrated methods of using a flashlight in advance. Do so exactly in the detailed ways taught in class and use your light very sparingly but at the right moments and for the right reasons.

The "Ice Pick" method pictured is very effective for blinding an intruder momentarily with a powerful light or for swift left to right, low to high, close to far scans of very dark environments if need be. When you shoot using the "Ice Pick" method align the flashlight with your jaw line.

The "FBI" method demonstrated in the next picture is great in extremely dark environments. The illusion is to make the bad guys think you are more over to the side if they attempt to shoot at you. Holding it 35 to 45 degrees up can also create a more confusing and intimidating look.

The "Harriers" position pictured last is a proven method for when you need to use the light not only for finding and identifying the bad guys but when you are forced as your last resort to shoot in self-defense or for the family's protection.

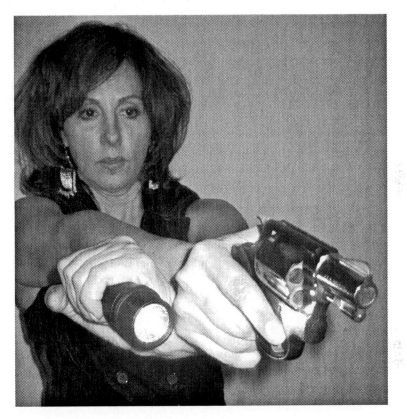

Practice smooth and swift transitions from the "Ice Pick" and "FBI" methods to the "Harriers" method. Use a rear switch thumb activated "tactical" flashlight for the best results and consider putting a short parachute cord wrist lanyard on it for retention.

You may need your hands free to reload, clear malfunctions, and restrain a prisoner or to provide medical trauma care. A red filter will help to protect your night vision and will reduce your overall light print visibility but it unfortunately does reduce your ability to see your red laser dot if being used together. It makes it difficult to see bleeding wounds and will reduce your lights ability to *"blind"* intruders; so red filters may be best left for special operations shooters. A blue filter is especially useful while checking a patient for bleeding if they are wearing dark or black clothing. I recommend you get a quality set of night sight goggles for dark environment use. They could save your life.

Ideally, under all circumstances and as soon as possible position yourself in the area of least light and remain still in the darkness. Let the threat move, make noise and become backlit but if at all possible, not you. Force them to move and to use a flashlight to find you. Hopefully they won't but if they do come after you then you, at your position, will be in the most advantageously tactical situation.

Even better would be if you are behind bullet proof cover and use night optics and night vision goggles. Remember, they may very well have night sight goggles of their own and most likely will. Anticipate for this and prepare and behave accordingly. When you are forced to move, be mindful that every dark area may conceal a threat who is observing you the way predators observe prey. Minimize their chances of seeing you. Use your light very sparingly, intelligently and effectively. Both your intelligent use of light and cover are critical keys to your survival.

Disarming a Weapon Threat

If you have to perform a disarming, know there is a very high probability that the weapon will fire. Disarming is very dangerous to perform but with enough training and practice it can be done effectively as a last resort option only. With this in mind and only if very well trained should you as a very last resort attempt this. Since you are about to be killed anyway try always honoring the following three principles:

1. Step out of the line of fire/knife attack and redirect the muzzle or blade into a safe direction.
2. Gain control of the weapon as a high priority and or the dominant weapon hand of the threat.
3. As trained, deliver a threat stopping action.

KNIFE AND HANDGUN DISARMING:

1. Step aside
2. Gain control
3. Strike the assaulter's throat with the outside of your forearm or with the leading knife like edge of your hand and or gain control of the weapon.
4. Immediately step back and with the weapon in hand, utilize the weapon to your best advantage. Refer to our training in prisoner control and legal responsibilities.

RIFLE DISARMING:

1. Redirect the rifle barrel's muzzle upward.
2. Punch the assaulter's throat with the Y or web of your hand. Use a forward step with some hip rotation and exhale to maximize the power of your strike.
3. Grab the Butt Stock of the rifle and dynamically pull it down away from the assaulter's shoulder as you step backward. Maintain a firm grip to take control of the weapon.

4. Powerfully and rapidly strike your assaulter with the muzzle. If the person is wearing body armor strike the face, if not then attack the solar plexus with a direct thrust.
5. Tactically shoulder the weapon and step backward creating distance from you.

If the weapon has a sling attached these maneuvers will of course become more complicated. It is possible to effectively use the sling in close quarters to choke the threat into losing consciousness in as little as 10 to 30 seconds. This technique is only selectively taught and given during our personalized advanced course.

Note: For extensive DVD training in highly effective and real world proven disarming techniques please see the CRI Counter Terrorism School DVD information set in the back of this book. It contains the world famous CRI CTS method and the exact techniques used by some of the most experienced and professional people in war fighting and the crime fighting industry. Please see www.critraining.com

Knife Fighting

You may be thinking; "No way, I could never cut or stab another human being." Well that is exactly what some of our former flight attendant students said at the CRI Counter Terrorism School. After just a little bit of training in our Counter Skyjacking Course we witnessed how a very peaceful, gentle and friendly female flight attendant became intensely aggressive and brutal when one of our CRI instructors charged their group with a (700 V) shock knife. She and the other flight attendants viciously cut and stabbed him. Afterwards they said, "They did not even realize that they were so brutal and effective in their defensive response". They also said, "That after the training, they will now do exactly the same thing if they are under the threat of a knife attack". Doron Benbenisty.

A knife is often easier to come by than a gun. When effectively used, a knife in trained hands can be a very efficient self-defense tool in any hand-to-hand combat scenario. A very practical solution is to carry a box cutter disposable #10 medical scalpel knife. It is a micro small tool, inexpensive and very intimidating. Carry a scalpel blade complete with handle. It is important to learn how to fortify and defend your personal perimeter of safety by learning hands-on how to slash and stab effectively with one and with two knives together. Only use a knife as your absolute last resort. You must be highly skilled with inward and backward slashing, as well as straight and angled stabbing thrusts with either hand or both hands in order to be highly effective with a knife. Let the knife become one with your hand, your mind and your entire body. Let it be an extension of your arm. You need to practice frequently using two knives and with a medical scalpel.

However, the use of a knife, box cutter or scalpel is not ideal. It should always only be the last resort. A shotgun or handgun is always a better family and self-defense tool in most situations. Martial arts' training provides a great foundation for knife fighting but on its own it is simply not enough in many instances. Know that I take no pleasure in teaching knife fighting, but consider it essential if you are to become an effective and adequately prepared full spectrum family defender.

Without some prior martial art training your foot work is most likely going to be clumsy and ineffective at first. A non martial artist will typically start off with a poor stance, with slow reactions and wildly swinging arms. This typically presents a vulnerable neck, fingers, chest, back . . .

However, most people can improve exponentially and get good at some of the key aspects with as little as one focused hour of coaching and sparring. Ideally, a minimum of one intense day, a weekend or better yet one week of quality realistic knife fighting will greatly improve your training. You will gain some useful skills, but mastery takes a lifetime of diligent study and practice. A minimal functional knowledge of knife fighting and even more importantly knife disarming techniques is an essential aspect of family and personal protection on the streets.

Knives are commonly used by street criminals. Sadly, some criminals have extensive exposure to the deadly Filipino martial art and knife fighting techniques known only to serious practitioners of Escrima, Arnis de Mano or Kali and other such fighting systems. To truly become an effective defender you first need to understand the ways of the attacker. To survive a violent street or in home criminal encounter where edged weapons are being presented you may be forced to attack proactively as the fight begins. Action typically beats reaction. The dangers and realities of knife attacks by multiple skilled street criminals are rather grim and at minimum people will get badly cut.

Knife fighting can only be effectively learned through hands-on training and lots of practice with rubber training knives, body armor, groin cups, helmets, and safety glasses. It is a very important aspect of ones overall training as a family protector and for self-defense. Knife fighting is extremely brutal and dangerous and should be avoided. If you are ever forced into an unavoidable knife fight, use two knives if that option is available to you. It will give you an intimidating and effective competitive edge. Hold the lead hand knife in a fencing grip and the rear hand knife in a reverse grip, or both in a reverse grip, hiding your knives behind your forearms. Use fast powerful 35 to 45 degree Samurai slashes or street fighter figure 8's by using two rapid two directional style slashes followed with direct fencing thrust like stabbing movements. Use your entire body when stabbing while applying good balance in a mixed martial artist stance. After stabbing, twist and cut in a deep and large crescent moon or C shape manner or in an L shape for larger wounding, greater shock and to retrieve the blade. Keep it simple and direct with three to five blade entries or less. In total privacy you might try your technique at least once on a large heavy piece of suspended raw meat. It may even convince you to never ever want to use a knife for real combat. However, should you be forced to do so, your experience will be of great value.

Become a serious student of the best foot and hand work strategies and tactics. Learn and know how to slash, block, trap and stab. Know how to use your breathing effectively and study the human anatomy to understand where the vital slashing and stabbing targets are and the best angles for attack on these artery, vein and organ targets. Utilize mostly fast, precise, multiple slashing actions aimed at the fingers and blood vessels such as the external carotid arteries that are 1.5 inches below the skin of the neck. Aim for the trachea, inner and outer thighs, the back of the knees or any other nerve centers, tendons and muscles. Reserve stabbing actions into vital organs such as the heart, under the armpit, lungs, kidneys, the spot between the anus and the groin, the base of the skull, the top of the head, or into the subclavian artery located around 2.5 to 3 inches down from the collar bone as a final act only. These actions are all incredibly dangerous to practice or to use in real life situations.

Therefore, please be aware that the author disclaims any liability from any injury or damage to the reader or to any third party. This information, as with everything in this book, is for informational purposes and entertainment or for novelty purposes only. The author assumes no responsibility for any use or misuse of any of this information.

Effective knife use is both an art and a science and requires diligent study and practice to master. Everyone should invest at least some time investigating knife fighting. Having said that, true professionals avoid getting into knife fights. When one is forced upon them they either just do a powerful disarming, shoot the assaulter or stab the assaulter with a sharp, carefully selected, well positioned knife using one or more direct vital organ stabs rather then slashes. Become diligent in knife disarming training and in building your fundamental skills along with some uncommon skills in both of these critical aptitudes toward family and self-defense.

In a popular film "Raiders of the Lost Ark", an adventurer named Indiana Jones played by Harrison Ford is confronted by a scimitar wielding attacker in the market place. He has been going AAPE to avoid capture just prior to the moment and has lost contact with his partner and is trying to locate her. Rather than confront this scimitar wielding Assassin head on with just a bull whip, Indiana Jones nonchalantly draws his .45 caliber revolver and from 25 feet puts down the threat before it materializes further. He then reassesses his new threat, the crowd, and in light of his actions, he immediately goes AAPE and continues his pursuit of his missing partner. Please understand that I am not recommending the shoot first ask no questions attitude because there are always laws and repercussions for any lethal action you might take, but even Hollywood sometimes gets it right. AAPE.

Knife throwing is also a beautiful art if done well and it has it's time and place in a full spectrum warrior training program. In 99.99% of the time, it is advisable not to throw your knife. This is especially important if it is your only weapon. Having said that, with frequent training and in some unique last resort situations it is still a very powerful option and should never be totally ruled out.

When forced into using a knife to stop a threat, it will be most effective to use a direct stab into a vital organ as opposed to slashing. Slashing the neck, the inside of the arms and inside their legs is the most damaging alternative. As a last resort, you can quickly eliminate the threat by stabbing a person in the face. You will definitely discourage the attack. A hatchet is also very intimidating.

It will serve you well to study the Asian views on knife fighting. Especially research the techniques of the Filipino, Korean and Japanese martial arts and knife fighters. As in all combat, armed or unarmed; the three core principles of combat remain the key. Apply surprise, speed and Wolverine like yet legally appropriate violence-of-action. Once you attack, maintain momentum in a loop of rapid consecutive slashes until you can close the loop with a threat stopping thrust stab and large C shaped cut. Gain training experience with both fixed and folding blades and with a variety of blade lengths and designs such as karambit type and talon shaped blades. Also practice with a #10 and #20 scalpel knife or a box cutter. A Japanese carpenter's cutter is an outstanding and inexpensive knife for self-defense.

More importantly than just studying how to fight with a knife, realistic practice in defense against a knife and specifically learning three to five proven knife disarming techniques are very valuable and highly recommended. Practice is essential to develop the required respect, balance, agility, defensive and offensive foot and hand work, angles, breathing style, speed, timing, accuracy, techniques, rhythm, mindset, experience, skill and confidence. There is no substitute for practice. One thing is sure. You never want to be up against multiple skilled knife fighters without a loaded gun in your own trained hands. Knives do not perform well in gunfights. Be the person with the gun, preferably two guns but have both a great knife and solid knife fighting and knife disarming skills as a last resort for back up.

Should you ever have to use a knife in a fight, keep things simple and focus your best efforts with a mindset of "controlled aggression" and flexible intelligence? Remember to keep your attacker fully visible and remember the keys to effective combat. They are surprise, speed and violence of action. If forced to do so to survive, attack the throat, eyes, top of the head, temple, inner ear, base of the skull, nose cavity, heart, torso and abdominal areas, the kidneys, groin or inner upper thighs and inner arms. AAPE the situation as best you can and either avoid it or get out of it ASAP.

Your mindset is very important. Think of your entire body as the weapon while using your mind, your feet, your elbows and not just the knife. Focus your *"controlled aggression"*. For most, keep your non knife hand close and turn your wrist inwards towards your body to protect yourself from incoming slashes. Use low, fast and powerful surprise kicks where the opportunity presents itself but only if you are very skilled as a result of frequent and diligent training. If you are not then I pray you have a gun and are expertly trained and skilled in its use.

The best knives for this application (close quarter defense and combat) surely include the James Williams Samurai inspired 13 inch Hissatsu blade with a long narrow strong point and thick spine. A sharp, strong battle hatchet, the true Japanese Tanto knife, the short Wakizashi sword, a 22 oz. or heavier 12 inch or longer Gurka Kukri, perhaps the Frontier / Cowboy / Pioneer style Bowie with its 10 ½ inch blade, the long double edge dagger with a thick spine, a quality boot knife, a quality neck knife, a Japanese Carpenters knife, a box cutter and only then a quality tactical folder. The U.S. Marine Combat / Utility Knife, the American, British or Russian Bayonet is also very, very good but essentially the Samurai inspired Hissatsu that many elite warriors use today is superior in close quarters combat and a Wakizashi or even two Wakizashi's will give a family home defender the most courage if ever needed as a backup to your twelve gauge pump shotgun and .357 or .40 caliber handgun. The truth be told, even a crappy knife, a sushi or steak knife or a cheap folding knife or a short sharp stick is better than any unarmed technique.

If you have instant access to it, and must do so to stop your immediate life-threatening assaulter, stab the vital organs directly while holding the knife edge up rather than simply slashing wildly or precisely. As stated, even a sharpened stick can do the job if it is with enough speed, force, intent and accuracy. Slashing with a knife is only occasionally used to open the path when needed or to scare someone away as opposed to stopping them dead. In a knife fight, you can never be pensive. Always be mentally prepared in advance to get cut and expect to see blood. It could be either yours or the attackers but when it happens, the situation can present itself as both an opportunity to escape and AAPE your way out of further harm or you may need to finish the battle. Either way, it remains a very nasty business and should only be considered as a last resort.

There are many, many great options in knives. In fact, there are literally hundreds of them, perhaps even thousands. Most though are designed for other purposes in mind such as hunting and skinning, as a utility knife or for survival. Very few are designed purely for fighting wars or purely as a quality personal defense type weapon. The British and American commando daggers are. So are the Japanese style Hissatsu by Williams. The Williams Hissatsu is the pinnacle of design. This opinion is also shared by some of America's Best and most experienced combat Warriors.

Ultimately, it is always best to have two handguns and a knife in your personal layered defense system for an emergency response, or at least one handgun and two knives. Better yet, a shotgun, two or three handguns and two knives available provides a formidable defense system. It sounds like a lot but most elite tier soldiers will carry a battle rifle or carbine and or a shotgun plus at least one handgun and at least one knife in spite of being supported by 1-12 carefully selected, highly trained and equally well armed buddies. Think about it. Even the police will carry similar weaponry and still rely on supporting officers. Do not ever assume that one layer of defense will be enough; especially if it is simply a
Stun gun, baton or pepper spray. Since I really want to make you a hard target then let's follow the example of a deep layered approach shall we?

Swordsmanship

IF firearms are not available to you, or if you want a powerful backup for your firearm/s or if you find firearms unacceptable, then I highly recommend you explore the study and practice of the ancient Samurai Bujutsu. Translated it means *"the art of the warrior or the art of martial arts or just simply, war"*. You should specifically at minimum study "Shinkendo", and also "Kenjutsu"—*"the art of the sword"* where you will gain extensive practical experience in Tameshirigi. You practice the cutting of water soaked bamboo mats and bamboo pole combinations or perhaps the cutting of large chunks of animal meat so as to become skilled with blade impact. A Wakizashi (short sword) can be a fear eliminating yet very powerful and effective and fear inducing family protection and self-defense weapon especially when in the trained and skilled hands of a person lodged in close quarter encounters.

The Katana is a much longer (29 to 35 plus inch blade), heavier and more powerful but may be too long for a modern confined space in asymmetrical urban combat. Therefore a 21or so inch blade such as the Wakizashi or even a 13 inch or longer Tanto knife blade is recommended for family protection and self-defense purposes. These blades are excellent as a backup for your 12 gauge pump shotgun with #6, # 7, and perhaps double 00 buck ammunition and your handgun/s of choice. Of course your awareness and based on that awareness; avoidance, remains your best overall strategy.

When you have a loaded shotgun, one to three loaded handguns and a sharpened high quality Wakizashi immediately available, and you and are highly skilled in the use of each of those weapons, you are certainly not a soft and choice target in any criminals mind. That is the core objective of my FEAR NOT system. If you are absolutely opposed to guns then I strongly recommend a quality high power bow and arrow/s or crossbow and a quality sword which is certainly much better to have during an imminently violent emergency than nothing at all.

The first thing to do is to study and embody the Bushido. (The moral code-of-conduct of the Samurai as it contains the soul and spirit of ancient Japanese Swordsmanship.) It is believed that each Katana (Japanese Sword) has a soul and that to become a true classical swordsman your soul and that of your sword must be in harmony as the sword becomes an integral part and extension of you.

A Katana or Wakizashi in the hand of a person who does not know nor obey the Bushido code is potentially very bad for all concerned. Therefore, before we continue, please allow me to first share the code. "Our goal is always to respect others, the sword and ourselves and to be safe and responsible people." We want and urge you to be good, kind, honest and non-violent citizens in a civil society.

All martial arts training should always focus first on making one a better, more kind, courteous, exemplary and benevolent person who will help to improve society. The correct perspective in Martial Arts is all about avoiding conflict through respectful etiquette, courtesy and sincere diplomacy but when conflicts arise; resolve them in the least violent, most respectful and kindest way possible. This is why martial arts training are so valuable in child development and especially for teenagers and young adults. A child who through example from an early age learns the philosophy of martial arts will likely engage less in fights but shine in respect, etiquette, courtesy, self-discipline, neatness, punctuality, loving-kindness, quiet and calm self–assurance, confidence, posture, balance, coordination, concentration, patience, goodwill, loyalty and more. All are great qualities to have in every domain of life.

The Fundamental Principles of Bushido

Respect life. Living with the right heart / attitude / mindset deeply rooted in a daily spiritual preparation can result in conscious and mindful living with the calm acceptance of death as a natural part of life.

> Bravery, daring guile in combat and wise valor

> Caring, compassion, benevolence and love for all people, everywhere

> Right action, justice, respect, etiquette, courtesy and excellence

> Total sincerity, truthfulness and responsible fairness

> Honor

> Loyalty, faithfulness and devotion

Martial arts instructors / masters first and foremost exist to help students become better people. They inspire and encourage students to strive for personal growth, improve their character and aim at perfecting their character into a lifelong practice. They always make a sincere and great effort to offer excellence to others and to be truthful and defend truth. Common traits are to respect, honor and exemplify etiquette and courtesy. They avoid getting into meaningless fights and contribute to the cultivation of a better society through ones daily living of spiritual values while practicing intelligence, self-discipline, internal power, calm self-assurance, courage, loyalty, virtue, trust, goodwill and etiquette. This is the true spirit of a real martial artist.

Can you imagine a world where we all subscribe to and practice that? A person who is sincere, wise and skilled in social etiquette yet who is kind, respectful, loyal and patient very seldom needs to fight. When one is guided by love, honor and caring in all of ones actions, good things normally follow but sadly not always. Even if you act with love, caring, respect, protocol, courtesy and etiquette; others may not.

So with that entirely in mind, let us explore the core fundamentals of Japanese swordsmanship for in my view it embodies and exemplifies all the previous traits better than any other. Sword skills are best learned in person from an honorable and responsible school and traditionally, sword skills are not taught to those of bad character. It is and should only be reserved for those who respect the art, their teachers, self, nature, life and society at large. I personally believe one should take a formal and ceremonial blood oath to only ever use one's sword and sword skills to protect or defend and never in anger.

A Katana or Wakizashi is a very potent and lethal weapon and with correct technique can easily cut a persons head, leg or arm off with a single cut or with two at most. In ancient Japan only a Samurai was allowed to own and wear a Katana and a Wakizashi. A Wakizashi with a 18 ½ to 21 inch or longer forged, folded steel blade made out of 1055 or 1560 carbon or original Japanese Katana quality steel will give you a deep sense of pride of ownership, emergency preparedness and confidence once you are skilled in it's use.

Select one with a handle that is long enough for you to hold comfortably with your two hands about 2" apart. A handle almost as long as your own forearm is ideal. The ancient Samurai slept with their swords right there with them and always ready to use when needed. They never went anywhere without at least their Wakizashi on their person, even if they were in the presence of the emperor. The Katana battle sword was their 7.62 x 51 mm weapon and the Wakizashi was their backup .45 side arm. You can find a quality, functional Wakizashi as a very affordable investment. Please be wary to not acquire a non battle ready brittle and low quality blade. Do your own research and due diligence. You will be glad you did.

Join a good martial arts school that teaches short sword technique and become a diligent and responsible student of sword philosophy, principles and technique. A 13 inch blade or Tanto style knife is easier to carry when you are on foot or in your vehicle and an 18 ½ to 21 plus inch blade Wakizashi is ideal for in-home defense. The short Samurai inspired sword-knife is making a strong comeback amongst elite modern day soldiers and has seen action in modern day Afghanistan in the hands of American warriors. The excellent CRKT© Hisshou™ is such an example. The Cold Steel© brand "battle ready" and " Warrior Series" O Tanto™ is also an excellent, intimidating and inspiring yet affordable choice as is their Wakizashi and Katana.

When using a Katana or Wakizashi you must be skilled in the proper grip, stance, foot movements and basic cutting techniques. Remain mindful that the use of any sword, as with all weapons, is potentially very dangerous and even lethal. A sword cannot guarantee you will be a hard target. That depends on your level of skill and each unique situation and circumstance. Also, federal, state or local laws may prohibit the possession or use of certain weapons and this may or may not include a sword. Do not train with or use a sword if your health or relevant laws do not permit you to do so in a safe, healthy and legal way.

Study sword etiquette before you handle any sword. For family protection and self-defense this is not so much our focus but we do consider it a very important aspect of swordsmanship. Honor all relevant safety measures just as you would with firearms and knives for a sword is lethal.

The Stance (Hohaba)

There are at least six to ten basic stances and also six basic movements to learn. They must be learned in person from a wise and skilled sword master. The most often used stance to posture and intimidate an imminent assaulter with and to fight from is the high ready with the sword in front of you. Stand in a short martial arts stance with good posture and hold the sword 45 degrees up with comfortably bent arms and the tip two inches below your eyes or at throat level just like you would with a battle rifle, carbine or handgun muzzle in a high ready position. Having said that, I personally prefer to keep the sword sheathed as long as possible rather than posturing with it.

The traditional Samurai way is to cut an opponent down directly from the draw of the sword with one clean cut to the throat, armpit or knee. Stand with your feet approximately 16 to 28 inches apart with 60 to 75 percent of your weight floating on and off of your front foot as you cut and move. Your rear foot should be positioned 45 degrees outward. When threatened in a combat situation lean slightly forward from the hips with your spine straight and your head aligned. Again, apply nearly 60 percent of your weight on your forward foot and increase the weight as you cut. Use the correct two handed grip. A close stance with your feet allows for faster movement. A good solid positioning yet fast stance is essential and fundamental to effective swordsmanship.

A more aggressive high ready stance is with the sword up, one fist above your head with the blade horizontal to the ground and ready to defend and cut.

Tactically, in a family protection and self-defense situation, you will not posture in this manner. When forced to do so by imminent assaulters with ability, means and evil intent and exhibiting lethal behavior in a "code black" kill-or-be-killed situation; you will in that moment of truth simply draw the sword and cut as an extension of your draw.

The Grip

Grip your sword with both hands. Your wrists must always be toward the top edge of the sword.

Grip the sword in the web of your hands, with your thumbs pointing down and your elbows positioned inward. Now, position your right hand at the top with your index finger one inch from the hand guard. Your thumb should be over your middle finger and your grip is accomplished mostly with your little finger. Your front hand grips at about 35% overall gripping strength and again, your little finger does most of the gripping. Your lead hand provides direction and accuracy.

Allow for one or two inches of space between your front and back hand. The more space between your front hand and the hand guard and between your two hands the more fluid you're cutting and defensive movements will be.

Your rear hand or left hand in a right hand grip has your thumb over the index finger. The rear hand grips harder than the front hand at about 65% of your overall gripping power and again you grip hardest with your little finger. The rear hand provides balance and power.

The Cut

When using the Samurai Katana, Wakizashi or Tanto style blades, the secret is to cut not chop! It is a sword with a razor sharp and durable cutting edge but not an axe. Use circular and drawing motions to cut. The front 9 inches of the Katana is its primary cutting edge. With the Wakizashi and Tanto blade, use the front half of the cutting edge. The secret to effective cutting is to cut at a 35 degree angle and to squeeze your hands inwards while exhaling sharply and locking your wrists. When you tactically use the sword blade to block another edged weapon, you use the back part of the spine or side. Having said that, it is best not to use the sword for blocking at all if you can help it. It is best to step out of your assaulter's line of attack and cut to his center quicker than he can cut to yours. Training and practice is essential. All cutting, both in training and in family/personal defense must be done from a pure and true heart that you have prepared through daily prayer and meditation. Practice frequently by cutting rice straw mats, (wara) and/or green bamboo stalks (medaka/madaka) practicing targets.

Basic Sword Handling

When handling the Katana or Wakizashi, begin with the heels of your feet together with toes out 35 degrees; so that you can be nimble and swivel 360 degrees around into any direction while keeping your eyes constantly at chest high level with a soft gaze as if you were looking at a distant target. We manage the *"tsuba"* hand guard of the sword with our thumb and provide control and security on the sword handle with a gentle grip from our other hand to be ready to engage instantly if necessary.

When handling your sword, maintain excellent balance and a good sword posture. Keep your head aligned with your spine yet still and forward for a good stance and movement but never up and back. Slide your feet to move and to pivot your body. Simply rotate from your hips if you need to circle swing at an angle to make one or more 35 degree downward cut/s with the front 5 to 9 inches of the blade. Stay light on your feet. When you slide step you want to place most of your weight on your front foot, facing forward. Keep your full weight mostly forward. Pivot with your back leg and foot. This is our foundation with the sword.

The Tactical Practice Drill

It is important to develop the habit of early morning daily practice. I urge you to master the following areas:

Calm mind and warrior spirit through spiritual practice
Stance and footwork including the sliding shuffle, the forward step and the back foot pivot
Grip
Distance, timing and speed
Accuracy and sword control (stopping precisely just beyond the cut)
35 degree angle cut

Stand in a neutral but balanced way with your feet shoulder width apart. Distribute your weight to start with at 60% on the forward foot. Place your tongue on the roof of your mouth and breathe deeply through your nose.

Unlock your sword sheath with your left hand thumb, tilt the sheath 45 to 90 degrees with the blade outward and inhale as you draw, step forward and cut sideways behind the knee, the upper leg, ribs, arm or neck as you steadily exhale. Sadly, if necessary, follow immediately with a second cut. This may be a 90 degree downward head cut or a 45 degree downward cut onto the neck or across the heart, into a wrist, forearm or upper arm. If necessary this may be followed by a direct stab into the heart. Exhale as you cut or stab. It is brutal, bloody and up close and personal. At this time, those who chose a sword over a firearm may rather wish they had chosen a firearm.

The traditional Samurai technique is a mid level side cut with the blade tip lower than your shoulder followed immediately by a downward cut to the top of the head and then both a functional and ceremonial shaking off of the blood to the side before sheathing the sword again and bowing to the sword.

A very effective technique is to step 45 degrees out to the side as the person attacks and then to cut through the assaulter's abdomen as you step forward while evading his or her attack. Then, if necessary, add a second step and a turn to cut into the back of the knee or neck if it is still necessary to stop the threat.

Sword Drills

Our first drill and technique is stepping 45 degrees or more off line and out away from center to your opponents weak side while drawing the sword straight at the threat target. Turn the sword at the last moment and cut 45 degrees up across / through his torso, followed by a second rapid, explosive 45 degree downward cut from his neck-shoulder connection down to his opposite hip. Keep your stance relatively short and your back leg foot very light so that you are constantly ready to move again in any new direction. Keep your eyes at high chest level and your tongue behind your front teeth and mostly at the roof of your mouth.

Our second and alternative drill is a traditional type drill. We prefer to be standing rather than kneeling. From here, as we draw, we perform a swift horizontal cut with the blade tip somewhat down followed by a two handed vertical downward cut. Occasionally we add two or more angled downward cuts in rapid succession as seen in masterful cutting demonstrations. Now, draw the sword **straight out** towards the target while keeping your eyes on the opponents high chest and bend into the target as you draw. Your off hand stays on your scabbard on your first horizontal cut as you draw. However, if necessary, use this hand to support and reinforce your sword hand in any unconventional manner. Cut from and to the center while dominating their center in a calm, focused, flowing, soft, relaxed way from a position of balance, truth and harmony. Keep elbows tight and very close to your body. The sword must go straight out from and to the center (Jinchuro).

As you cut, grip strongest at that moment. Learn to grip mostly with the bottom two fingers of your cutting hand and strongest with your little finger/s. Exhale as you outwardly extend. Use a small dynamic hip rotation with speed and reach your most powerful exhale at the point of contact to give power to your cut. After the initial horizontal or 45 degree upwards and outward cut from the draw, shift the grip to the front two fingers as you bring it up and grip with both hands for your vertical downward cut to the center.

As an example, these are some of the core fundamentals that we are interested in. We recommend you study, practice and teach carefully and diligently with the sword as with any weapon. We train and practice to be fluid with it. In so doing, it will help to build your warrior spirit and confidence in it as an art form and as a functionally effective weapon should one ever need to use it during an emergency response to protect your dear ones and / or self against any live threat. If this resonates well with you then you will love my Kusemono-(Bu)-do Full Spectrum Martial Arts System.

The reasons why we recommend the Samurai sword as opposed to other swords are; due to the curvature of the blade itself, it will draw quicker from the scabbard, the blade will stay longer in the cut causing more severe damage and it transfers less shock from impact into the hands. We consider the Samurai blade to be a superior battle specific sword.

Note: A swordsman with a Katana, Wakizashi or Tanto can be both a formidable family protector and lethal assaulter yet a sword is not a good match for a gun. Having said that, a person with a sword in hand can close a cap of 30 feet or so in just a little bit more than the blink of an eye. If you have a firearm and miss hitting the person with a sword; they potentially can now cut or stab you within a second or two. As you see, this course of action works both ways. You need to become proficient with any weapon of your choosing. Better to be aware, AAPE and avoid all dangerous and potentially violent situations through your awareness and etiquette.

The Bottom Line on Edged Weapons and Edged Weapon Fighting

A 12 gauge pump shotgun, 7.62 x 51 rifle or heavy caliber handgun is considered better to have than just a knife when a really bad emergency requiring weapons does occur. However, at times in close quarter combat type situations where there is a risk of shooting someone you care about; a knife can be even better than a handgun. I teach this at advanced levels in my Kusemono-Do martial arts system as a counter gun disarming technique and can potentially refer you to the works of a master on this.

A full size fighting knife or a Kukri is generally better than a small knife. A double edged boot knife and often a straight or curved blade neck knife can be better than a tactical pocket folder but a folding knife is certainly better than nothing. A Japanese carpenter cutter or modern box cutters are very inexpensive and highly effective edged weapons. In a certain kind of man's hands a hatchet (Tomahawk style battle axe) or even a commando spade can be a powerful edged weapon but so can something as common as a medical scalpel.

When you have the benefit of some distance, a 35 to 50 pound or heavier hunting bow with 125 and 165 grain hunting broad tip arrows are very lethal. A cross bow, a spear or a 29.5" to 35" long blade such as the Samurai Katana sword may be a valuable addition if no firearms are available to you.

Should you ever end up having to protect your family or defend yourself with a knife of sorts you will be better off with a sharp, long, thin blade that has a strong spine or perhaps a short Samurai inspired sword such as Wakizashi. We recommend you carry two or even three knives; one high, one low and one in deep concealment. Depending who you are, who your assaulters are, where you are, why you are there, your personality type, the training you have had etcetera should dictate the number and type you may wish to carry.

Professionally trained Military types prefer to conceal their knife/s behind their forearm/s and mostly deploy it blade up with straight hard and direct stabs to your eyes, throat, armpit, clavicle area and down into your chest or heart. Another effective thrust is a 33 to 35 degree up stab into the kidneys in a very calm, methodical and effective way. Street fighter types tend to prefer having the knife highly visible and constantly move it around and slash at your hands / fingers, elbows, legs, knees, feet, face, neck, arms, torso . . . while using deception and by being highly opportunistic. Remember to notice patterns and deny them noticing your pattern or system. The details of both these two approaches are best learned in a hands-on training experience. Skills and training experience in both styles are very valuable.

In my view the very best modern day option is to have at least a 13" or longer Samurai inspired tactical fixed blade knife such as the one's designed my master swordsman James Williams. Space permitting, you could use a short Samurai Wakizashi * sword with a 19" or shorter blade. Back up either with a quality 7" or longer fixed blade fighting knife or a 5 inch plus blade boot knife and a quality tactical folder with a 3.75inch to 5.5 inches or longer blade. Remember, a folder needs a highly reliable multi safety function system to keep it from closing on your hand under high impact. **My BEST advice yet is to never be in a knife fight!**

* Footnote The *Wakizashi* with a 13 to 20 inches plus *Nagasa* blade is also sometimes called a *Shoto.* (Short sword)

The even shorter 9 / 10 / 13 inch *Tanto* blade and even shorter *Aikuchi* Japanese dagger without a hand/sword guard *Tsuba* is also worth considering as additional or alternative and excellent self-defense back-up / close quarter tactical knives. The Samurai inspired *Hissatsu* available from Bugei.com is the best modern day option for 90 degree and 35 degree stabbing and even 35 degree slashing. It is primarily designed as a knife for stabbing in lethal close quarter confrontations where using a carbine, shotgun or handgun may not be your best tactical option.

In my Kusemono-Bu-Do (Real Man / Warrior Way) comprehensive emergency response martial arts system we teach more in this regard. We draw inspiration and example from both sword masters; Obata Toshishiro Kaiso, Shodai Soke, the founder, headmaster and chief instructor of Shikendo which translates as the "true sword way", at the Honbu Dojo in Little Tokyo in Los Angeles, CA. and seven times All Japan Battodo / Tameshigiri (cutting) champion and holder of a total of a combined 75 dan–black belts in the sword and numerous other Japanese martial arts.

Also, James Williams, Kaiso, who is an extraordinarily accomplished sword master and specialist tactical trainer specializing in Samurai inspired edged weapons and designer of the powerful *Hissatsu*. Should you ever be forced to fight with an edged weapon, you most ideally want a *Wakizashi, Hissatsu* or *Katana,* or a sharp high quality battle hatchet in your own trained hands depending on your environment and how much space you have.

Tactical Communication

Communication in the tactical arena can be with oneself, one's partner and/or children if applicable or other people and more specifically also with the threat, the 911 operator and/or law enforcement officers. Remember to especially keep your commands and all your communications short, clear, accurate and timely. Calm yourself and speak slow, clear and deliberate. Be brief. Avoid yelling. Role clarity and clear communication during navigation, tactical movement, threat location, threat identification and threat engagement as well as during trauma medical care are all vital aspects to clarify and rehearse. Regarding hand signals, generally only use pre-planned and well rehearsed signals while communicating with your partner and family. The same goes for all your coded verbal communications with them.

Self Communication—As a whisper or where tactically acceptable communicate out loud with yourself depending on your unique environment and situation. Talk yourself through your first contact action drill to boost your courage and to focus on the highest possible quality execution of the drill. It may be as simple as saying or shouting single words such as *"Go", "Cock", "Reload", "Retreat"*. . .

Sad to say, but you may be forced to use some deception in an extreme circumstance where you are alone, at a high imminent risk and potentially outnumbered. For example you may shout *"John, get the other shotgun. It is loaded with buckshot and slugs"* or *"John, call 911 and cover my back with the shotgun."* You might also pray in a whisper or out loud. Self talk can be very useful when wounded and help you to maintain your focus while implementing methodical protocols and systematic procedures for yourself, family or buddy care. This is provided you can do so without compromising your position behind cover in the eventuality there is the presence of additional threats.

Partner Communication—Typical partner communications when on foot and a threat has been positively identified could be as simple as shouting the nature of threat and the direction in which the threat is being observed. Examples include *"follow me and do as I do"*, *"knife left"*, and **"pistol front"**. Other examples in law enforcement or war zone environments may include *"loading"*, *"magazine"* or *"peel off to the left/right"* for partner bounding and *"Go, Go, Go"* as taught for a dynamic single room entry. Once your zones are clear, declare appropriately *"left clear"*, *"right clear"*, *"all clear"* and *"roger that"*.

Silent communications may include hand signals such as holding up a fist just above your shoulder to indicate *"stop"*, and/or pointing with two fingers at your two eyes and then in the direction you want your partner to look toward and provide cover. When you are ready to move forward, a simple series of forward motions such as three consecutive times with your index finger is practical. Ideally you should connect with brief eye contact and a brief, mutually confirming nod. Prior to a room entry, the point person can nod his or her head when ready. The second person in the rear then squeezes the shoulder of the point person with her or his non-dominant hand and the point person nods again before immediate entry.

Threat Communication—Your communications with the threat should be minimal, forceful, clear and understandable. For example, *"Stop!"*, **"I do not want to fight but will if you force me to do so!"** *"Drop your gun"*. Shouting too loud will just make you less understood. Project a calm, confident manner best you can.

Victim Communication—Talk injured family members through each step of our medical trauma protocol and procedures ahead of actually implementing that particular step. This will help you to focus methodically, systematically and decisively. It will also reduce the uncertainty of the injured person. This is very important and we encourage it so as to reinforce the injured persons will to live. Use the persons name frequently but sadly you should also be ready, willing and able to eventually guide them in a transition during a crossover into eternal life prayer if need be.

Doron Benbenisty states—*"Be advised, that the bad guys are smart and very resourceful. If they cut your power line and activate a frequency dropper device they will effectively not only disable your home phone but also your cell phone. You will be completely disconnected from the outside world with no way to communicate for help. You must have an emergency response plan of action in place that will enable you to survive at all cost even without a telephone at hand until the police arrive. You must be prepared and decisive. Your life is a gift. Do not let anyone take it away from you."*

Prisoner Management

Y ou must first rapidly secure the prisoner/s before you can begin any medical trauma care. The following is the best procedure for doing so.

Stand with your back into a corner or at least backed up against a wall. Firmly and clearly verbalize your commands. Use short commands only. Shout them out!

Use simple commands such as: **"Stop", "Drop your gun" , "Turn around", "Kneel", "Lay down", "Look away", "Ear on the ground", "Spread your legs wide/ cross your ankles", "Spread your arms and fingers", "Turn your palms up", "Stay there; If you move I will see that as a threat and shoot."**

Do not go close to the criminal/s! Command them to immediately drop their weapons. With their hands held up high and away from their bodies, order them to step well away from the weapon if space permits and preferably direct them backwards away from you. Sending them as far as 30 feet or more back from your and their weapons would be best. Be mindful that a motivated and well trained person can cross a distance of 30 to 35 feet in about 2 or so seconds from a standing start. They could then disarm and strangle you or stab you with a knife or shoot you with your own gun.

To avoid this occurring, command them to turn around. Warn them you will shoot if they make any sudden movements or ignore your commands. Tell them to spread their fingers wide and to keep their arms up high and visible while they kneel down. Do this one knee at a time and on your command. Command them next to lie face down and look in the opposite direction away from you and each other with one ear on the ground, with their wrists turned palm up and with their fingers spread wide. If nobody in your family has been hit and you are not wounded and bleeding, this may be sufficient. Call 911 ASAP. Have your spouse or neighbor do so if they are able and willing. Call for help at your earliest and safest opportunity to do so.

If you need to begin trauma care on a family member or yourself, collect their weapons ASAP if you can do so safely. It is important to control their weapons and to unload them immediately. At minimum, remove the magazines from pistols, carbines or rifles along with the bullets from revolvers and keep it all under safe control. Remember never to block your firing position while keeping them covered. Do this only with very reliable help and great caution.

Until help arrives and only in the event where you cannot continue to supervise them very closely should you attempt to bind them? Let a strong competent helper, or two or more helpers provide cover for you as you restrain, bind and secure them one at a time with tuff-cuffs. Avoid this at all costs if you can.

If not, then first secure their wrists behind their backs with their hands facing outwards. Next secure their crossed ankles using *"flexi/ tuff-ties"*, rope and lots of duct tape. Then, head up to high ground. Get on a truck bed or car roof, your staircase or somewhere at least above them and away from them. Control them from the darkest area protected behind solid cover if it is available.

Remember, only attempt restraint if the police are delayed and only if you have lots of powerful yet competent help. You should restrain the prisoners by using great care. Ideally, avoid the need to do so. It is better to keep a safe distance and remain on hyper alert.

Should it be necessary to restrain them because you need to provide trauma medical care to your own or yourself then once again, make sure you tie their hands facing outwards and secure them with those ankles crossed? If competent and powerful help is not available then let it be. Do not involve weak or frightened and inexperienced people and place them in any risk. Keep your distance and you may want to say to the threat if it serves your purpose; *"I am going to count to five. As I count, I want you to run away. After five counts*

I never want to see you again." Use your own common sense and best judgment as to what is the safest and best thing for you to do.

If the prisoner is heavily wounded provide basic first aid care to them. It will be safest and perhaps enough to just instruct them to self-administer direct pressure or hold a tourniquet or a chest seal as may be necessary. Provide what they need. It is the right and humane thing to do but only after your family and yourself have been taken care of. Otherwise, do not go close to the prisoners.

If you do not have substantial and very competent help covering you then do not personally provide medical help until they have been secured with flexi-cuffs and perhaps even hogtied with some Para cord and this could also depend on how *"bad-ass"* they are. Even so, be very cautious and just perhaps let them self-administer their own basic medical care.

In the chaos of a riot or war zone this may not apply. There you most likely will simply retreat to a safe place. Remember, we are all about preserving lives first. Our own, our families and even that of those who trespassed against us but not at the risk of your family or your own life.

This should be as far as you will go to assist. Practice extreme caution so as not to be grabbed, overpowered and taken hostage by them at this or any other point.

Professional quality super heavy duty *"flexi-cuffs"* are very valuable to have in addition to a shotgun, handgun, night vision goggles, powerful flashlight, medical trauma kit and a tactical knife. I recommend having at least three sets of *"flexi-cuffs"* ready for use. I once heard of a man breaking two sets of these like twigs so be careful.

Having a note book and a writing instrument is also very valuable for recording facts and information such as suspect identification descriptions. Your detailed description of suspects that ran away will be of great value to the police. Be a good citizen and get those facts on paper. Shock and fear may temporarily affect your short term memory. This happens at times but will return after a little emotional caring. If emotional support is not available then sooth yourself as best you can. Take control and get your self control back the way we teach in class and with meaningful prayer.

When the Police Arrive

"Follow the directions of the police completely and without arguments. Remember they are responding to a situation they are not familiar with. Allow them time to gather facts."—Wes Doss

Call 911, ASAP, again. If they are already not still listening in, give the operator or police a brief updated situational report. Again, first tell them exactly where you are, then next what you and your family look like and finally how best to locate you. Hang a blue light up/out as a marker. When they enter you should be facing them with your hands up, weapons already made safe and placed in a clearly visible area. Expect that they may first send a police dog in and that they may body search you at gun point. Do not react to this! Reacting may get you bitten or shot. Stand totally still and just breathe deep and slowly. If you need to move, do that slowly but not towards the police unless they clearly command you to do so.

Remember that you do not legally have to speak. Simply thank them for showing up and coming to help you. At the very most, tell them truthfully how you were directly attacked and feared for your families and your own life. Share that the bad guys intended to kill you and forced you through their imminent actions to take a threat stopping action as a last resort. This was due to their *"means/ability, "distance/privacy/opportunity"* and *"jeopardy / clear intention"*. You had no way of avoiding their assault or retreating.

Thank them again for coming to your rescue. Then remain silent. Do not give advice, make requests, argue with them, insult them or question them. Just say thank you for coming to help us/me. Thereafter do not volunteer any more information.

If you feel compelled to talk and know you are 100% justified, respectfully tell them that you are in shock and please choose to remain silent until after having had legal counsel and representation.

Be clear with your legal counsel that the threat was life threatening, that you did all you could to prevent this from happening and be able to back that up with verifiable proof. Indicate how you retreated right up until shooting was the only way left to stop the threat and state clearly that this last resort was forced onto you by the imminent actions of your violent and dangerous assaulters. This is very important. Choose your right to remain silent. In general, minimize your communication with law enforcement officers. Only express your gratitude and provide useful facts regarding any escaped suspects.

Remember that the job of law enforcement officers is to assign blame. They are there to enforce the law and they do not want to be shot while doing so. They want to return to their families and are also simply human with their very own fears, hopes and dreams. Most police officers are very nice, decent and good people, but they have a particular job to do and according to very specific orders, protocols and procedures. They could and most likely will handcuff you and they will/may take you in for questioning; especially if any bad guys were shot by you. All of this will first have to be validated.

You should know that after seeing your surgical shot placement and especially after seeing how securely and professionally you tied your prisoners up that they will be very suspicious and cautious of you and therefore perhaps even edgy and aggressive. If you used hoods on your prisoners the law enforcement team is not going to be nearly as comfortable with you. If you are wearing body armor, have night vision goggles, a tactical knife, a battle hatchet, a specialized and professional level medical trauma kit etcetera, they will be very nervous around you and very suspicious. This is normal and to be expected. Avoid this best you can.

Yet, without some advanced preparation you would have been a soft target. Finding the right balance is our challenge. As far as most law enforcers in most countries are concerned they would prefer you to have one humble handgun or basic shotgun and a few band aids in your possession. The problem is that in most real world violent encounters that may not be enough to protect your family and defend yourself.

They might also treat you harshly. Initially, they will have no choice but to hide the fact that they are in awe and highly impressed but will still have to treat you like a very dangerous suspect. Respectfully, and in a medium soft tone of voice, sincerely thank them again for showing up. Too soft of a voice and calm of your vocal tonality will also alarm them, possibly scare some and make others edgy. Also understand that the average police officer in most countries does not have nearly the level of training and skill I am explaining here and most do not get issued the level of weapons and medical gear I am recommending.

I think it is better to be well prepared to protect your family and defend yourself and explain it to the judge later then to have your children kidnapped, your spouse raped and yourself killed. How about you? I think dealing with the legal system is considerably better than being kidnapped or raped or dragged off in some holocaust to a prisoner camp or hostage house while being held for ransom.

This point is tremendously important. When the police arrive they will have to treat you as a suspect. They will take control of your weapon just like you did with your prisoners. In a just, honest, fair and non-corrupt system this is totally okay. That is their Standard Operating Procedure (SOP); so let them and have a good attorney to defend you. Cooperate 100%. Make your weapon safe and lay it down before the law enforcement officers enter your room if it is safe to do so. Do not make any sudden moves. Do not argue and never turn the muzzle of your weapon in their direction. Follow their orders exactly. Address them respectfully as Sir or Ma'am as may be appropriate. Only make soft and gentle eye contact while moving at a slightly slower than normal pace. Avoid looking directly at their weapon systems. Expect to spend hours under arrest at the police station for fingerprinting, photographs, report questioning, or even to be jailed in a police cell for a few days until bail has been arranged.

Initially, this may not be an option. They will likely search your residence, confiscate all your weapons and even restrict your family's access to your home or at least the area where the shooting occurred. You can imagine the inconvenience, cost and family trauma involved. Even if you are totally innocent they will suspend your concealed gun carry permit, hold on to your weapons until after the court case, and leave your family and you unprotected against a revenge attack. Depending on how the facts are interpreted, you could and most likely will face a criminal trial and possibly a civil suit. Even after being found blame free, some people in your family, your circle of friends and neighborhood may treat you in unfriendly and unkind ways and avoid you altogether while gossiping about you.

You can see why I am training you not to shoot if you can at all avoid doing so. This is exactly why the second A in AAPE stands for **Avoidance**. You should know the laws wherever you are and how they may affect you. Simply talk, buy or run your way out of trouble if that is an option. Do not hurt anyone if you can escape and retreat without doing so. Move neighborhood, city or country if that is what it will take to get further away from potential conflict and high crime. If that is not an option then I'd rather you prepare more than most think is necessary. Surprise the bad guys with how well prepared you are. Be the granny, mom or dad skilled in a special technique or two for that moment of imminent danger. But again, I'd rather you please avoid all fighting and retreat without engaging if it is at all possible.

Can you see how dangerous, how inconvenient, and how severely unpleasant all the above criminal actions and police investigations will be for your family and you? It is hardly ever worth the sacrifice. Prevention and deterrent measures are infinitely better. Make your family and self a less attractive target. You can and must do that starting today.

Do more good in your community and country. Join "United Way®" or any helpful organization and do more for the poor in your area and country. Be an honest good person and only keep honest, good company. Do not exploit or cheat people. Avoid any conflict. Be a law abiding conflict avoiding citizen. Do not show off. Do not flaunt your wealth and status and think retreat and safety at the first sign of possible danger. I hope you can now see why I have over and over repeated that you should not engage, unless totally forced to do so. Failure to take heed of my recommendations can increase your families and own risk of being kidnapped or murdered. Set an example as a good person doing good things and for what is right. But remember in order to avoid trouble you need to prepare well for any eventual conflict and always AAPE your environment and situations.

Having said all that, it is as equally important to act without any hesitation in that terrible crucial time when you have to escape or engage. Study this integrated system as a drill. Understand it and ingest it in detail. Immerse yourself in it. Acquire and carry your required key items everywhere you legally are allowed to do so. Carry a .40 caliber pistol and a .38 Special revolver or back up compact or subcompact 9 mm pistol or .22L pistol along with a neck knife, tactical folding knife and thumb knife, a tourniquet, two tampons etcetera. A G-19 pistol is a great back up choice. What you carry from my various recommendations and check list really depends on who you are, what you do and where you are on the planet. Always carry at least one weapon with you. Get professional training and coaching. Nothing can replace in-person training and coaching. Reading alone is not enough. One mistake can mean death to a loved one or yourself and years in prison or sitting in a wheelchair for the rest of your life.

Remember, *"Proper preparation prevents poor performance and a casual approach leads to casualties"*.

With proper preparation you will build skills few other women or men have. You will authentically be able to protect your family as their defender under circumstances that will make others freeze, faint or vomit out of sheer terror, angst and fear.

The combination of our AAPE method, foundational 2.2 on-foot drill, in-vehicle drill and in-home system will make you well prepared. AAPE is the key to being able to deal with rather intense situations and circumstances across the most likely spectrum of possibilities. This tactic followed by our necessary first contact drills whether for in-home, in-car or on-foot situations will help you survive violent criminal attacks, professional kidnapping attempts or to even escape from a civil unrest, riot or unfolding war battle. Potentially, you could now help your family, forum buddies, neighbors and yourself to survive.

Trauma First Response Care

Here are the six greatest causes of preventable trauma induced deaths after shootings, gun and knife fights.

1. Bleeding.
2. Blocked airway.
3. Chest wounds and abdominal wounds, an open "sucking" entry wound, plus an exit wound, and or a tension pneumothorax.
4. Shock.
5. Trauma induced hypothermia.
6. Infection.

Mastery of the protocols and procedures relating to the rapid and correct treatment of these six killers can save your or a loved one's life. Begin with a swift head to toe front, side and back check. Be systematic, methodical, decisive and proactive.

Cut clothing if necessary to get to a wound. Remember the greatest risk and therefore our highest priorities are massive blood loss due to leg or arm wounds, internal bleeding and organ destruction, low blood volume, airway obstructions, torso wounds resulting in a sucking chest wound, tension pneumothorax, a flail chest and shock or a trauma induced hypothermia.

Here is what is most important to do. Do as much as you possibly can within the first two minutes of a wounding and immediately beyond. In extreme yet unsupported and life-threatening situations your failure to do so will result in certain death or severe long lasting and crippling injury. Ideally this should only be done by suitably qualified medical persons but if they are unavailable or delayed you may be forced to provide self or buddy care until help arrives or is reached. Become trained, certified and qualify yourself. This is for informational purposes only. Remember that some of these medical protocols and procedures may be illegal to perform by uncertified individuals in various countries such as America.

You must treat and stop all bleeding in less than 2 minutes or ASAP after an extremity wounding. Self administer a tourniquet procedure if needed. Then pack the wound first with gauze before you use a blood clotting product be it granules, a sponge or clotting gauze, or use a combination of all three of these proven blood clotting *"agents"*. It is important to get wounds *"packed"*, covered and tied off ASAP once the threat has been stopped.

You should preferably use gloves, nitrile rather than latex, and absolutely do not inhale any of the *"dust"* from the granules. Use medical masks if available to protect the patient and yourself. Work fast! Once the human body goes into trauma induced hypothermia it will be much more difficult to stop the bleeding. You have to stop the bright red bleeding in less than 2 minutes. Use two tourniquets if need be. Improvise by using tampons and sanitary pads if need be to pack any wounds to stop the bleeding. Direct and indirect pressure should be your very first response followed by a tourniquet plus the use of wound packing and blood clotting items and products. Include an Israeli bandage/battle dressing. Stopping profuse bright red bleeding is our highest priority in saving a gun shot victim from death. Practice doing this swiftly and with mastery.

Remember to write the time on the tourniquet itself showing when you applied it and mark the person's forehead and clothing with a T and the time. Do not cover up the tourniquet with any clothing. In fact, cut all immediately surrounding clothing open or off with large blunt nose medical shears.

Here is our step-by-step protocol and procedures for emergency responses immediately after a shooting or gunfight. Use them just as soon as it is safe to do so.

1. Perform a swift, methodical and systematic full body search from head to toe, front, sides and back using a blue chemical light stick or if safe to do so a white light. We use blue to see bleeding better without creating a large light signaling your position to other potential threats. Cut clothing with a large blunt nose shear if need be.

2. If bleeding is present stop it ASAP. Give priority to profuse and bright red bleeding located especially in extremities and in particular the neck and upper legs and chest. Immediately use intelligent and appropriate direct or indirect pressure and if needed one or even two tourniquets on limbs (arms and legs) only, as we demonstrate in class. Place the first high on the limb and the second closer to the wound. Record the time of application on their forehead. Leave it in place for a maximum of two hours. Check and release very slowly after an hour if safe to do so and continue to monitor.

3. Pack open wounds preferably with sterile gauze or stop the bleeding with tampons or a sanitary pad if it's available or as an improvised solution if you need to do so.

4. Use blood clotting agents such as clotting granules, sponges or gauze to further control the bleeding. Use nitrile gloves and do not inhale clotting agents. Combat Gauze™ is a great product. Press it down onto the wound for at least one but hopefully three or four minutes with direct pressure before wrapping with an Israeli bandage. The victim could perhaps do so while you move on to the next step.

5. Wrap a bleeding extremity wound with an Israeli wound dressing bandage or a pressure wrap if available.

6. With stomach wounds, avoid contamination and wrap to support and contain intestines but do not push hard to get organs back into the body.

7. Reinforce the will to live, keep the person warm and treat to avoid infection.

If the victim suffers from a blocked airway, use a gloved hand to sweep the mouth and airway clean. While holding the head to the side, pump it clean with a bulb pump bag. If no *"c-spine"* injury is suspected after pinching individual toes for a response then gently perform a *"jaw tilt"* and further mouth sweeping in a *"recovery position"* or perform the *"Heimlich maneuver"*. If the victim is still unable to breathe or is choking, perhaps roll the person into a *"recovery position"* or insert a breathing tube such as a nasopharyngeal airway 30 F nose trumpet. If all this fails you may have to cut a surgical emergency airway as taught in our advanced classes. This is best taught and learned hands-on and in-person.

If a person has been shot or stabbed in the torso and has an open chest wound, always gently check for an exit wound. Wipe the surface blood away and fit an occlusive chest valve ASAP. Use a HALO™, HYFIN™, Asherman™, Bolin™ or similar type brand name product or improvised system as demonstrated in our classes. Seal the exit wound as taught. Our class teaches you to improvise if you must with the entry wound seal packaging and medical or duct tape. Seal the entry wound on three sides if improvised materials are being used and the exit wound on all four sides.

Be especially concerned if the victim experiences chest pain, demonstrates panting while breathing or an asymmetrical chest pattern. If they are in the late stages they could start turning blue while exhibiting a bulging jugular and a migrating trachea as a tension pneumothorax develops. First sterilize the area as taught in class and then without delay insert a 10 gauge, or a 14 gauge catheter decompression needle on the affected side into the second intercostals space above the third rib at the mid clavicle line. The safest entry is high and well above the midway point between the nipple and the collar bone and away from the heart while staying well out on an outside line between the nipple and collar bone. Make sure you point the needle away from the heart. Once the needle is in, remove the needle part of the system and leave only the catheter in. Cover the catheter with an Asherman™ valve to protect it. Listen for any distinct air release sound. Sitting the victim up may better facilitate breathing. Legally, very specific training is required for proper use of a decompression needle and typically may only be recommended for use by a physician or under his or her supervision.

Remember it is very important to insert the needle into the second intercostals space, over the superior edge of the third rib from above, on the anterior chest and specifically at the mid clavicle line of the injured side after first cleaning the insertion area with a antimicrobial swab. Insert it directly through the skin at a straight 90 degree angle. Monitor the persons breathing closely.

For realizing shock, as taught in our classes, first pinch a finger hard for 2 seconds and check the time for the blood (color) to return. Reinforce their will to live.

To check ones spinal status and nervous system injury, ask the patient relevant questions while you pinch two different toes. Squeeze one on each foot and let them identify the toes pinched without their looking but responding only by sensation. If no *"c-spine"* injury was found, elevate the legs eight to sixteen inches to help manage shock.

Preventing trauma induced hypothermia is accomplished by keeping the person warm. Proactively facilitate the gradual warming or continued comfortable warmth of the patient as taught in our hands-on training. Provide and preserve warmth around the neck, head, heart, kidneys, thighs and feet. Applying monitored heat generating chemical pads on the heart, kidneys, neck and thighs can be very valuable. So can the introduction of a 'thermal wrap" and / or a blanket. Warm the person gradually and constantly monitor their status.

This combination of tactical drills and medical procedures must be learned and practiced in hands-on training scenarios as a full spectrum and integrated system for family and personal survival if ever attacked by violent criminals, you get kidnapped or have to survive and escape a riot or war zone battle. Testing your skills and overall effectiveness through in-person and continued coaching for further skill building with procedural validation and continued skill refinement are also very valuable endeavors. It may save your life. It is my prayer that it will do just that if unfortunately you ever need to use this system.

So lets take one more review and slightly expanded look at the real world application of our medical trauma system for when external help is delayed and or very unlikely to at least arrive in time, if ever, to even save the life of our loved ones or ourselves. May good always prevail over evil?

The 2.2
Medical Trauma Systems

Because this is so important in saving lives and making you and your family very difficult to kill, let's summarize the medical protocol and procedures once more and in even greater detail to be sure you understand what will be required in an extreme situation. As I am not writing to impress literary experts and want to be sure you get what you need, I would rather be redundant in the eyes of critics than letting good people down by not providing enough repetition to reinforce this information. It takes both tactical combat and medical trauma first responder knowledge and skills to survive violent criminal encounters and when you, as a civilian, are unfortunately caught in the crossfire of urban and other battle zones you could be the only resource available.

1. AAPE the situation first from a tactical perspective and only after can you then assess for life-threatening injuries. Focus on identifying all bleeding, airway and torso challenges plus shock and trauma induced hypothermia. Prioritize the bleeding wounds and then swiftly manage each priority.

2. Use the safest route with the best cover to reach the victim. Use 2 second dashes. It is best to remain below knee level at all times. If there is heavy fire then crawl if you must or sprint in a zig zag pattern if that would be better.

3. Return effective fire if forced to do so.

4. Command and encourage the casualty to either crawl to better cover, help you fight back, or to begin self-care depending on the unique situation. Use all or part of these instructions if any of this applies and if able to do so. If not, the person must perhaps fake being dead to avoid attracting further attention. You may have to drag, roll or carry the person into or behind cover. Prior

training is important for everyone in your family. In the case of a severe externally bleeding wound, use self-care in the form of a proximal to the wound tourniquet and or apply direct pressure which is vital as immediate field care. Your priority is to control and stop all bleeding within 2 minutes or soonest possible. If there are multiple casualties, ideally focus on those who are still breathing and talking first then also simply open the others' airways at this time.

5. When you reach the victim, first perform a very rapid evaluation and treat external bleeding with a second tourniquet three inches above the wound, pack the wound/s with sterile gauze, add clotting gauze and pressure and finally wrap the wound/s with an Israeli battle dressing. You must stop the bleeding and prevent the onset of serious hemorrhagic shock. Specifically level 11 and 111 blood losses are where there is a loss of more than 20% to 35% and blood pressure drops dangerously low.

6. Perform a quick jaw-lift if needed, and clear the airway if required with a swift and thorough finger sweep. If need be progress to the use of a nasopharyngeal nose trumpet and if all three of the previous procedures remain ineffective consider performing a surgical cricothyroidotomy with a # 10 scalpel blade or special kit if adequately trained to do so. Only attempt it as a very last resort in an extreme emergency or if the person will certainly perish if you do not do this.

7. Apply an occlusive dressing/chest valve over all open sucking torso wounds caused by gunshots, stabbing etcetera. Also check for exit wounds and cover completely if present. Should the casualty suffer from a developing tension pneumothorax as evidenced by progressive breathing challenges (panting) proactively use a 14 gauge, 3.25 inch decompression needle/ catheter system and after cleaning the injured side of the chest, insert it into the second intercostals space on the injured side while pointing away from the heart as you insert it. Be sure not to insert the needle medial to the nipple and or close to the heart.

8. Monitor and treat shock by reinforcing the will to live. Lift the legs if no spine injury is present and keep the person comfortably warm and safe. Proactively prevent or at least manage trauma induced hypothermia. First reduce and minimize exposure to cold by providing warm cover to rest on. Replace wet clothing if applicable and add dry warm layers, a skull cap, and chemical heating pads. Then place them in a rescue bag/blanket in a recovery position. Reevaluate tourniquets continually and avoid keeping them on for more than two hours if at all possible so as to avoid tissue damage. Ideally apply gauze wound packing and Combat Gauze™ with direct pressure for three to four minutes and wrap the wound in an Israeli bandage. Prior to slowly releasing the tourniquet/s, first check for a positive overall improvement. Look at the patients overall mood and mindset while you search for a peripheral pulse, especially if severe bleeding and shock has occurred. If bright red bleeding begins again or as yet the bleeding did not quite stop and remain controlled then you may need to apply one tourniquet directly onto the skin, three inches above the wound and tight enough to stop the distal pulse. Remember to mark a T on the person's forehead and shirt or trousers with the time when the tourniquet was applied. If problems persist then move the second tourniquet or use a third so that you have two very tight tourniquets right next to each other three inches above the wound on the injured limb.

9. The casualty will certainly need intravenous fluid if in shock. Ideally, a (.9) 500 cc Saline or Ringer's lactate but preferably a 500 cc Hespan™ if available. If no longer in shock, still conscious and able to drink, then induce fluid resuscitation using small sips of water. Medication may be necessary if in shock.

10. If available, consider giving medication such as 500 mg of Tylenol™ every 8 hours or 15 mg Mobic™ once every 24 hours. Especially if no professional care or help is scheduled to arrive anytime soon. Specialized infection blocking medication will be very useful if available. Please research this.

11. When you can get a message out requesting help, be very accurate and specific about information such as your location and exact urgency of injuries; help required, special gear needs, medical requests, a marking signal at the sight, terrain information, security risk information and number of injured persons.

12. If available, place a clearly visible casualty card or even an improvised card on the patient. Record information regarding injuries, times, treatments given and medications provided. It is wise to have a tactical vest, jacket with oversize pockets, backpack or a briefcase with medical trauma supplies ready for emergency response use and also get certified ASAP.

When all are safe and help arrives but it is dark, simply shine your flashlight briefly in their direction if you are sure they are friendly force helpers that can be trusted. If there is a lot of smoke, rubble and confusion; it may be necessary for you to increase your visibility by vertically swirling a chemical light stick on a string in front of you. This creates a bright and highly visible light circle in the darkness. In 99.9 % of cases it will be best to simply shine your moving flashlight intermittently and low in their direction without blinding them.

"Again I urge you to avoid trouble and resist upsetting or hurting people. I pray that good may always prevail over evil and we should all have faith that in the end it will."

The Bottom Line

Regardless of whether you are in your home, a hotel, your car or anywhere on foot including an unfolding war zone, be alert and if attacked AAPE faster than your imminent threat can adapt to your actions. AAPE is always your master key. Use it with intelligent flexibility. Act immediately and with a trained mind and trained hands.

Do all you can to avoid the threat and to escape unseen or at least to deescalate the situation as soon as possible. If that is not an option then meet the threat with force. Should you be forced to counter attack in defense, you then focus some serious intensity into shocking, discouraging and creating confusion in the mind of your threat. Respond with trained and effective actions. Be proactive and decisive. Be ruthless in the critical moment if that is what it will take to stop the threat. Maintain a very high level of situational and environmental awareness. Notice each person entirely and zoom in on their hands. Use the best possible cover and the darkest areas to your advantage. Try to expose as little as possible of your own body. Stay low in and behind cover. Use high ground selectively. Do not dead end yourself. Become a very hard target. Constantly AAPE!

Get a heavy caliber weapon such as a .40, .45 or if you so prefer a quality 9 mm pistol or a 12 gauge shotgun, in your own well trained hands and go into dark cover as soon as possible or exit out into your least likely, best and or closest escape route.

Scan constantly from left to right and 360 degrees around with your weapon muzzle 45 degrees up and your sights just two inches below your eyes. Let your muzzle follow your eyes as you scan from a dark area behind good, solid cover. Scan dark areas where threats may be lurking. If you are discovered and forced to engage then do so with surprise, speed and controlled aggression. Become a lighting bolt that strikes from out of the darkness. Be surgical, smooth and effective with semi-automatic fire only.

Be mindful of both threat and friendly fire. Overload the threat with a brief burst of ruthless chaos as you become the Wolverine who bites their jugular and strikes at their testicles, heart, lungs and brain stem with surprise, speed, 7.62 x 51 or 12 gauge or .40 caliber rounds, a sharp knife, a sharp hatchet, trained hands and feet.

Stick with combinations of the simple, effective drills we teach in class executed with intense *"violence of action"*. Maintain momentum and at the peak of the chaos created make your escape. Vanish and go into hiding. Take three deep, long, slow, silent breaths and become stillness. Study and memorize this segment very well. Integrate the philosophy, principles and core practices described here and it will serve you very well.

Let this be the core of your emergency response system for close quarter first contact battle and all that may evolve from it. These are the fundamentals that will best get you and your family out of the killing zone in a time of imminent danger or at least give you the greatest chance of survival in any combat zone. Remain unorthodox, unpredictable and not too pattern attached. Change your pattern and change direction. Use deception if you must. Have some gear ready to go. An example is to keep a three layer system of a shotgun, a pistol and or revolver and a knife or at least any two of these weapons depending on who you are, where you are and what threats are most likely.

Most importantly, have a ready soul. When forced to shoot, shoot the most imminent threat first. I recommend firing three shots and more if needed. Aim for the heart and lower brain. Three shots, two in the heart and lungs and one in the lower brain is an effective pattern. After stopping all the threats, immediately scan around and conceal your firearm in a low ready position. It is best to know one primary response pattern with a few alternative drills depending on your environment and threat behavior.

Once mastered this generic strategy system and our three specific at-home, in-car and on foot drills will make you as effective tactically as some of the best war-fighters in the world and give you a competitive edge when fighting off criminals. This will be especially true if you are wearing a bullet proof vest with front, back and side plates, and have a 12 gauge pump shotgun with a reflex sight or a well zeroed 7.62 x 51 battle rifle, 3 large caliber handguns, night vision goggles, plus a tactical knife, or a battle hatchet and medical trauma kit on you and are masterful in their use.

However, armed with the wisdom and knowledge of the 2.2 system and just a 120/125 lumens tactical flashlight, .40 and 9 mm pistol or even just a .22 L pistol with a spare full magazine or .38 Special revolver with an extra full speed loader, a tactical folding knife and a tourniquet and / or wound bandage you will be in a better position to defend your family and survive then 97% of the worlds people. This combination of specialized knowledge, family protection with self-defense tools and medical trauma first aid supplies is what will give you an edge.

Be a nice, kind, gentle, humble, non-violent, law-abiding and respectful person. Be a good person. Sadly, I still want you to also be a very prepared, competent, proficient family protector capable of ruthless efficiency in a gun and/or knife fight when forced upon you.

Remember our focus is always to first avoid all risks and violence. If we cannot avoid the danger then we try our very best to talk our way out, buy our way out or run our way out to safety. If that is not possible then we choose if applicable to use a non-lethal method such as pepper spray, a stun gun or some non-lethal martial arts technique to stop the threat and give us a chance to retreat and escape. If this is not an option or likely to be ineffective due to the power of the threat then we present our primary selected weapon.

If death or severe injury is imminent with no further preclusion because of the immediate and severe risk; then we engage with a lethal option such as an intense head twist, knife slash and stab combination or shotgun or handgun response as you have been trained. This is where we fire two or more rapid and accurate shotgun rounds or three to seven fast and accurate handgun rounds or more.

If wounded, first stop the threat then stop all bleeding as soon as possible. Apply direct pressure, pack the wounds with gauze and wrap them with bandages. Apply a tourniquet if necessary. Use other specialized medical items as needed and based on your own availability, expertise and level of training / certification.

APPENDICES:

Here in the appendix are 20 of the most important and fundamental things to know for acting within your most likely, safest and best legal limits when using firearms. Please study all of these appendices in detail. They contain very important legal and safety considerations. I highly recommend all the books pictured below as they all provided me with ideas and reinforcement for my own knowledge as a bibliography for my own research and as a reference for **FEAR NOT**.

Weapon & Personal Safety

1.   Know the laws of your nation, state, county and city. Always act only within your legal boundaries as required for justifiable homicide. The best thing to do is to avoid shootings through high awareness and active preventive measures. If you do become involved in a shooting, your best legal position is not to leave the scene of the shooting and to be very swift and diligent in calling 911. Give a fully honest and unhampered report of the situation without disclosing too much until you have spoken to your defense attorney. Be safe and stay clean. Do not shoot anyone or anything unless absolutely forced to do so.

2.   Always try to retreat and disengage first. Retreat to a safe, dark area. If that is not possible, deescalate. When no further options are available to escape death or be crippled if you don't do so intentionally take aim but only with the intention to stop the threat but never to kill the threat. Select, train with and carry quality gear you can rely on.

3.   Value awareness, threat avoidance and preparedness. Always carry some tactical tool even if it is just a knife or G-19 or .22 L pistol or .38 Special revolver and some medical trauma supplies. We prefer and recommend heavier calibers as a first choice. (.45, .41, .40, .44, or .357) Even carrying just two tampons for EMT are better than nothing. Remember, tampons and sanitary pads make for great improvised blood stopping dressings. However, avoid carrying any too aggressive and too professional gear as it will make you look like a cold hearted killer. Only carry and use what is legally authorized and justified. The legal system requires you to be *"the average reasonable guy"* even though in most cases it is a mediocre, lame sheep and totally under prepared kind of guy that is the standard that legal folks measure by. Do not exhibit, carry, wear or use any *"Rambo"* or too *"Bond"* or gangster type of gear, clothes or techniques. Even grim reaper images like the one shown in the photograph

on your 1911's grip can reflect negatively on your mentality in court. A smoke grenade and lots of spare magazines with powerful self-loaded or non-standard ammunition may also be seen negatively.

4. If tactically safe to do so you should always issue a loud, clear and authoritative verbal warning first and allow a reasonable time for a response. Say clearly and purposefully *"I have a loaded shotgun and will shoot you if you are a threat to us. The police are on their way. Leave immediately while you still can. Run now. I will not shoot if you run!"* Realize that although it will aid your legal position, it could also get you killed as it will compromise your location. When you speak, do not sound like you are panicking. Do not brandish a gun around to intimidate a potential threat and do not fire a warning shot. Both of these actions are illegal.

5. Shoot the absolute minimum number of shots that it will take to stop the threat. Preferably and effectively always only fire carefully aimed potentially survivable threat stopping shots.

(Sometimes in life you may unfortunately need to reconsider this advice and to survive one may be forced to be a little less kind and a lot less conventional in order to stop a motivated threat.

6.   Do not carry or use customized weapons. Stick with a standard weapon, preferably identical or similar to what the local police officers use. Especially do not use a super customized very sensitive trigger. Use only standard factory loaded ammunition, similar to what your local law enforcement officers use. Typically heavy grain hollow points or expandable full metal jacket rounds, where hollow points are not allowed in public, will serve you well and reduce any over penetration risks.

7.   Avoid all potentially dangerous people, places and situations. Retreat and escape at the first sign of possible danger. Always strive to deescalate all inescapable violent encounters. If forced to engage be better prepared, better trained and better equipped than your assaulters. Go AAPE on them faster and more effectively than they can on you. Get and stay ahead in the AAPE loop and constantly observe for danger using all your senses. Scan 360 degrees to maintain security. If your family is with you and trained, then form a tight 360 formation. Be mindful of how immediate your threat is. Are the conditions favorable to kill you? Do they have the *"ability/means, opportunity and clear intent/mental state/jeopardy"* to kill your loved ones and you? Where is the closest or best cover and escape route? Who poses the greatest risk in each moment? What is the status of your weapons? Should you escape or engage? Can you hide or run, talk or buy your way out?

8.   Keep your weapons, knives, and ammunition locked away from children and all unauthorized people. Teach your children gun safety awareness as taught in our classes.

9.   Keep your weapon on safe, unloaded and in your holster as much as possible.

10. Always treat all weapons as loaded, no exceptions, ever.

11. Never point your weapon at anybody or anything you are not consciously selecting to kill or destroy.

12. Keep your finger out of the trigger guard and off the trigger until you positively identify the threat or target with the full intention of shooting within a second or less.

13. Always assess and know what is beyond and close to your target. Use only factory loaded, law enforcement strength, expanding full metal jacket and hollow point ammo to prevent over penetration and shoot at 35 to 45 degree angles. Kneeling unconventionally and firing from rear prone or with a high-elbow position when standing can help to avoid over penetration or miss problems causing secondary injuries.

14. Place your weapon back on safe before holstering or first unload your weapon completely depending on your situation and who you are, where you are and why you are there.

15. Lock weapons and ammunition away from children and from all unauthorized persons. It is your personal weapon. Do not let others touch it. It is your sole responsibility.

16. When doing dry drills, remove all ammunition from your area of practice. Lock all ammo away and lock the door of the room in which you practice.

17. When you draw your weapon from your holster keep your trigger finger out of the trigger guard. Pivot the weapon and with accurate pointing aim your weapons muzzle by pointing directly at the stopping zone of your target. Only disengage your safety once your weapon's pointed at the target and only once on target does your trigger finger go onto the trigger. After shooting, immediately take your finger off the trigger and out of the trigger guard and engage the safety immediately. You are responsible and accountable for every round you fire and

more specifically for whatever you hit either intentionally, in self defense or accidentally. Be it a person, animal, car, building etcetera. We cannot afford to miss shots we take in a tactical family protective environment. Nor can we have any uncontrolled discharges. The consequences may be death to a family member, some innocent person or yourself. Therefore, both marksmanship and safe gun handling are critical skills to master.

18. Never take an unclear shot and never take any pleasure in shooting any being whether human or animal. If you must fire to protect or feed your family or to defend yourself, be sure to make a clean accurate shot. Shoot only out of necessity. Wounded humans tend to fight back as do some wounded animals and rightfully so. After each shooting burst, scan left to right, and as soon as possible also scan 360 degrees around for further threats. When you withdraw, retreat only far enough to be safe and as a law-abiding, responsible person immediately call in a situation report of the incident to the police.

19. Call 911 ASAP. Report the incident immediately and responsibly. Report no lies, no deception and no tricks, ever unless escaping from a riot or war zone.

20. Do not leave the scene before the law enforcement personnel arrive. Be ready to be okay with the surrendering of your firearm/s to them and be arrested by them even if your use of force was totally justifiable.

I recommend you get adequate professional training from men like Doron Benbenisty, Wes Doss, Ken Haan and my team and I before you need to use the skills mentioned here. Practice safe, effective and efficient gun handling, marksmanship and our in-home, in-car and on-foot-in-the streets drills under low light and assimilated stress and shock conditions. Remember, our goal is to always stay out of all fights, guns and otherwise. If that is not possible our next objective is to deescalate the situation and withdraw and escape without engaging a second longer than what is safely possible. If we must engage, then it is legally best to issue a clear verbal warning first. Be very careful in making that decision because tactically silence may be the better option. What the law requires and prefers and what is tactically best is not always compatible. Stay legal and safe.

If the bad guys still show clear *"ability/means"*, *"opportunity/ distance"* and *"jeopardy/intent"* to kill or cause severe bodily harm and the threat is an *"imminent defend-or-be-killed"* situation with no possible *"preclusion"* to avoid it without a force-on-force response, then we engage for only two or so seconds with our first response contact drill. If a non-lethal response will stop the threat, use it. If a non-lethal response will not stop the threat then and only then as you're very *"last resort"* use *"equal lethal force"* as needed in your unique situation. You want to be willing and very able to shoot if forced to do so, but also at all costs first avoid doing so for moral and legal reasons which could include a criminal trail, civil suit and all the emotional trauma and financial expense that may be involved.

Although I continually urge you to avoid all fights and encourage you rather to retreat and escape; be mindful that sadly if you are forced to fight by violent criminals don't just respond with minimum action. I also absolutely want you to know that if forced by criminals to protect your family and defend yourself you must be able and willing to be devastatingly effective and, even if only briefly, be as intense as a Wolverine who has been done wrong.

After using your firearm in any civilian tactical situation, kneel down low or stay on your back if applicable for a few moments and immediately place your weapon in a concealed position while you scan from left to right and 360 degrees around for further threats. (Doron is demonstrating in the photograph.) This can prevent a situation where someone who arrives on the scene and sees a person shot may see you with a gun in hand and suddenly shoot you. To immediately place your weapon in a less visible low ready is a valuable technique I learned from Doron at the CRI Counter

Terrorism School. Should you suddenly be forced to engage again it will also help you with an element of surprise?

Weapon and Shooting Fundamentals

If you are new to firearms handling, this is a very important must study segment for you. Even seasoned professionals can always benefit from a reminder.

Remember the wise words of Thomas Jefferson, one of the founding fathers of this great nation of the free and the brave.

"Those who hammer their guns into plows will plow for those who do not"

Legal considerations

Get professionally trained in weapon safety, weapon handling, marksmanship and tactics from professional sources I recommend or use a reputable school or an individual of your own choosing. You need to be proactive and a diligent student of our national constitution. Study all relevant laws relating to legally responsible firearm ownership, carry, storage and their use. Please read extensively. Know the subjects of gun safety, responsible gun handling and marksmanship and other related topics which include mental preparation, medical trauma care, unarmed self-defense and both urban and wilderness survival. Check your federal, state, county and local municipal gun laws and requirements regarding the safe storage of firearms and ammunition. Observe registration and compliance regarding both open and concealed carry and use. That is your own responsibility.

To be justifiable in terms of legal use, it is very important that you did not cause the encounter. You must be 100% an innocent victim of any violent, unavoidable, unprovoked, lethal and imminent criminal behavior. This is based on the *"reasonable person"* standard the law goes by. When compared to the threat and the ability of the assaulter/s you must only have used *"reasonable force"* after making significant effort/s to retreat without engaging. This also applies even in your own home/dwelling where the *"castle doctrine"* could make some allowances for you so that you need not have to retreat. The principles of fearing for your life and imminent danger with no other choice for survival usually apply. Armed attacker/s with the ability and clear intention to kill or commit bodily harm onto you or your loved ones, and are within range to do so, constitutes such a risk.

When practical, store unused firearms unloaded with their trigger locks secured. Separate them from the ammunition in a heavy and bolted down gun safe. Absolutely ensure that all your firearms are inaccessible to your and any visiting children. Having firearms for family defense but putting your children at risk is an unforgivable mistake. All firearms must always be under adult control.

I say it again; please remember that to be justifiable in terms of legal use, it is very important that you did not cause the encounter. You must be 100% an innocent victim of any violent, unavoidable, unprovoked, lethal and imminent criminal behavior. This is based on the *"reasonable person"* standard the law goes by. When compared to the threat and the ability of the assaulter/s you must only have used *"reasonable force"* after making significant effort/s to retreat without engaging. This also applies even in your own home/dwelling where the *"castle doctrine"* could make allowances for you not to need to retreat. Never *"brandish"* a weapon, meaning waving it around as a threat. Do not ever fire a warning shot. Both these actions are illegal. Only present a weapon as a last resort and if there is clearly no further *"preclusion"* for retreat or avoidance of an imminent lethal threat. Do seek additional detailed information for a more thorough understanding from a local attorney in your county jurisdiction regarding the legal ownership, storage, carry, transportation and use of a firearm for family and self-defense.

21. **Safety** Again, get professionally trained and certified in gun handling. The NRA™ is great for this and I hear outstanding reports about the professionalism of the "Front Sight"™

organization. Be sure that your firearm is safe to operate. Store and carry your weapons safely and be responsible. Keep your weapons out of unauthorized reach yet easily accessible if needed for an emergency response. A finger print scan safe with a backup power source may be a great option for you to consider. Treat all weapons as loaded and when you load your firearm be sure that you are always using the correct ammunition. Point only at a legally justified target as a last resort measure and never ever in jest. Never leave an unsecured firearm in an unguarded vehicle, by your bedside or any other easily accessible place while there are children around and / or when not at home. It is also not safe or wise to keep a loaded gun under your pillow, your bed or on your nightstand. Just locking your doors and leaving a light on while traveling is not nearly enough to prevent a home intrusion and weapons theft. When you handle your weapons, keep your finger off the trigger and out of the trigger guard until it is time to shoot. Always know what is beyond your target.

22. **Weapon Selection** The most important considerations in selecting a weapon are first what weapon fits your hand best, then ammunition availability and only then what caliber you should choose if ammunition is readily available. It is really your marksmanship skill that counts and your ability to place shots accurately into high value areas which are proven to stop threats. Shot placement more than anything else is what determines your ability to stop a threat with any weapon. Accurate shooting ability is foundational and essential.

We prefer pistols because of their greater magazine capacity, smaller muzzle flash, faster reload and better concealment profile. However, revolvers are very reliable and best for body-to-body contact encounters and therefore totally worth carrying. Revolvers are an American classic and have a long and outstanding track record of reliability. I think you should carry one of each, a revolver and a pistol.
A .45, .40 or 9 mm caliber pistol matched with a .38 Special revolver, or even a small .22 L pistol or .32 revolvers and

or a quality tactical folding knife or neck knife are all great choices. This depends on who you are, what you do, where you live and where you go, as well as on your willingness to be professionally trained and to practice frequently.

For most I recommend a heavy caliber revolver and .40 or 9 mm pistol. I like "Glock™", "Colt™", "Heckler & Koch™", "Sig Sauer™", "Browning™" and "Smith & Wesson™" as great brands worth considering but there are many other reliable brands. A "Remington™ 870" or "Mossberg™ 500" 12 Gauge pump action shotgun or perhaps a submachine gun or carbine will be a great home defender addition. For in and around your home using the shotgun may be the very best single choice. For other all around home, car and on-foot use; having one to three quality handguns are recommended.

Again, depending on where you live you may even want to consider a 7.62 battle rifle or if on a ranch perhaps a long range rifle such as a Sig Sauer™ SSG 3000 sniper or a 7.62 or similar high powered hunting rifle. In very rugged environments, a civilian semi-automatic American M14, or Chinese SKS type 63 rifle slightly modified to accommodate AK 47 magazines and the Russian AK 47 assault rifle are all excellent choices, provided you have enough ammunition or easy access to additional ammunition when it is needed.

Soldiers will typically first use their sniper rifle, battle rifle or carbine, then their shotgun, then their pistol and then their bayonet or tactical knife in that order. In contrast for family protection, self-defense and general criminal home intrusion defense we will typically recommend use of a shotgun or handguns and especially if you live in an urban area. Most modern day pistols are very accurate with training, light to carry, simple yet fast to operate and very reliable. Many shoot great with standard factory ammunition and can easily be fitted with an even more accurate after market barrel.

Few are likely to jam on you if well maintained and if used by trained and experienced hands unless subjected to extremely sandy or muddy conditions. Should a malfunction occur, fix it as trained or transition to a backup weapon. At a minimum, I believe you should carry a handgun and or tactical folding knife, a powerful 120/5 lumens flashlight and a cell phone. If you expect real trouble I recommend you also get a shotgun. A shotgun with no 6 birdshot ammunition remains your best single family at home protection and defense weapon.

I just love this little story that is going around. Apparently an old sheriff and Texas Ranger were attending a function where a lady commented on him having an unconcealed handgun on his hip. She asked, *"Sheriff, I see you have a handgun, are you expecting any trouble here tonight"*. He replied, *"No Ma'am, if I were expectin any trouble, I certainly would have brought me a deputy, my double barrel shotgun or my trusted old .44 lever action rifle. How bout you Ma'am?"*

Whatever your choice, buy the very best quality you can afford. Sadly, far too often these days many Alpha-hole company owners in the ruthless pursuit of profit shamelessly design their products to fail after just some use. You do not want to be the victim of that. You want top notch weapons of professional quality with a proven track record of reliability, as well as a backup weapon.

Two handguns, two flashlights, two knives, two spare magazines would be the minimum choice of a real professional person. Should you settle for less? Redundancy is essential in intense family and self-defense arenas and during severe fire fights. Just as underwater cave divers carry three sources of light, use a detailed checklist and only use a third of their oxygen on the way down, so should you have backup gear on hand, use a check list and be modest in your use of ammunition but always depending on the situation. Back up gear is also great for equipping other people such as perhaps your spouse/partner during a suddenly, unexpected emergency response.

23. **Concealment** Get a legal permit for concealed carry for each weapon. Practice drawing from concealment. Carry up to 2 or 3 concealed weapons as a fully integrated and layered defense system. Wear loose fitting dark colored heavy fabric clothing to conceal your weapon/s if you body carry. Carry your primary handgun ideally on your strong side hip. Tactical holsters should be right on the hip, right behind your hip or slightly forward according to your personal preference. A vest is a dead give away. Wear instead a loose, light and long jacket. Place a .22L pistol or a spare magazine, tactical folding knife, small tactical flashlight or even a few extra loose rounds in your dominant hand pocket for weight which helps with a better clearance as you draw. For ladies, a purse holster is very useful or a cross draw holster. An inner thigh holster works well when wearing a dress or skirt. I prefer leather and polymer holsters. Leather is softer to carry and silent when you draw. Polymer is fast and offers quicker access. Shoulder holsters, inner thigh holsters and even purse holsters all work great in cars and when you sit on a toilet. Hold your purse holster on your lap.

24. **Stance** Establish your own best firing stance. Ideally, we suggest you mostly use the proven Israeli military stances and tactical shooting positions we teach, and at times the high ready stance as used by the US Navy SEAL's. A personalized Weaver stance can be highly effective if you are well trained and practiced in it. Realize though that it may make you a more at risk target since side wounds are very lethal and may involve damage to several organs from a single shot. Carefully use a personalized Weaver stance or better yet stick with proven combat stances such as the ones taught in this book and in our classes. If you insist on using the Weaver stance then modify it adequately so as not to turn your body too far sideways. Use the Weaver or perhaps an Isosceles stance for long distance shooting when you are at less risk and have solid cover. The Weaver stance does offer great recoil control. Lock your shooting elbow and bend your non shooting hand elbow just slightly.

Here are the most important basics. Balance your weight about 50 / 50 on the balls of both feet, shoulder width apart. Scan for threats with your head up and keep your lead (front) sight 2 inches below your eyes while keeping both eyes open. Always keep your head up and both eyes open while scanning for threats over the muzzle. Scan left to right, low to high, close to far. Keep your mouth slightly open with your tongue against your upper teeth and both hands on your weapon as often as is practical. Keep your arms half way to two-thirds extended and remember to keep your front sight 2 inches below your eyes. Hold your finger off the trigger and against the trigger guard until things go code high red or black. Then take up a little trigger slack and only shoot when on target.

I personally prefer a low tactical kneeling position for many applications and I like the highly effective US Navy SEAL high ready position most for while on the move and for high risk, gun in hand ready to shoot situations. Should I personally have to first draw my weapon in a real world tactical situation I love the Israeli method as a proven, simple and highly effective stance and system.

If you come under fire at short range while armed with a handgun you may want to use the rear prone position. The classic Weaver stance is well proven and excellent, and typically best used for target shooting as it totally enables great accuracy but the Israeli standing and also the SEAL methods are in my view the best for aggressive, fast moving, high speed close quarter combat situations.

Once you have some marksman experience at high levels with the classic Weaver stance; move on to a personalized version of the Weaver as it is especially effective with a few modifications. Then practice the more tactical Isosceles and ultimately focus on mastery of both the SEAL version of the Isosceles and the Israeli methods. Do exactly as taught here unless someone truly outstanding and reliable tells you differently. The bottom line is use the stance you trust and are best trained in but please do consider the counseling I've given above.

25. **Draw** First, rapidly press down into your holster to get a solid grip. Draw the weapon smoothly from a quality holster and high quality gun belt. Use a high yet firm grip. Your shooting finger only enters the trigger guard half way up and forward when going up and forward onto the threat target sight picture, but only if you are already committed to shoot after AAPEing and have made a don't shoot/ shoot decision. Only once you are 100% sure of your threat target and on target should you engage the trigger. If you are not 100% sure, then keep your trigger finger off the trigger until you have clarity.

26. **Firing Grip** Get a good firm high grip around the front of the grip stem as you draw with 3 fingers of your firing hand. First push down as you take your grip then present the weapon smooth and fast in a straight line with your threat target. Keep your trigger finger on the outside of your trigger guard. Wrap your non-shooting hand around the side and front over the shooting hand. Grip a little harder with your non-shooting hand than you do with the shooting hand.

Overall, develop a strong grip yet sensitive. Also develop an agile, flexible, strong and functional body. Be *"Mogadishu ready"*. It is a great asset. Kettle bells, dumbbells and yoga are ideal for strengthening. So is mixed martial arts practice and my Alpha F3 Functional Fitness System. Other natural body weight only exercises such as pull ups, press ups and sit ups will also benefit more than just your grip.

27. **Sight Alignment and Sight Picture** Shoot with both eyes open 99.9% of the time. The other .1% shooting with your dominant eye open while you center and level your front sight into the rear sight. Focus on the top tip of the front sight. Targets will be slightly blurry as will be the rear sight. I recommend you install Crimson Trace™ laser technology grip sights on your handguns

and perhaps a Holographic, or a red dot sight for your carbine or battle rifle, and ideally a Schmidt & Bender™ 1.1 4x20 short dot scope for your battle rifle if you have one. Learning to use your standard iron sights correctly for sight alignment, sight picture and breathe control use is best learned in-person from a professional trainer and remains most important. Do not rely too much on technology. Your lead sight is of the highest importance.

28. **Trigger Control** Only place your trigger finger onto the trigger just prior to shooting and remove it as soon as you are done. This prevents any accidental firing. When taking up the trigger slack, the trigger pressure should be equal or less than the weight of the weapon. Squeeze only with the front pad of your trigger finger. Squeeze smoothly with no movement of the weapon, especially while holding the front sight motionless and true. Visually follow through on each shot and count your shots to remain magazine status aware. (If you have small and not strong hands, perhaps have your trigger just slightly adjusted to about 3.5 pounds of pressure. Be mindful of the potential legal interpretation of such a choice. Four to eight pounds is fine for most people and a standard trigger weight remains your best legal defense.)

29. **Tactical Firing Positions** Practice standing, kneeling and prone positions along with the unconventional positions we teach for shooting at safe angles. Also master using the high ready position.

a. **Dry and Target Practice** Always use ear and eye protection when you do live fire training and practice. An electronic shooting timer is also very valuable and so is a great coach. Take all appropriate and responsible safety precautions. Practice in both day and in low light but more often in low light. For confined areas, practice with your pistols or a revolver of your choice along with a shotgun and then later with a carbine/s. Familiarize using various knives such as a neck knife, a tactical folder, a throwing knife or a spike. Practice firing three rapid shots with good accuracy in less than 2 seconds from 3, 7, 15, 25 and 50 yards with your weapon of choice. Try this mostly in low light but also using a 120/5 lumens tactical flashlight. Often practice firing between 5 and 9 shots per target and shooting random numbers of rounds on multiple targets set at random and varying heights and distances. Practice aimed shooting as well as both point shooting and close quarter instinctive shooting. Always do weapon transitions and magazine changes as you go. Remember that a loose cluster in your groupings may be more fatal than a tight shot group. Aim to hit the spinal cord, heart and brain (brain stem) if you can but only with the intention to stop, not kill the threat. Under stress and battle chaos most shooters will miss with several rounds.

History tells of elite operators shooting a man multiple times with their high powered rifles then using top of the line heavy caliber pistols before he went down. Please realize that when you are no longer shooting at targets, one, two or even three 9 mm rounds will not instantly stop everyone. In fact, it almost never will. When dealing with multiple attackers you may only have time for shooting one bullet in the heart, lungs or brain per person. Go for the torso first. Police records show it can take 5 and up to 20, 9 mm or .38 Special, rounds to stop a motivated or hyper drugged man and that three out of every four rounds fired by police officers miss the target. Most attackers can close a 7 to 10 yard gap in less than three seconds. Sometimes, if they are fatally wounded, they can still get a knife into you or squeeze off two or more deadly shots before they die.

Therefore, there is merit in opening your protective and defensive response with a .357 revolver or .45 caliber pistol as a first choice or a heavy load shotgun if available and if it is safe to do so. Chamber #6 or #7 birdshot in most situations, but for extreme circumstances and for outdoor protection I personally would prefer the loading sequence to be slugs first, followed by buckshot and then backed up with birdshot which will then come out first in the firing order. For legal purposes I recommend you use birdshot only. My first choice combination may be seen as premeditated behavior. It's better to be cautious and perhaps stick with only # 4, 6, 7 or 8 birdshot.

With your handguns, study the grouping on your targets after a live fire round and focus on self correcting your accuracy. Where are the majority of your rounds landing; high, left, right, low, tightly grouped or spread out? Use shooting correction targets to improve before going back to more vital organ target shooting. If your grouping is too high and wide like it is for many new shooters and out of practice folks, slow down to first build accuracy. Focus more on the top of your leading sight, and then lower it a little in the rear sight notch. This will ensure better overall alignment. Hold the weapon still and avoid pushing the low part forward in shot anticipation and during actual firing. Aim again after each shot but recover from the recoil first. Ultimately, get more practice under expert supervision and coaching. Video and watch your performance in slow motion with a great coach.

Follow a safe, frequent, dry run practice drill schedule. Practice your draw and presentation skills, your magazine changing skills, and your weapons transition skills in standing, kneeling and prone positions. Then practice while on the move. Use shooting correction, vital organ and hostage targets to practice. Ensure total safety for dry drills. Always unload all weapons and lock the ammunition away. Control the environment. Ensure privacy. Verbalize out loud as you make the weapon safe for your dry drills and when you load it again afterwards.

30. **Weapon Cleaning and Safe Storage** Maintain your weapons and other tools to a very high standard. Preferably use only non-corrosive ammunition. To clean your or any other handgun, first remove the magazine and then cock it and do a visual safety check. Field strip it using safety glasses while removing and fitting the recoil spring. Apply copper bore solvent inside the barrel and let it sit for a while. Wipe, dry brush and wipe again the rest of the firearm body and parts. Clean and lightly oil the outside of the barrel. Brush the inside of the barrel with

long smooth strokes using a copper brush while using more barrel solvent. Wipe the inner barrel down well with some clean dry patches pulled through. Finish with a light oil patch and another dry patch. Lightly lubricate all the rest of the weapon. Concentrate especially on oiling areas showing wear and where there is movement such as the receiver rails on you pistol. Do not oil the trigger. Simply dry wipe it. Wipe the external areas with a light dry or light silicone based, antirust lubricant, and then dry wipe it thoroughly.

Now holster, carry or store your weapons responsibly in a bolted down safe out of the reach of any unauthorized person but especially criminals or children. A finger print safe with a reliable back up power source by your bedside is worth considering. When transporting a gun by vehicle or aircraft there are specific requirements in various locations. Please check with your local authorities and any chosen airline. As a general rule for transport in your car, if it is not on your person with a concealed carry permit if applicable and available in your state; then it should be unloaded and locked away in a gun box in the trunk of your vehicle. Ammunition is stored away from the gun. A trigger lock may also be required. With all airlines, your guns and ammunition must be declared, unloaded and locked in an approved container. They may not be taken into a pilot and passenger seating area within the aircraft. Not even in a locked box in your carry on. All weapons must be checked separately.

31. **Training** The points covered here are only the fundamentals. Time and opportunity permitting, there are finer points we prefer to only selectively teach live and in person to law abiding people. Please understand that it would not be wise or prudent to give every advanced technique and tactic to everyone in receiving a publication such as this. Master these fundamentals and execute them faster and better than your assaulters in order to survive. What is covered here is substantial and at a higher standard than what many people will ever be exposed to, let

alone master. Quality training with frequent, safe, dry practice runs is what will give you the edge when needed.

There are three key areas to master:

(1) *Gun Handling and Marksmanship*
(2) *First Contact, Tactical Drills*
(3) *First Responder Medical Trauma Protocol and Procedures*.

This is the gunfight survival triad and it all begins with the fundamentals of safe, effective and responsible gun handling along with justifiable, safe and accurate marksmanship. Keep a training log and journal and set very specific improvement goals for each training session if you are serious about improving. Be sure that the training you receive covers the safety and legal aspects of gun handling and gun use and is designed to give you real emergency response skills and not just false confidence through methods that will increase your legal problems and or get you killed after such use. Your training must include intense yet realistic real-world scenario type simulation. It must integrate both tactical and medical trauma training. This is best done through systematic and methodical training culminating in intense high-speed, force-on-force scenario based activities. Your training must stress aspects such as shoot/don't shoot decision making, muzzle and trigger discipline, the correct use of darkness, light and cover, surprise, speed, justifiable force of violence and intelligent cornering and room entry.

Become trained by a reputable, professional school and if in doubt seek the guidance of an NRA certified instructor. The NRA™ offers numerous training programs such as "Choose Not to be a Victim©", the "NRA Basic Personal Protection©" in home course and several others for safe, responsible, defensive firearm use. The NRA is at the forefront of promoting the practice of responsible gun ownership and the protection of gun rights for law-abiding citizens. Please visit their website at www.nra.org. For world class and highly specialized but more advanced training, take a really good look at using www.critraining.com. It is an outstanding school to learn professional quality tactics and for scenario based training. Frontsight® also has a great reputation and my team and I also provide training to carefully selected individuals and groups. There are also several other outstanding individuals and schools I am happy to recommend.

32. **Defensive Real World Shooting** When forced to shoot and as a very last resort, use the proven Israeli methods if you are well trained in them. That process will at the absolute minimum require at least two days of intense training but ideally much more. Some fundamentals can be learned in four hours but realistically more training is always better than less training.

Handle and fire the weapon with both hands on it but be willing to be unorthodox when necessary and also practice weak hand only shooting under very low light conditions. Preferably always use an aimed firing approach. At distances of less than 3 yards you may need to use an unorthodox instinctive firing approach. Another advantage is a weapon fitted with a laser grip sight. When available, shoot from behind solid and well protected cover. Fire 3 to 7 to 9 plus rounds depending on how the threat responds while aiming at whatever visible *"center mass"* is available. Find your threat target in the triangle between the upper 30% chest and lower brain/brain stem above the upper lip and brow. Only shoot with the intention to stop, not to kill. This may require shots to the pelvis, heart and lungs or at minimum the upper thighs; central nervous system located in the spine and into the brain stem and lower brain between the upper lip and middle of the head.

After a shooting, break from your *"tunnel vision"* by scanning from left to right, low to high and close to far. As soon as it is safe to do so, scan in the same manner 360 degrees around while taking long, deep breaths and exhaling silently and slowly. After shooting, improve your position behind cover in a dark or darker shade and behind bigger, stronger and better positioned cover and call 911 immediately when it's safe to do so. Reestablish the threat and go AAPE again while being prepared to repeat constantly if necessary. Real world use of cover, weapons handling, marksmanship, tactical drills, tactical weapon loading, malfunction corrections, weapon transitions, prisoner control, etcetera is best learned practically from a highly dedicated, professional instructor, and not only from a book or DVD. Both are great and important supplemental sources for learning but inadequate on their own. You need all three; in-person training, books and DVD's to develop total full spectrum mastery with depth of knowledge.

If you are going to avoid or resist being kidnapped, raped or murdered; resisting with the use of a firearm in your own well trained hands is the best deterrent and way to minimize your risk of severe injury or death. If you cannot avoid, prevent or escape a violent criminal assault it is likely that only the skilled use of a firearm or at minimum a stun gun, pepper spray, tactical knife, a hatchet or a scalpel knife will give you a reasonable chance of survival. Without weapons and training you are a lamb on the slaughter altar and at their mercy.

If nothing else, it will make you a much harder target. Without these tools and skills we have been discussing you will be an easy, attractive and very soft target for violently predatory gangs or individual criminal wolves willing to kidnap, gang rape and kill any individual. History and police records are testimony to the fact that a firearm in the trained hands of a law-abiding citizen can save lives. Sadly, a non-violent response will in most cases not stop an aggressive kidnapper, rapist or murderer. The surest way to survive is to go **AAPE**. Always be ready to respond with a trained mind, hands and body as a best resort in any imminent life-threatening situation. When it comes down to defend or be brutally raped or murdered, you have to be ready and also willing and able to fight if forced to do so. Until then, do everything you can to always avoid all high risk people, places and situations and get as much training and practice as possible.

Remember, shoot to stop threats but not to kill. It bears repeating; to stop threats you must aim at the centerline of the body, from the pelvis up. Direct your attention mostly at the upper third of the chest and at the brain stem and lower brain above the upper lip and below the mid forehead. Accurate shots fired into these targets may cause the threat to lose function in 3 to 8 seconds while standing. Once the threat falls down, he or she may recover for 3 to 25 seconds due to a brief increase in blood pressure thus creating a further risk of the threat shooting you. Always regard the threat active.

Realistic practice is required. Train and practice across the full spectrum of basic to advanced shooting skills and use of a flashlight, knife and medical trauma drills. Practice under realistic low light conditions in an environment that is very similar to the most likely real world conditions that you will truly need to operate in but be aware that when bad guys strike, they will choose the time and place best suited for their interests.

33. **Use of Light** In indoor settings a 120/125 lumens flashlight may be very useful if used correctly and very sparingly but be mindful of after burn. When outdoors, a light of 250 lumens to 1000 lumens may be better if used intelligently with only briefly effective usage and again with great care and mindfulness of the after burn effect. A 120/125 lumens rear switch activated flashlight is ideal as an illumination tool for family protection.

Training in the correct use is highly recommended. Always position yourself in the darkest cover possible. Immediately after you use your light you must move to a new position. You sometimes can attack your threats eyes with a second of blinding white light. If you are at very close range you may strobe your threat or sway the light like a pendulum but only briefly and only if well trained and practiced in this technique. Use your flashlight as sparingly as possible. Flash, move and escape or flank and attack if possible. Attack if need be but only as a last resort. Become a diligent student of the best intended use of a tactical flashlight in a defensive role as a family protector. Learn to understand and avoid *"after-burn"* problems and how to smoothly transition from the *"FBI"* method to the *"Ice-pick"* and *"Jaw-hold"* methods to the *"Harriers"* method. Practice aligning your eyes, light and weapons front sight and your threat target in various degrees of low light. Practice is vital to avoid task overload problems such as *"hand confusion"* and accidentally shooting under stress due to *"sympathetic supporting hand contraction"* of your trigger hand. This is why trigger finger training and discipline is so important.

34. **Malfunctions** Follow the drills we teach in class. With a pistol, cock the pistol as taught and fire. If that does not work then turn the weapon on its side and look again at the ejecting port. Sweep the stuck shell away if applicable, drop the magazine three inches or so, cock, reinsert the magazine and cock again. With pistols, most minor stoppages can be fixed with a quick cocking action and or brief inspection plus a fast and forceful cocking action. If it is an option and at all available fix malfunctions only behind good cover. If you are caught out in the open with a malfunction and the cocking procedure alone does not fix your problem, transition immediately to the back up firearm. Do not ever hesitate to AAPE. Avoidance is always better than defense.

Ammunition

Warning: Keep all ammunition out of reach of children and unauthorized individuals. Observe all safety rules and know the power and limitations of all the ammunition you choose to use. When using live ammunition, always be extremely diligent to maintain the highest standards in muzzle, safety selector and trigger finger discipline and safety. No exceptions.

As a responsible full spectrum family protector and defender you need a good supply of carefully stored, selected, *"fresh"* ammunition for any eventuality, be it a violent home invasion or a situation where you need to escape a riot or war zone.

Typically, in most criminal encounters where there is a shooting involved you may not need more that 3 to 10 rounds at most. Now having said that I would rather have 3 to 10 extra rounds and more than I need available to me than need more ammunition and not have enough available. How about you?

Three 10 round magazines loaded with 8 or 9 rounds each should be sufficient for most weapons and for most people in most circumstances. So should a bandoleer of 5 to 55 shotgun rounds. After having said that, keeping several 20, 30, 50 or 70 plus round magazines full of ammunition is very valuable when things get really crazy in condition red or black situations. It gives the one who has the ammunition for his / her firearm in hand increasing confidence. Remember; do not load magazines to their 100% capacity. Always load one or two short to improve feeding and minimize the risk of stoppage.

For training, non-lead ball ammunition may be the best and most cost effective and the healthiest option. For real world gunfight / shooting situations, lead hollow point or expanding full metal jacket ammunition is recommended.

Always be mindful of over penetration risks. Hollow points and expanding full metal jacket and all variations of *"soft tip"* ammunition is generally better for stopping violent kill-or-be-killed threats. In an urban environment where missed shots or exiting bullets may harm the innocent, including your loved ones, the soft tip is better.

This is why we ideally recommend you only use a 12 gauge pump shotgun with #6 or # 7 birdshot ammunition for in-home family defense. If you live in the country, then we also recommend you have several rounds of 00 buckshot and a few shotgun slugs for backup ammunition during more extreme situations. On an approved and safe shooting range, fire each of the types of ammunition you own so you see and understand how it fires, what recoil to expect, become acquainted with the sound, the spread of the shot, its trajectory and pattern, what impact to expect, etcetera.

I once had the unique good fortune to ask in person a Colonel from an elite Tier One Unit, who had extensive operational experience; **"What his first and top choice weapon recommendation would be for a family and home defense." He recommended a 12 gauge pump with #6 or #7 birdshot**. A senior U.S. Navy SEAL NCO along with a top former Israeli special operations operative also recommended a 12 gauge pump. I agree whole heartedly and in my book the experience of those three elite warriors settles it, so let's take a look at some other specific details.

Shotgun Ammunition

First establish by reading on the barrel of your shotgun if it is designed to fire 2 3/4 inch or 3 inch shells or if both are fine for safe use in your shotgun. Three inch shells have a more powerful load but for in-home use the 2 3/4 inch loads are fine.

Please take care and always stay safe by only using a firearm that is in good condition and only use shells designed with the gauge and length that it was intended for. Read all the fine print details of the safety warning on the ammunition box before use and if possible immediately wash your hands well after handling ammunition. If they contain lead you could especially avoid potential cancer, birth defects or harmful reproductive injuries to your health.

Also familiarize yourself with the use of chokes for your shotgun and what effect they have and which ammunition is best used with what choke.

Slugs are traditionally not used with chokes. It is not necessary and that combination may cause severe injury to you and extreme damage to your shotgun barrel. Beware and please read the details on your barrel and or the details on the ammunition box for information regarding the use of slugs.

Plastic shells rather than paper shells are recommended. Here are my top 3 choices:

 # 6 Bird Shot contains 100 or so tiny lead or steel pellets weighing 1 oz in total and can be used with or without a choke. (*It is a lethal load and recommended for very careful and responsible in-home family protection use. It is ideal for scaring and chasing most threats away and that is our primary and ultimate goal. Soldiers shoot to kill. Family protectors only need to stop the threat and chase them away.*) May I recommend you look at the Winchester brand "blind side" steel load shot shell. It has six flat sided, hexahedron shaped pellets, allowing 15% more pellets per shell and it causes greater wound damage. Please also research hypersonic loads. Still, # 6 and #7 are your best in-home family defense options.

Double 00 Buckshot is a very powerful and lethal option. It contains 9 polyethylene / lead pellets and can be used with chokes. 00 Buck can cause some serious damage and easily kill a person but so can just about any load from a shotgun. 00 Buck is my first choice for any riot zone and war zone exfiltration.

1 oz. Lead Slugs are also a very powerful and lethal round and should be used discriminately and with great care. Be sure to know what is beyond and close to all of your threat targets. I recommend you have some slugs available to you during emergencies.

00 Buck and then 1 oz. lead slugs are my personal first choices in that order. From surviving a riot or a war zone to the use of a shotgun if you live in an isolated country environment that has powerful predator animals and other potential threats, a full and correctly loaded shotgun can be an especially effective deterrent.

Please be careful and observe all relevant safety rules. Do not rely entirely or only on the safety device. Maintain safe muzzle discipline and only point the muzzle in a safe direction or at a legally justified threat or target. Maintain impeccable trigger finger control and trigger safety at all times.

Handgun Ammunition

Know that the majority of handguns can fire a round through almost all modern building materials and structures including sheet rock walls, ceilings and doors (not brick). Therefore most firearm instructors recommend hollow point and / or expanding full metal jacket but not ball / full metal jacket rounds for family and self-defense. Rounds that *"splat"* or fragment are safer to use if there is any risk of innocent, non-threat individuals being hit unintentionally.

You need a caliber and type of round that can stop most threats with two or three well placed rounds. The larger the caliber the more likely this is to happen. .45, 44, .357 or .40 calibers are the most reliable for stopping power but ultimately it really depends on your accurate shot placement to the threats heart, spinal cord and lower brain. A 230 grain, .45 caliber ACP *"Hydra-Shock"* round or 125 grain, .357 Magnum semi-jacketed hollow point is a good choice for threat stopping power.

If you have and prefer the popular .38 Special revolver, a 158 grain +P round or even a 125 grain round may perform well with wise and accurate shot placement.

9 mm pistols have gained enormous popularity amongst law enforcement and civilian shooters and are even in service with the military. Many soldiers can vouch for their value and effectiveness

however; many experienced and elite soldiers prefer to have a .45, .357 or .40 caliber as their primary handgun or at least as a backup handgun. That tells us that they do not fully trust the 9 x 19 mm caliber to do the job in extreme life and death situations. If you choose to carry a 9 mm your accurate shooting skills must be of a very high standard and you must always be ready and willing to fire at least 3 well placed 115 gm + P ,or +P+, or 124/147gm + P jacketed hollow-point or standard hollow point, or 9mm NATO high pressure ball rounds per target threat when using your 9 mm. (Put 2 in the heart/lungs and one in the brain/face if forced to do so as a last resort when in extreme and imminent danger.)

Practice mostly with less expensive ammunition but also get familiar with the more expensive loads. You want to be familiar with how your choice of ammo performs. Observe the persons response and keep shooting until the threat is stopped. Remember to carry at least two extra loaded magazines since you may need 3 to 7 plus rounds to effectively stop some threats.

Having said that, shot placement is what determines shot volume. Even a .22L handgun can stop a threat if used effectively by a highly trained, skilled and versatile person. It all depends who you are, who they are and where and how many times and at what distance you shoot them. You are the weapon. The gun is just a tool in your well trained hands. Your selection of firearm type, caliber and ammunition grain and quality all matter very much but your proficiency as a shooter is inevitably what matters most. Firearms skill must be developed through quality and frequent training with qualified and skilled coaches.

Quality firearms and ammunition can give you an edge but is insufficient in and by it's own in a real world violent and armed confrontation with prison-hardened, psychopathic criminals. As I believe that immersion and repetition are essential to learning, please allow me to remind you to become highly proficient at using the combat modified Isoceles, the Israeli and Weaver stance with both revolvers and semiautomatic pistols. Ultimately based on your own research and experience select the one system (*stance, holster type, ammunition type, breathing and trigger system . . .)* you most believe in for you may live or die by the very consequences of your choice. Flexibility and versatility remain important.

Practice correct low light shooting, tactical magazine changes and firearm transfers. You should also familiarize yourself with standing or kneeling and in both front and rear prone firing positions. Practice slow, accurate shooting and safe rapid response shooting under instructor induced stress conditions that also requires you to make wise *"shoot / do not shoot"* decisions at a variety of distances. Practice with a variety of ammunition types, including the exact type of ammunition you intend using in a real emergency response. Be careful not to shoot too closely at metal targets and other hard objects. At the most fundamental level, master you're shooting ability as accurately as what your genetic potential will allow. Practice drawing from various holsters, from concealed carry and from a bent arm high ready position.

Rapidly and smoothly align your firearm with the target as you punch it out onto the threat targets heart or brain and take up the trigger slack as you align with your target. Notice your front sight on the target and drop it into the rear sight and let the shot fire as a planned surprise and follow through on your shot as you reset on the trigger and acquire the front sight again to repeat the process for the next shot.

At the end of each shot string or *"battle lull"* scan left and right and prioritize to look at the places a threat can most likely shoot from. Be mindful of shooting angles. Remember, in real world situations you will need to stop the threat/s, then head for the darkest spot, behind the best cover on the highest ground and secure your position 360 degrees around and phone 911 or radio for help. While you wait continually scan left to right, close to far and low to high to search and identify the best and most likely threat shooting locations such as doorways, windows, far side car front wheels and chimneys on rooftops. *"AAPE"*

Be an intelligent, mindful, proactive and wise observer. Constantly avoid getting into fights of any kind, especially gun fights. Position yourself in the tactically most advantageous and superior position with the best cover, best concealment and best angle to defend and break contact and retreat / escape from. (*Remember Col. Boyd's OODA loop*) When you see somebody, first notice the entire person, then the hands, right and left, check each hand twice and make your *"shoot / don't shoot"* decision based on the imminent or not imminent threats *"ability"*, *"opportunity"* and clear *"jeopardy-intention."*

If in doubt as to what ammunition to use; ask for recommendations specific to your firearm/s of choice and your needs at your local gun store and / or your local law enforcement offices. Avoid excessively heavy and hot custom made loads when selecting ammunition for civilian family protection and self-defense purposes.

Remember; always treat all firearms as loaded. Always perform a careful visual inspection with the muzzle pointing towards a 100% safe area such as sand. Look twice to be totally sure. Be sure that the muzzle never crosses over or points at anything but a safe target or legitimate imminent threat. Keep your trigger finger off the trigger until you have to take up the trigger slack and shoot based on a wise and well informed decision to do so. When practicing, please protect your eyes and ears and ask others around you to do the same.

When performing dry practice drills check each firearm 3 times and verbalize out loud as you perform the safety check in a locked room free from any ammunition. All ammunition should be locked away, preferably in another room during your dry practice. That is the only responsible and professional way to dry practice. Only use safe, dedicated, special dry practice specific ammunition for dry practice.

Store all of your ammunition in a cool, dry, safe place and locked away from children and everyone else. Write the date of purchase on each box. Use your oldest ammunition first for live fire practice.

The wise selection of a quality 12 gauge pump, (*perhaps a quality American or European M14 M1A or FN or H&K or other 7.62 x 51 rifle or a reliable Russian or Chinese or Eastern European 7.62 x 39 SKS and an AK-47 or a American or Italian or other carbine of your own choice*), plus one, two or three heavy or medium caliber handguns (*.45, .357, .40. .38 Special, 9 mm*) with magazines loaded with the ammunition recommended (*125 to 230 grain expanding jacketed hollow point*) above in quality leg or hip and shoulder holsters, plus quality training in a *"controlled aggression" "combat mindset"* accurate and proven marksmanship skills course based on a foundation of dry practice habits and keeping with the FEAR NOT In-home, In-car and On-foot tactics you can expect be better prepared than most so you can FEAR NOT. The combined information in FEAR NOT has the potential when trusted and applied diligently and correctly to make one a formidable family protector and self-defender.

Ideally master the use of three (3) to preferably five (5) weapons. (*A quality zeroed 7.62 X 51 mm rifle or a carbine of your own choice, a quality 12 gauge pump, a quality handgun, (with carefully and intelligently selected ammunition*) a short 13" blade "Samurai" sword-knife or longer "Wakizashi" or a 12" blade, 22 oz "Gurkha Kukri", or a sharp high quality battle hatchet, and a tactical knife, or a Japanese Carpenters cutter) I am sure you will agree that once you master the tactical drills along with the medical protocols and procedures offered within **"FEAR NOT"** that your self confidence will soar. It is my belief that most career criminals will also agree that any person whether a man, woman or couple that is armed and skilled with these five weapons loaded with 125 to 230 grain jacketed expanding hollow point ammunition is not a soft target. They would rather run away and seek out easier and softer targets to prey on. Just imagine facing a well trained man and woman parent team in a tactical high / low position with a *"combat mindset"* ready to defend their children or grandchildren while armed like this. That is my vision for you and your partner should hardcore *"bad guys"* ever show up at your home. My concern is that unless you take life this serious you may or will potentially be in a very bad position if several *"tough guy's"* select you as their prey.

Use several outdoor and indoor dogs, binoculars, external movement detection lights, surveillance cameras, alarm systems and specifically alarm doorstops, metal security gates and our AAPE system to forewarn you. It will give you a little bit of precious time to rapidly *"dress"* for their visit and to swiftly retreat and escape the threat. If forced to do so as a last resort take up a well planned, fortified defensive position behind solid and prearranged cover and with excellent concealment. Many if not most people may think or say this is totally *"over the top"* and that is understandable, but when the brown stuff hits the fan big time *i* am sure most will wish they were this well prepared. Just, imagine how safe you will feel if all four or eight or twelve plus of your immediate neighbors took family and home security this seriously. I certainly would not want to mess around in a neighborhood like that if I was a criminal. How about you?

Now, schedule yourself to go and purchase some fresh / additional quality ammunition as recommended and relevant to the firearm/s you own. Also check your trauma medical kit once more and be sure to have at least several tourniquets, sterile gauze, six inch wide hemorrhage (*severe bleeding*) control bandages for trauma wound dressing, occlusive one way valve chest dressings, 14 gauge chest decompression needles, a nose trumpet, burn dressing, pain control tablets, a blue filter light or chemical light stick and several chemical heating pads in it. Remember a quality and comprehensive trauma specific combat medical kit is as essential as any quality weapons and intelligently selected quality ammunition specific to your needs for any most likely threats.

When really *"bad guys"* show up in your life having machetes and revolvers and shotguns with both armor piercing and tracer rounds, you will be glad *i* insisted you take several advanced medical first responder classes and prepare a superior trauma medical kit, in addition to mastering 3 to 5 weapons and acquiring guaranteed quality and proven ammunition. I suppose with my having grown up in Africa where rape, kidnapping and murder is a daily reality and where good people are almost always *"outnumbered"* by violent criminals, it gave me a different perspective on how prepared one needs to be. Feel free to adjust as necessary but be careful not to adjust and adapt this so much that you end up underprepared.

Trust me when I stress your need for *"situational awareness"* and a *"combat mindset"* with a tactical first contact drill plan and system. Keep a 12 gauge pump shotgun with at the very minimum five # 6 birdshot rounds handy along with a handgun and 6 to 20 plus expanding or hollow point rounds. At the very least your medical supplies should include a tourniquet, sterile gauze and a wound dressing or several tampons and sanitary pads to be used as improvised wound dressings plus the knowledge and skills for all their uses. Anything less is irresponsible from my and a family protection / self-defense perspective.

It is my / our goal to make you a very hard target to rape, kidnap or murder and my sub objectives are to equip first time gun owners with very useful, better than average information and to make a valuable contribution to the knowledge of highly experienced gun enthusiasts who want to become an even more capable family protector and self-defender. It is also my/our hope that all or some of this will prove very useful to *"good"* law enforcement officers and that it will continually help keep soldiers on the *"good guy / our"* side alive whilst inspiring them to be the best combat ready soldier they can be.

Our distribution controlled **FEAR NOT Special Report** companion to this book is specifically offered with only serious professionals in mind. It is also for carefully screened civilians who wish to take their personal standards to the next level.

If you are a serious person in regards to maintaining your families security and personal defense along with establishing emergency zone survival and evacuation tactics, you may want to consider some of the gear which I consider to be a few of my personal favorites. This is what I would love to have in an extreme emergency if they were available to me and recommend for you if these are legally available options for you. An M14 M1A, or SKS or in an urban setting rather a 12 gauge shotgun in your hands, an AK47 or 12 gauge shotgun worn with a double sling somewhat similar to that of a back pack, or a M6 .22L & 410 shotgun combo folded down into a small rucksack, a concealed Scorpion machine pistol, extra ammunition, a 13" YK-30 steel blade James Williams designed and Samurai inspired knife, or short 18.5" to 21" blade Samurai sword, plus a Tom Brown heavy duty bush craft and survival knife and / or a hatchet, a yard of 550 Para cord or commando wire saw potentially used as a garrote, a compass and a flint fire starter.

These items are obviously for very extreme emergency evacuations only. I realize that ammunition for these weapons may be hard to acquire depending on who you are and where you live. Therefore, the 12 gauge shotgun that I have recommended throughout FEAR NOT along with a popular caliber handgun such as a 9mm, .40 or .45, and your personal favorite hunting rifle may remain as your best option.

Rules of Engagement

The ultimate and number One ROE was written by Moses on God's command; *"Thou shall not murder/kill"*.

Here are our seven core ROE's:

1. "Though shall not kill (murder)"—God.
2. Avoid all places, situations and circumstances where you may become involved in a shooting or gunfight.
3. Always attempt to retreat and escape without engaging. Even if you are in your own home, retreat if at all possible instead of engaging in a gunfight. Based on the *"castle rule"* and as a direct result of the threats clear *"ability/opportunity* **and** *jeopardy"*, (behavioral and or verbalized intent) you may have a full and legally justifiable right to use lethal force if under imminent assault in your home. Yet, go with God's command as your first and overall guiding principal. Retreat rather than resist if escape is possible. To take a human or animals life is a very personal decision we should all congruently make prior to facing a violent, criminal encounter.
4. Always de-escalate all situations the best you possibly can.
5. If due to the threats direct behavior you have no other choice and are forced to engage out of fear for your family's and own life only then engage briefly but intensely with one 3 or 7 to 9 round burst of semiautomatic fire. Then AAPE, reassess the situation and make a new and committed attempt to retreat.
6. Avoid reengaging after the first lull in fire. Battles pulse with action. Use the first break in action to improve your tactical position behind cover. Endeavor again to retreat tactically from the danger zone. If necessary engage a second time if once again as a result of an imminent threat and with no preclusion you are forced to do so. Again work to ideally improve both your cover against fire and sight. If it is dark and you do not have sufficient cover then move immediately after shooting and or upon using your flashlight. Your primary goals are always

and shall remain to not engage, not escalate and not get your family or self shot or taken. Our focus must be and remain on taking good cover, then retreat without engaging at the earliest possible opportunity. You can accomplish this by using stealth, surprise, distraction, speed and prayer.

7. Should retreat be totally impossible because you are trapped in a kill zone and pinned down under heavy fire or fully exposed to a direct criminal attack, then engage immediately with one quick burst of 3 or more rounds. Briefly and very intensely create sensory overload and shock for and in them through effective fire and controlled Wolverine like aggression. Do not pursue the evil doer's if they run away. Let them go. Do not follow them or attempt a citizen's arrest unless you become stuck with them as prisoners. Create a suspect identity description for the police and let the authorities deal with their capture. If forced to manage prisoners until the police arrive, keep a safe distance of at least 30 feet if possible and maintain strict control and supervision. Always operate according to our prisoner control drill and with the use of healthy common sense.

3 Fundamental Principles Of Combat

The three fundamental principals of combat are surprise, speed and violence of action which should be used to gain an advantage if or when needed to protect your family and defend yourself.

1. Be proactive and confidently evolve the situation just like any elite fighting units would. Defend by counter attacking immediately, be fully integrated and forward. Action is better than reaction in combat. Use surprise. Defend by attacking with simple, unknown to them, defensive battle tactics and combat survival techniques. Where needed, use superior firepower which includes greater speed, more accuracy, higher volume, superior weapons, larger calibers, superior tactical firing position and better cover if available. Be the person with the largest caliber weapon and the most weapons on you in the fight. You must be the person with the best body armor, best tactical position and best cover plus have the best 12 gauge combat shotgun or 7.62 x 51 caliber high precision battle rifle as well as the two or three .45 or .40 caliber pistols and 7 plus inch tactical knife and tourniquets, wound bandages etcetera. Be the best equipped and best trained person in the fight. Be the most skilled and most intense yet coolest person in the fight.

    I can recommend several outstanding individuals and organizations, including the NRA™. I have also heard good things about Front Sight©™ (For moral and legal reasons, only use lethal force to protect life when fearing for loss of life or extreme bodily harm. We'd rather you always avoid getting into a skirmish or fight and try at least to retreat and escape unseen without fighting or without fighting much if at all possible.)

2. Stay as much as possible on your feet to remain mobile. Do not cluster under fire. Control your aggression and remain

focused while you spread out into a tactical flare and when moving intelligently and dynamically forward. Use surprise, speed and controlled aggression in violence of action. (If alone, use cover and darkness more carefully and more often and routinely stay below knee level.) Use your light very carefully to locate, identify and blind your threat and to reduce their ability to gather useful Intel about you. **DISRUPT THEIR AAPE LOOP** by observing and anticipating. Create chaos and use that chaos and their confusion to escape the battle zone. Avoid obvious pattern detection by the threat to figure you out but do notice your threat and assaulters patterns.

3. Have three to five weapons on you. Do not stop fighting just because you are wounded or to help the wounded. First eliminate the threat by fighting forward but only if a safe retreat and escape is not possible. With protective detail drills we shoot running back or sideways into cover with the person we are covering and protecting. Our goal then is 100% to get away from the fight. As family protectors we'd rather choose to retreat to safety if possible instead of attacking

Throughout this publication we took the defensive position to avoid shootings, knife and gunfights. We did our best to recommend you deescalate rather than escalate various situations. That is the moral and legally best thing to do.

However, should your family and you ever be assaulted by a group of armed thugs or professional killers then be willing to be ruthless, unconventional, intense and even lethal. In the midst of a real world attempt on your lives or a *"slaughter-or-be-slaughtered"* encounter you must be willing to do whatever it takes.

Battle conditions are fast and deadly and sadly that is what you will need to be in order to survive. There is a time in battle to be proactive, to become the assaulter, to be the wolf and not the sheepishly helpless victim if your family and you are to survive. Never take any pleasure in killing. Only become ruthless and cunning to survive if you are absolutely forced to be. Remember that in your training and if you

259

are ever in any high risk situations. Train and practice often to be skilled in the use of a tactical flashlight, knife, handgun, shotgun and most of all in the use of a trauma medical care kit.

AAPE continuously and constantly. Observe and process information and unfolding conditions or circumstances to prevent and avoid high risks. Constantly assess your situation and position with high situational, tactical and operational awareness, cultural understanding, and situational evidence. Swiftly place yourself into the safest escape route available or rapidly orientate and position yourself in the best possible cover and darkest area possible to APPE from. As a last resort in an imminent fight-or-perish situation intelligently unleash your inner Wolverine.

Surviving a Kidnapping

If you are taken, you may get treated very kindly, gently and respectfully, **OR NOT**. You may be restrained, isolated, humiliated, beaten, degraded, stripped naked, abused, gang raped . . . or even killed. These are the key things that you can do if you are taken:

1. Avoid eye contact.

2. Do not look at their weapons.

3. Act very scared. Initially raise your shoulders, breath in a shallow panting fashion and slump your posture.

4. Cooperate.

5. Focus on your family's love and need for you and your love for them.

6. Learn in advance how to deal with getting tied up so that you can increase your chances of success. After being blindfolded and tied up for an extended time your hands will be severely swollen and you may have sight problems. Once you are tied up, they can have their evil ways with you anyway they want. I prefer to fight back while still on my feet.

   If you are sure that all they want is ransom and you are from a very wealthy family with a large K & R (Kidnap and Ransom) insurance policy; the typical law enforcement advice of not to fight back may or may not prove to be wise. If you are not in such a privileged position then fighting back at first contact could or also could not be the best option. The decisions are made on the spur of the moment and believe me when I say your chances are improved infinitely from your training no matter what you decide. It will be dangerous and training is essential.

Every situation is unique. Relying on being rescued is also risky. Global rescue statistics do not look too positive. The Israeli's have a formidable track record but for most it is a very risky business. I believe the best plan is prevention and to not be taken. **AAPE** is your key. Also know that the Police recommend you do not resist or try to escape and that you should wait for them to rescue you. That sadly does not often work out too well for each situation is very complex, unique and risky.

7. If you get forced into a car trunk, do whatever it takes to free your hands and feet. Pull out the tail light cables of the car to attract law enforcement attention. Knock or kick a rear light out and then stick your arm out and wave like crazy to attract attention. Be ready to go AAPE when they stop. At the very least you may legally have a .22 L pistol in deep concealment on your body and ideally also at least a neck or thumb knife as our training suggests. This can give you an element of surprise and save your life. If you get the opportunity to run away, remove bright or light colored clothing but do not expose more skin. Grab what you can that is dark colored to cover your skin if you are light skinned. Sprint away while changing direction often. Find a crowded area, yell for help and run in amongst groups of people.

8. If your kidnappers force you to drive, look for a law enforcement officer and do what you can to attract their attention. Actions such as carefully failing to use your indicator or safely and visibly running a red light without endangering innocent lives may get their attention. Pray, hit the horn or as a last resort consider almost causing a (very) minor crash with a police cruiser, ambulance or another car. Attempt this only as a very last and desperate resort and with great caution so as not to kill or hurt anyone, damage government property or any other property.

9. Master our AAPE System and our In-Home, In-Car and On-Foot first contact drills. Build your proficiency in everything offered in this information guide. Where it is legal to do so, carry at

least one concealed handgun or a high powered pepper spray and a folding knife and or neck knife and a thumb knife. Ideally have two or three blades on your person for family protection and personal defense. Be a hard target. Be more unpredictable in your daily patterns. Take the required and recommended precautions. Get more training and practice frequently. By not training and practicing you will make yourself a soft target that is very easy to kidnap rape or murder in civilian life or simply kill in a war zone. The choice is yours. With adequate, professional instruction, training and coaching it is indeed entirely possible to become uncommonly proficient at AAPEing your way around, through and out of very dangerous environments.

10. Learn the fundamentals of escaping from captivity and of unarmed combat and knife fighting. Certainly learn gun handling and carry one.

11. Master at least the most important medical procedures for increasing the survivability of gunshot and knife slash or stab wounds. You must be totally proficient in treating massive extremity bleeding, sucking chest wounds, tension pneumothorax, airway obstruction, shock and trauma induced hypothermia. Master at a minimum how to make improvised bandages and how to use an Israeli bandage to dress wounds and or as an improvised tourniquet. Please realize that the right gear can be a wonderful help but the more gear you have the more training will be required. Too much gear can quickly become a hindrance. Stay nimble and sharp.

12. Remember that your survival in all tactical and medical emergencies will always depend on how you think. End results show how you made decisions and how you went about implementing your decisions. This is determined by the quality and depth of your training and the system you are trained in. The CRI Israeli method is outstanding. Further, the AAPE system is your core guide. Use it decisively. If your family is at risk and if it makes moral, legal and ethical sense to do

whatever it takes, then do it immediately and with intensity. Always remain motivated to escape if the opportunity to do so safely presents itself. Be proactive in evolving and developing situations. Adapt constantly. Be willing to be unconventional and audacious. Use creativity, innovation, diversion, disguises and deception as well as intense lethal force to create chaos, disorientation and confusion for your assaulters. Be physically, mentally and emotionally ready to seize opportunity and to evolve situations. Use surprise, speed and violence of action. Keep your escape plans simple. Trust your instincts and training and also pray silently with your eyes open.

Once on the move use shadows for cover, maintain momentum and change your direction often. This is where your training will make a huge difference. You need a simple, effective system based on real world experience and execute it methodically and systematically without emotion. Constantly observe. Scan left to right, low to high, close to far and beyond items. Seek the best cover and superior position with proactive initiative and be swift in exploiting your threats weaknesses as they become clear. Continually scan for threats in windows, doorways, along edges, rooflines and on roof tops. Note moving shadows, muzzle flashes and other threat indicators. Hide in the darkest areas behind the best cover, observe often and be ready to move. When you are ready to move, expose yourself to the risk as briefly as possible.

Get a weapon in hand such as a spade, axe, rock or stick. Employ anything that could cause severe injury if used with a determined mindset and *"controlled aggression"*. Use it smoothly, swiftly and powerfully when in imminent danger or where you fear for your life. Create total chaotic sensory overload for your assaulters. Interrupt their ability to AAPE you and seize the opportunity to escape further away while they are in shock. Expect a positive outcome and continue to maintain your momentum. Realize that if they recapture you they may get very nasty with you. Failure at this point is no longer an option available to you. Keep evolving the situation using all the information you gained from studying this book and all the skill gained while training with us and other specialists. Stay an arms length off of walls. Never give up. Take long deep slow breaths to calm yourself down and to clear your thinking. Exhale twice as slow as you inhale but silently. Keep scanning left to right, low to high, close to far and both into and deep beyond cover and 360 degrees around. Keep AAPEing. This is how you stand the best chance of getting away alive. Think like a Tiger or Wolverine and train with that kind of intensity. Recall the well known US Navy SEAL saying *"The only easy day was yesterday"*. Tomorrow is not guaranteed to be easier than today so do your best, expect a positive outcome and be ready for those tough days that are intermingled with the good ones. That is the nature of life!

Training to Survive
Real World Kidnappings

Training with a realistic kidnap situation in mind and being very diligent in your prevention are both very important.

"The CRI Counter Kidnapping courses on how to survive execution attempts as well as assassination attempts are being considered by high level experts to be two of the best courses of their kind in the world. Thousands of people have been trained during the last ten years using these methods and many lives have been saved"—Doron Benbenisty.

Please be encouraged to check out what I feel is the best and most intelligently and effectively designed real world counter kidnapping system of training in the world. The real secrets of counter kidnapping and how to train for such an eventuality must be learned in person from Doron at the CRI academy.

1.   **www.critraining.com/counterkidnappingcourse**
2.   **www.critraining.com/survivingexecutioncourse**
Warning: it contains violent graphic beheading content and is not suitable for children or sensitive viewers. **Do not click on the video link.**

The following is only an introduction to some of the training you should expect. Ideally one must train with at least three men grabbing you with no warning and in low light conditions. Place one on each side while a third grabs your legs and lifts you off the ground. Train in the kind of clothes and shoes you are most likely to wear when abducted. Get some practice in fighting back both as they grab you and once they have you off the ground and carry you away. Fight intensely, totally freestyle with the combinations we taught you for at least 15 to 90 seconds at a time in real time high speed mode. Use protective sparring gear for all. Keep everything super realistic and fight hard to test your abilities so that you may never develop complacency and a false sense of confidence. If what you plan to use in a real world encounter does not work in a full speed sparring scenario then find a better way because it will also not work in a real world kidnapping.

Training must reflect real world intensity and always end at a point where your family and you are 100% safe. Use only rubber training weapons or Airsoft™ guns along with boxing gloves, adequate eye, neck, torso and limb protection pads, helmets, groin cups, knee pads and elbow pads which are highly recommended so that you can up the intensity and attack the head and groin etcetera. Practice at about 60 to 80% power and intensity but remain careful with necks, eyes and joints. This type of training should only be done under highly experienced supervision and only with adequate and proper training under controlled conditions since this type of training could result in death or severe injury.

When fighting, keep you chin tucked in, you mouth closed and your tongue against the roof of you mouth away from your teeth. Breathe through your nose.

Be especially diligent in your practice of escaping from restraining holds. Also be careful in your practice of knife avoidance and both gun and knife/edged weapons disarming techniques at full contact intensity. Become masterful at grabbing a wide variety of weapons from several opponents of all sizes in a low light, confining and realistic real world environment. It is important to practice disarming with a variety of people bigger than you. Work on stepping out of harms way, grabbing weapons smoothly and accurately, closing the gap with your assaulter swiftly and effect striking them and taking them down without ending up on the ground with them.

Remember, most fights do end up on the ground and the reality of life is that both men and women get brutally raped in the real world. For women especially this is a definite risk. How will you deal with such an eventuality? Will you fight back and win or simply submit and be a victim? If this is a fear of yours then learn and train how to avoid it and how to fight your way out of such situations. Train how to fight standing and when on the ground or every other possible position. Have strategies, techniques and a simple workable plan ready to activate. More importantly, do all you can to avoid any and all high risk areas? Hands-on training in escaping from captivity is absolutely important and a very high priority. When in training I will ask you again to always remember another US Navy SEAL saying; *"Losing one pint of sweat in training is better than losing a pint of blood in combat".*

Avoiding Kidnap and Rape

To avoid becoming a kidnap and or gang rape victim you must become a master at the AAPE system. You must also become a formidable unarmed fighter with uncommon skill in at least 3 to 10 or more proven self-defense techniques. Some effective strategies, tactics and techniques are:

1. Avoid going out alone. Only go in a large group. If you do go out alone, do not dress too revealing or at least not while traveling to your destination and back. Please cover up. Modesty is better. Check to make sure you are not being followed. Drive around the block if you want to be sure. Do not stop if someone crashes into your fender. Drive to the nearest safe, crowded area or police station. If forced to do so be ready to use my **FEAR NOT** 2.2 System in-car and on-foot first contact drills described in this publication. Please be alert and very careful. Act decisive and with surprise, speed and cool controlled aggression when forced to do so.

2. Always carry at least a powerful pepper spray and a stun gun, folding tactical blade, box cutter, scalpel knife, revolver or pistol with easy access ability and be ready to use it. Most importantly, be skilled in using these items. Use them swiftly, confidently and with precision if assailants show the ability, opportunity and intent to kidnap, rape or kill you and if escape is impossible and a serious and imminent felony assault is unfolding. If they use a pepper spray against you, immediately use your hands to cover your eyes and look away for a second. Close your mouth and hold your breath for a second or two and then explosively fight back the best you can as taught in this book, in CRI's DVD or our hands-on class.

3. Avoid as best you can dark deserted areas such as parking lots, staircases, alley ways, backstreets and clubs in high risk areas.

4. Always keep your car and home doors locked.

5. Always check for intruders hiding in the back seat area of your car before you enter, then immediately lock your doors and drive away. When you get home be especially careful to AAPE around your garage where an ambush is very likely.

6. Always have your mobile phone ready to dial 911 and do so at the very first sign of perceived trouble and potential or real danger.

7. If attacked, get your back against cover and fight back with Wolverine intensity especially during the first 15 to 90 seconds and do not stop until you are safe or can escape. Kick low and powerfully or grab the attackers head and forcefully twist it up and sideways. Use your elbows, knees, finger nails, bite viciously, attack their eyes, groin, throat and scream extremely loud and run away at your first opportunity. Please get trained. Remember to have a friend with you when you go out and please carry at least a pepper spray, stun gun or a .38 Special revolver, .40 caliber pistol, 9 mm pistol or at the very minimum a .22 L pistol and a cell phone which is within easy reach. When really bad trouble finds you; you will be so glad you did!

Mentally rehearse how you will deal with a rape attempt where three attackers or more are present but do not dwell on this possibility too often or for too long. You do not need or want to kinetically attract this to yourself. Be prepared without obsessing over it. In person hands on anti-rape training is very valuable. Get as much as you need and as soon as you can. Acquire the best defensive hardware affordable and accessible. Prepare well and continuously. Train hard with the most demanding instructors in the most difficult and specialized schools so that you and your family will **"FEAR NOT"**.

Citizen Witness

The law enforcement community needs good citizens to help them keep an eye open for potential criminal and terrorist activities. Our help to them can make a great difference. In a fair and non *"Gestapo"* like free society and just system, they need that advantage and we should provide it willingly. Their new anti terrorism motto is **"See Something, Say Something"**.

The first thing to do is to remain safe. Do not try to be a hero. It is too dangerous and the police frown on citizen's being too *"gung-ho"* and heroic. The bottom line is that in an emergency response there is a risk of being killed along with the risk of too easily overstepping your legal boundary. Police guidelines include making no attempt to use any weapon of any kind and to not engage in any attempt to overpower or arrest anyone. Simply observe carefully and record what you witnessed. What the police want and need is a living, accurate and talking witness as a source of information, nothing more. That is wise and good.

Look twice or more times to confirm accuracy. Immediately write down what you see and hear. Be systematic and methodical but keep your head down. Key information for your suspect ID chart and the information that the police will need and want include the following:

Height
Weight
Sex
Skin color
Hair color and length
Eye color
Facial hair
Voice pattern
Build
Scars & tattoos

Estimated age
Number of violators
Weapons, handgun–pistol or revolver, long gun–rifle or shotgun
Civilian or military
Jewelry
Clothing, hat, shirt, jacket, shoes + anything said
License plate number
Type and color of vehicle
Estimated age of vehicle
Direction they left in

Remember; **DO NOT** pursue the bad guys. You could get killed and you can get into legal trouble. That is the work of the police. Let them do it. Love and respect them for it and support them in the service they so bravely provide which is often under very difficult conditions. Do call 911 ASAP for emergencies, and 311 for non-emergencies in the United States. Stay alive and be a safe witness for a safer world. Take Care, Be Safe and G-D Bless.

The Soul and Way
Of the Real Warrior

A real full spectrum warrior and master of battle-craft does not love war, combat or violence. True warriors do not take pleasure in killing, not even killing an animal for food. When he must, he oft times offers prayers of gratitude just like the wise Native American Indian hunters do. The Ultimate Warrior knows that war and armed conflict of all sorts are dark, horrific and disgusting. They know its filthy, evil, greedy underbelly far too well to want to glorify war. They love peace rather than war and strive for peace and harmony. The real warriors only engage in justified war craft to prevent evil people from doing evil things to good and innocent yet possibly weaker people.

The Ultimate Warrior is not a gun, war and macho image fanatic. They are not boastful and they are not bullies. True master full spectrum warriors do not support bullies or serve to uphold tyrants, dictators and oppressive murdering warlords. You see these kinds of tyrannical people down through history and even today operating throughout the world.

True warriors are respectful masters of their craft and choose especially to be kind, loving, discreet and gentle to the poor, the meek and the disarmed. They will often serve, teach and protect.

Their training is often hard and enables them to be strong capable warriors that avoid violent choices and violent people. They broker peace and always prefer not to engage in combat if that is an option. Sadly though if forced into action and to engage, they can become as ruthless as a Tiger or Wolverine and be just as systematic, methodical and decisive as would any fully trained yet unconventional family protector and defender. They develop the warrior within and they are willing to slaughter the wicked opposition and those who prey on the weak. Ideally, they have a transcendent belief or cause and

273

protect the weak *"sheep"* like people and will fight to help free the oppressed.

Some warriors like those that are found amongst good and just law enforcement officers, were born with the instincts to protect like a pure bred *"sheepdog"*. Yet, there are often others who see themselves as ex-wolves turned *"sheepdog"* that felt called upon and ultimately destined to use their lethal skills to help protect good people from danger. Because the ex-wolf knows the ruthless ways of the wolf, he sometimes can teach how to protect and defend your *"flock"* against the dangerous wolves in society. Forgive my analogy, but I could think of no truer instance in nature to express my point than that of the ultimate protector himself.

Society needs positive and good warriors, not just negative warring and drug lord types. We need those who guard against ruthless and evil intentions and maintain those healthy boundaries in society.

Please be encouraged to prepare wisely but do not obsess over weapons and weapon craft. Master the art of the 5 weapons, the sniper / hunter rifle, the battle rifle, the heavy full size handgun/s, the short Samurai sword and the tactical knife. Any of these could be the one that makes the ultimate difference. Yes, I absolutely recommend you master your weapons.

It has been said that one can live by the sword but I also suggest you cultivate a garden patch or a fruit tree to feed various people, especially those in need. Do honest work, help the elderly, teach others a valuable skill or craft, set a positive example for the younger aspiring warriors and care for their soul. Speak into their hearts, challenge them to become great men but also continually test, validate and celebrate them. You could help them find their way and possibly their life's purpose which may only be revealed within their relationship with Source.

Teach them to be useful and caring yet fruitful and direct them on how to best serve their family, community, nation and humanity. This is the true way of the warrior. He uses his warrior strength and image to attract and inspire younger men but then he teaches them to be soulful, non-violent, respectful and noble while still being chivalrous, good, kind, protective and compassionate.

We first teach them skills as a foundation so we can bond, test and assess them. Then, by example we can train them to be a giver, a lover, a contributor and a gentle yet tender person. One can always be capable, wild, fierce and lethal with the 5 weapons but yet easy to approach and generous, just, fair and good.

The real ultimate warrior is confident. He / she create more connection while seeking to include instead of excluding people. They will seek to restore things to wholeness.

Superior training and knowledge can bring chaos to the evil doers and show how to restore order when there are attempts to bring chaos to good people. The warrior uses surprise, speed and controlled and appropriate violence-of-action in combat to dominate from the high ground and the darkest of shadows. As he loses the element of surprise, the ultimate warrior increases his speed and violence-of-action with a controlled aggression combat mindset but still can be systematic and just as methodical as in a practice drill. He also knows how to de-escalate situations, how to defuse them and how to prevent things from becoming an all out fight. Sadly, they are also willing and skilled in taking the fight to the bad guy's when necessary but prefer not to fight if a fight can be avoided at all.

The Warrior looks to continually co-create more good opportunities with and for many good people. Be encouraged to seek out great mentors and if possible to be one yourself. You could very well be a great coach. Make your own unique contribution. Be a great elder one day. Give younger men your blessings, your admiration, an initiate their rite-of-passage perhaps in a wilderness ritual. Express your unique gifts in your own unique way and the best way you can but also try to team up and cooperate with others. You can oft times contribute more together than you simply ever could when contributing just by yourself to your community and the greater world. There is an old and wise saying. **"There are limits as to what you can do but there are no limits as to what others can do for you."** Always broker peace, bring healing, and in all things strive to contribute to the greater good of all.

Most cultures and a majority of peoples teach to communicate and work from your heart. They listen with their heart and give from the heart. Open yours. Build love. Work hard. This is the true way and the true path. Embody this as a warrior, a lover and as a leader for the benefit of others. Think of all of those brave former old soldiers who toiled and worked hard cultivating the land and doing honest humble work while living simply, quietly and peacefully. All the while, they were pouring their warrior strength and faithfulness into the soil to feed others. Your fathers and mothers and there's before them and now you are that very soil.

As a warrior, cultivate your personal relationship in gratitude with Source and fear no one but God. Love and respect Source. Nothing is more important. Respect our planet; respect other people, yourself and all living beings including animals, and respect individual freedom and choice. That is a solid and sustainable way of living.

The warrior understands that we must all die and that his turn may come soon. *The true journey of the warrior is always a spiritual one.* That big ego, hard core *"gun guy"*, who is constantly spouting *"my this, can beat up your that"* immature, alpha-hole attitudes have no place in the heart and soul and life of the true, mature, ultimate warrior. Rather than an ineffectual parade of foolish bravado, one should be practicing non-violence, honesty, caring, love, patience, joy, humility, tenderness, gentleness, forgiveness and the valor and compassion to evolve situations and restore them to order, to wholeness and to non-violence. Please be that man / woman for a better world.

I understand how war and combat is sometimes necessary to restore order but the truth is; most wars are more about resource control and power than what is usually said to be the reason. Ultimately, war is horrific. Killing is bad and fighting has proven over and over to never be the wisest nor best long term solution. Sadly, it still today remains the way that power, control and resources are gained in most parts of the world. As long as there is greed exploited by tyrants and bullies there is and will be a need for warriors that are highly skilled in recon, man hunting, tactics. We need those who can call in a bombing run, grab a hostage or effect a hostage release operation while still being efficient enough to engage the evil ones with the choice of their 5 weapons. Remember, the wise and true warrior is discerning and does not kill randomly, if at all!

As long as there are violent and armed criminals on this planet right down to being in your neighborhoods, you need to be a skilled family protector and self-defender. *i* wish it was not so, but it is. Make an effort to be that person, that warrior with a soul and who has honor the way we have discussed here. *i* hope you will practice being as non-violent as you possibly can be but never be afraid to be a formidable foe when the situation is forced upon you. Let us choose peace, love, caring, and non-violence. Peace is with you.

About the Author

David Fabricius is a former army and SWAT guy.

He volunteered for military service in a classic Special Forces unit born directly out of the famous British 22nd S.A.S. (Special Air Service). They specialized in reconnaissance and full spectrum (sea, air and land) asymmetrical warfare.

He went on to receive additional specialized training and eventually worked as an instructor in a Police Special Operations Unit. This special operations task force was responsible for urban hostage rescue operations involving commercial aircraft, buses, trains, ships, oil platforms, and various buildings. They also trained and provided service as sky marshals, airport security, bomb disposal, V.I.P.

protection and were instrumental in anti-terrorism enforcement and capture in urban environments.

David Fabricius also later provided security training in the private sector for a tier one missile development corporation. He also participated occasionally as a private security contractor.

He has maintained a life long interest in martial arts which commenced at an early age. After winning numerous medals in competitions; he owned and operated his own successful karate school.

Today, David is known as a lecturer on leadership, life balance and works with men's initiation and soul. He also promotes and advocates personal safety and family security for elite audiences around the world. He is a global figure and he now resides in the United States.

David Fabricius is a JCI World Senator, the recipient of the Key of Freedom from the City of Miami, Florida and numerous other national and international recognitions for selfless service to humanity. He is also the founding Father of a Men's Movement. (www.menofthecode.com)

References and Bibliography

The author would like to acknowledge and express his gratitude for the influences many other trainers and authors have had on his knowledge and perceptions. This includes people from both around the world and across the USA. Influencing him foremost has been specialist trainers in both the military and the police units he trained with.

I want to also recognize American authors / teachers/ trainers such as Doron Benbenisty, Joel Martinez, Paul R. Howe, Jeff Gonzales, Don Mann, Ken J. Good, Lt. Col. David Grossman, Massad Ayoob, Eric Lawrence, James Williams, Toshishiro Obata and many others. A special acknowledgement is owed to the British SAS and SBS and the men who came from there and served as my instructors.

I remain indebted to everyone and every source listed below for the profound influence they posed toward my knowledge and understanding. This list can never be a complete list as there have been so many sources; some of which can no longer even be remembered by name. My appreciation, respect and gratitude go out to all. Books such as SEAL OF HONOR, THE MISSION, MEN AND ME, US ARMY RANGER HANDBOOK, and WEAPONS OF DELTA FORCE also provided inspiration, references, insights, reminders and validation.

The following books and DVD's along with many others have been consulted as references:

LEADERSHIP AND TRAINING FOR THE FIGHT / MSG Paul R. Howe
Authorhouse™

The Gun Digest® Book of Combat Hand Gunnery, 6th Edition / Massad Ayoob Gun Digest® Books

THE MODERN DAY GUNSLINGER / Don Mann, U.S. NAVY SEAL
Skyhorse Publishing Inc

Combative Fundamentals, an Unconventional Approach / Jeff Gonzales Trident Concepts LLC

TACTICAL PISTOL SHOOTING / Eric Lawrence
Gun Digest® Books

NRA GUIDE TO THE BASICS OF PERSONAL PROTECTION OUTSIDE THE HOME The National Rifle Association of America®.

ARMED RESPONSE / David Kenik
Merril Press

THE CONCEALED HANDGUN MANUAL / Chris Bird
Privateer Publications
THE STRATEGIES OF LOW LIGHT ENGAGEMENTS / Ken J. Good
Strategos International

MODERN HAND TO HAND COMBAT / Hakim Isler
Tuttle Publishing

SHINKENDO / Toshishiro Obata
SHINKENDO TAMESHIGRIA / Toshishiro Obata
International Shinkendo Federation.

THE ART OF JAPANESE SWORDSMANSHIP / Nicklause Suino
Weatherhill

CUTTING TARGETS WITH THE JAPANESE SWORD / Richard W. Babin M.D. with Sensei Bob Elder
Paladin Press

IAI The Art of Drawing the Sword.
Darrell Max Craig
TUTTLE PUBLISHING

SPECIAL FORCES / RANGER-UDT / SEAL HAND-TO-HAND
COMBAT / SPECIAL WEAPONS / SPECIAL TACTICS SERIES,
KNIFE FIGHTING, KNIFE THROWING FOR COMBAT / Michael
D. Echanis
Black Belt Books

MILITARY KNIFE FIGHTING / Robert K. Spear
Desert Publications

KNIFE FIGHTING, A PRACTICAL COURSE / Michael D.
Janich
TACTICAL MEDICINE / Ian McDevitt
Paladin Press

DVD's

The SYSTEM OF STRATEGY / EDGED WEAPONS USE FOR
COMBAT
NAMI RYU LAI JUSTU, SWORD ART OF THE SAMURAI
Bugei Trading Company Inc

WARRIOR'S EDGE, EDGED WEAPONS TRAINING
Cold Steel Inc.

VIKING TACTICS®
Rifle Drills DVD #1 and #2.

The author acknowledges that this list is incomplete and apologizes
in the spirit of healthy masculinity and for the sake of any significant
source that may not have been explicitly acknowledged.

PRODUCTS & TRAINING

To order additional copies of FEAR NOT or other publications and products that we recommend to help protect your home and family, go to www.menofthecode.com and investigate our CATALOGUE.

To order an additional copy of FEAR NOT or copies in volume for your business or organization, please contact the publisher at www.authorhouse.com or call 1-888-728-8467
and ask for the Order Department at Ext. 5030.

To book a seminar series, an interview, a speaking engagement, or a training session for a group or organization with David Fabricius and his team of professionals, we also suggest you use www.menofthecode.com and follow the link for SEMINARS AND TRAINING.

PRODUCTS & TRAINING

To order additional copies of FEAR NOT or other publications and products that we recommend to help protect your home and family, go to www.menofthecode.com and investigate our CATALOGUE.

To order an additional copy of FEAR NOT or copies in volume for your business or organization, please contact the publisher at www.authorhouse.com or call 1-888-728-8467
and ask for the Order Department at Ext. 5030.

To book a seminar series, an interview, a speaking engagement, or a training session for a group or organization with David Fabricius and his team of professionals, we also suggest you use www.menofthecode.com and follow the link for SEMINARS AND TRAINING.